WILHELM MEISTER
AND HIS ENGLISH KINSMEN

WILHELM MEISTER
AND HIS ENGLISH KINSMEN

APPRENTICES TO LIFE

BY

SUSANNE HOWE

AMS PRESS, INC.
NEW YORK
1966

Reprinted with the permission of the
Original Publisher, 1966

AMS PRESS, INC.
New York, N.Y. 10003
1966

Manufactured in the United States of America

FOREWORD

Grateful acknowledgment is made to Professor Ashley H. Thorndike, of Columbia University, for his helpful interest in the progress of this study, and for his unfailing kindness and patience in reading and criticizing its various chapters. I am also glad to mention my indebtedness to Professor Robert Herndon Fife for many valuable suggestions concerning the German material involved. Thanks are due to Professor G. C. D. Odell and Professor Ernest Hunter Wright for criticism of the manuscript, and to Professor Emery E. Neff, one of whose lectures originally suggested the subject. The notes for Lewes's "Apprenticeship of Life" and some useful information about Lewes were kindly supplied by Professor Anna T. Kitchel, of the English Department of Vassar College.

S. H.

New York, 1929

CONTENTS

CHAPTER I

MAN and his meeting with the world, *Mundus et Infans*, has always been good fiction material. Goethe was not the first to discover it, though no careful biographer of Goethe may be caught napping in the shadow of that admission. Even the eighteenth century did not discover it, although it sounds suspiciously like one of those good, solid, mouth-filling abstractions such as the eighteenth century loved to fasten its teeth in—Life and the Individual, *Geist und Welt, le Génie et l'Ordre Éternelle* —and the like. It seems that, long before men's minds began to work in capitals on such antitheses, the latent story material in the subject appealed to the eager author, perhaps because it implied the gaining of experience—usually the author's own—at the hands of the world, and therefore it involved action, travel. Even the younger Cyrus, that pert young Persian with an autobiographical Xenophon hard at his elbow, has to leave home to serve his apprenticeship as a soldier before he can rule a kingdom. After all—putting aside for the moment Miss Austen's *Emma* and a few other magnificent exceptions—no one can learn much of anything at home. Going somewhere is the thing. And there—in all sorts of tempting variety—is your story. You cannot come

1

to grips with the world and be balked and disappointed and disciplined by it, and finally reach the Celestial City or become a Master in the art of living, or make your choice of life and return quietly to Abyssinia, without at least doing the grand tour and having a few adventures. It is in the certainty of the adventures that the lure of the theme lies, and later there is the passionate interest in individual human experience—if the writer's own, so much the better—which John Bunyan as well as Goethe knew he could count on. No one said to Goethe's Wilhelm Meister in the forthright style of Mr. Worldly Wiseman, "Hear me; I am older than thou: thou art like to meet with, in the way which thou goest, wearisomeness, painfulness, hunger, perils, nakedness, sword, lions, dragons, darkness, and, in a word, death and what not. These things are certainly true, having been confirmed by many testimonies."[1] No one ever spoke to Wilhelm as plainly as that. But Wilhelm too hears plenty of warning voices, and Worldly Wiseman appears to him in several guises. The apprentice formula is a good one. For we know this young man will go on just the same, and who will refuse to follow the fortunes of a pilgrim hero whose path is to be so delightfully checkered? There is the pleasing suspicion too that all this would scarcely be worth while if he were not to emerge triumphant, adjusted to life in terms of the author's own conclusions about it, but what of that? It may be a tame conclusion enough; Candide learned only that one must cultivate one's garden, but what a series of profound shocks that phlegmatic

Westphalian was exposed to first! There is plenty of time along the way for discussions on all sorts of subjects—repentance, criticism, beauty versus wit, the best of all possible worlds, the relative miseries of the married and the celibate, the proper way to present *Hamlet*. Then too, if experience is the thing, it must include all sorts of people and ways of living, and so we get the *Weltbild*, the background of a whole period sketched in as Goethe and Fielding could do it —almost deliberately in each case, if we may judge by Goethe's words about *Wilhelm Meister* and Fielding's apostrophe to Experience in one of his great mock-heroic introductions. And against this eighteenth-century background certain typical figures begin to stand out, not labeled as plainly as Evangelist, Christian's watchful companion, or Good Counsel who browbeats the pleasure-loving Iuventus of the morality play into repentance, so that he may be raised by Merciful Promises. But there are mentors like Eubulus and Thwackum and Square and Mr. Allworthy and Imlac the sage and the Abbé, who try to guide the young apprentice, whether he be of the gay, irresponsible type, inclined like Euphues and Tom Jones to sing with Lusty Iuventus:

> Why should not youth fulfill his own mind,
> As the course of nature doth him bind?
> In youth is pleasure!

or of the more serious-minded seekers like Christian and Rasselas; or, like Goethe's Wilhelm, a little of both. These figures, old and young, much modified

it is true, are alive in the novel today. The very
titles of such novels as *Youth's Encounter*[2] and *A
Candidate for Truth*[3] testify that Goethe's theme, not
new when he came to it, has gone on through the
variations of the nineteenth century and into the
twentieth, partly on its own literary merits, and
partly from the fresh impetus that *Wilhelm Meister*
gave it.

The idea that inspired the name and the story of
Goethe's hero, Wilhelm Meister—the idea that living
is an art which may be learned and that the young
person passes through the stages of an apprenticeship
in learning it, until at last he becomes a "Master"—
is one which has had a long and complex history in
the novels of two nations, Germany and England.
They are preëminently the novels of youth. The
adolescent hero of the typical "apprentice" novel sets
out on his way through the world, meets with reverses
usually due to his own temperament, falls in with
various guides and counsellors, makes many false
starts in choosing his friends, his wife, and his life
work, and finally adjusts himself in some way to the
demands of his time and environment by finding a
sphere of action in which he may work effectively.
This is the apprenticeship pattern in the barest
possible outline. Needless to say, the variations of it
are endless. The following study attempts to trace
only the main line of the development of this theme in
fiction, from its source in some German novels of the
late eighteenth century, notably Goethe's *Wilhelm
Meister*, through the changing fortunes that befell it
in the English novel of the Victorian period.

The hero of such novels, whether German or English, is heir to several literary types and traditions, and may be an ingenious and bewildering compound of all his inherited and acquired characteristics. Hence his progress through the world is seldom a simple affair. His kinship with the recalcitrant hero of the moral allegory makes it necessary for him to meet certain abstract vices and virtues, often but thinly disguised as human beings, who tempt or warn or advise him. The picaresque hero, like Françion, Gil Blas, or Tom Jones, is another near relative who lends him a taste for carefree, rambling adventure of a realistic and often amorous sort—a tendency to go on long journeys and see the world, meeting in the course of his travels a motley array of characters who insist upon telling the hero their life-histories and who represent all sides of the social structure of the time. The "universal man" of the Renaissance, bent on developing all his gifts to the utmost and welding them into an artistic whole, is another part of our hero's complicated family tree, and over all this variegated group of apprentice heroes there falls, though ever so palely, the shadow of a still more remote ancestor, Parsifal, "the brave man slowly wise" through experience, learning painfully from the blows the world deals him, but a dedicated spirit destined from the beginning to reach the goal of his quest.[4] For these heroes are, after all, the elect— a little feeble, impressionable, vacillating, perhaps, but endowed with exceptional powers of mind and spirit, though it takes them a long while to find it out.   They are more sensitive and more gifted than the average young man; their perceptions are sharper, their failures more heartbreaking, their struggles for adjustment to the world more desperate than those of their fellows, but their ultimate victory is assured.

All these elements, with the addition of some others such as Pietism, peculiar to eighteenth-century Germany, went to make up what the Germans called and still call the *Bildungsroman*, the novel of all-round development or self-culture, of which *Wilhelm Meister* is the archetype, and which flourishes today in countless modern German novels.   Because it came into England chiefly through the influence of *Wilhelm Meister*, we may call it, for convenience, the "apprentice" novel, but it never assumed in England the importance of a group classification or a type.   The German passion for categories, as opposed to the English preference for vagueness in these matters, has enabled the *Bildungsroman* to remain in Germany something distinct from the more definite *Erziehungsroman*, the pedagogic or education novel, like *Émile*, and Pestalozzi's *Lienhard und Gertrud*, which have a definite intent, partly practical and partly philosophical.   It is distinct also from the *Entwicklungsroman* which has a more general scope and does not presuppose the more or less conscious attempt on the part of the hero to integrate his powers, to cultivate himself by his experience, which is essential to the *Bildungsroman*.[5]

Although the so-called apprentice novel in England was derived mainly from the German *Bildungsroman* as represented by *Wilhelm Meister*, this book is not primarily a study of the influence of *Wilhelm Meister* on the English novel. Certainly the apprentice form is most clearly developed by those English writers who had either spent some time in Germany, or were familiar with German literature and thought, especially Goethe's, from their reading. But except when definite parallels with *Wilhelm Meister* present themselves, as in the case of Bulwer-Lytton, the question of Goethe's influence is far too complicated and vague to trace here. The line at which the direct effect of *Wilhelm Meister* ceases, and independent English variations on the theme begin, is blurred and uncertain. Two languages and literary traditions, and two national cultures during a complicated period of their history, have helped to make it so. Our main undertaking here is rather to trace the growth and modification of a set of literary ideas that passed from Germany to England at the end of the eighteenth and the beginning of the nineteenth centuries—a set of ideas that shows because of its very comprehensiveness the changes which man's outlook on the world was undergoing during one of the most changeful periods of the world's history.

In England, furthermore, the course of the apprentice theme in novel writing is modified by other factors than *Wilhelm Meister*. Its autobiographical tone is in part due to Rousseau and the "confession" literature that followed in his wake, and in part to *Werther*, which was itself affected by the *Nouvelle Héloise*. *Werther* undoubtedly had something to do with the world-weariness, the supersensitiveness, and the introspective tendency of many of the English apprentice heroes. At any rate, the creators of these heroes develop a skill in self-analysis and a power to expose its results in fiction that has grown steadily from the ardent effusiveness of the romantic confession to the relentless machinery of the new psychology. It is a far cry from Les Charmettes or Julie's garden at Clarens, from Werther and Charlotte at the window watching the storm clouds, to that formidable day in Dublin exposed to us by James Joyce. Between the two extends the long chain of British young men whose more or less intimate histories will occupy us here. Their *Sturm-und-Drang* periods and learning from life by a kind of trial-and-error method, are all in some degree confessional of their authors' own experience, from the sorrows of Carlyle's Wotton Reinfred up the ascending scale of subtlety in method to Meredith's Richard Feverel and Evan Harrington. The impulse to "tell it all," in one form or another, has become more compelling, apparently, as life has grown more complex and there has been more to tell. It may be objected that these later writers are simply ringing the changes on old subject matter, that man's soul and his own interest in it have been from the beginning, that there is no more to "tell" about it now than in the days of John Bunyan or Henry Fielding. But the machine age of nineteenth-century industrial England, the growth of large cities, and the progress in transportation have surely not been without their effect on the quality of the experiences that fiction heroes undergo. The possibility of sharp contrasts, the more sensitive social conscience, the "speeding-up" of life in general, have added to their self-revelations an intensity and variety, a sharpness of outline, and an immediacy of appeal that has gradually deepened if not widened the province of the novel. The confessional quality of these apprentice novels may also be connected with Byronism. Their heroes are often misunderstood and badly adjusted young men, unappreciated by their families, and full of loud complaints against the world. But the chief Byronic contribution to their make-up seems to be a more healthful one. A dash of Byronic pride and fine theatrical frenzy, something of his sense of the vanity and futility of all things in heaven and earth, is often just the thing that saves them. They are not, as a rule, conspicuous for their sense of proportion or their sense of humor, but an ironic defiance of circumstance sometimes takes the place of it and proves to be a safety valve. *Childe Harold* and *Manfred* have given them, also, a taste for roaming the wild waste places of the world. They take to the road with reassuring ease; even Carlyle's hero in *Sartor*, who did not hold with Byron, "quietly lifts his Pilgrim-staff . . . and begins a perambulation and circumambulation of the terraqueous Globe."[6] Bulwer's heroes are drawn to Italy, and Disraeli's gravitate toward the mysterious East, while Butler's Ernest Pontifex gets only as far as the alien world of the London slums, but finds it far enough. "Any road," as Teufelsdröckh, using the words of Schiller's *Tell*, discovers, ". . . will lead you to the end of the world."⁷ Our heroes have a romantic, Byronic preference for stormy landscapes; even Teufelsdröckh, who was no believer in view hunting, gazes, in the course of his wanderings, "upon a hundred and a hundred savage peaks."⁸ All this does distract them—however gloomily, and however much they may still be a prey to moral reflections— from the torments of their ill-starred love affairs, so that Byron not infrequently saves them from the typical Wertherian *dénouement*.

With only the Werther-Byron strains and their inheritance of self-analysis from Rousseau, however, they might well come to grief—*zu Grunde gehen* as the more sonorous and suggestive German phrase has it—more often than they do, were it not for the admixture of *Wilhelm Meister* and the Gospel of Work which Carlyle derived from it. Without these, in fact, they would not be apprentices at all and certainly not masters of the difficult art of living in their English setting. Through Carlyle the sane and corrective power of action was the moral lesson that *Wilhelm Meister* taught its English readers and imitators, and Goethe's eighteenth-century *Bildung*, or harmonious self-development motif, became subsidiary. Our heroes became too busy finding something to *do*, to envisage life very clearly as an artistic creative process. Thus the English apprentice heroes, often derived only indirectly from Goethe through Carlyle's translation of *Meister* and his interpretations of Goethe in general, pass through their black period of Wertherism and Byronism to the Carlylean conviction that they must find something to *do* in the world, and do it whole-heartedly.

It is in the variety of things that they find to do, that the interest of this hybrid, transplanted apprenticeship theme chiefly lies. These German-English heroes, looking about them at their English world swept by industrial confusion, political reform, religious doubt, and imperial expansion, solve their common adjustment problem in strange and manifold ways. They may finally find the right woman to marry, and then settle down to a wise and beneficent rule over their ancestral estates. They may choose a career of public service as members of Parliament, or become, after many false starts and choices, successful doctors, reformers, or writers. The conclusions are as diverse as the personalities and careers of the different authors themselves. But the fascination of this whole array of novels consists in the fact that, by their very nature, they show life and philosophies of life as something moving, changing, dynamic. These authors and their heroes grow into an expanding and deepening consciousness of human experience, an increased awareness of living. Even when the hero settles down to his vocation, we get no sense of smug completeness. None of them has solved the problem; the best thing about most of them is their sense of their own inadequacy in the face of it, and of man and his destiny as an eternal mystery. Two expressions of this idea that form an interesting and perhaps somewhat significant parallel may be found at the conclusion of Carlyle's *Sartor Resartus*, and in the

closing chapter of H. G. Wells's *Tono-Bungay*, both
of which are, in a sense, apprentice novels.   Carlyle
writes:

> So has it been from the beginning, so will it be to the end.   Genera-
> tion after generation takes to itself the Form of a Body; and forth-
> issuing from Cimmerian Night, on Heaven's mission *appears*.   What
> Force and Fire is in each he expends: one grinding in the mill of
> Industry; one hunter-like climbing the giddy Alpine heights of
> Science; one madly dashed in pieces on the rocks of Strife, in war with
> his fellow:—and then the Heaven-sent is recalled; his earthly vesture
> falls away, and soon even to Sense becomes a vanished Shadow.
> Thus, like some wild-flaming, wild-thundering train of Heaven's
> Artillery, does this mysterious Mankind thunder and flame, in long-
> drawn, quick-succeeding grandeur, through the unknown Deep.
> Thus, like a God-created, fire-breathing Spirit-host, we emerge from
> the Inane.   Earth's mountains are levelled and her seas filled up, in
> our passage: can the Earth, which is but dead and a vision, resist
> Spirits which have reality and are alive?   On the hardest adamant
> some footprint of us is stamped-in; the last Rear of the host will
> read traces of the earliest Van.   But whence?—O Heaven, whither?
> Sense knows not; faith knows not; only that it is through Mystery
> to Mystery, from God and to God.[9]

And Wells, on his epic voyage down the Thames in his
new destroyer, speaks in strangely echoing accents,
though he speaks for the modern world:

> . . . The Hills of Kent fall away on the right hand, and Essex on
> the left.   They fall away and vanish into blue haze, and the tall slow
> ships behind the tugs, scarce moving ships, and wallowing, sturdy
> tugs, are all wrought of wet gold as one goes frothing by.   They stand
> out, bound un strange missions of life and death, to the killing of men
> in unfamiliar lands.   And now behind us is blue mystery and the
> phantom flash of unseen lights, and presently even these are gone,
> and I and my destroyer tear out to the unknown across a great grey

space. We tear into the great spaces of the future and the turbines fall to talking in unfamiliar tongues. Out to the open we go, to windy freedom and trackless ways. Light after light goes down. England and the Kingdom, Britain and the Empire, the old prides and the old devotions, glide abeam, astern, sink down upon the horizon, pass—pass. The river passes—London passes,—England passes. . . . Through the confusion something drives, something that is at once human achievement and the most inhuman of all existing things. . . . I have figured it . . . by the symbol of my destroyer, stark and swift, irrelevant to most human interests. Sometimes I call this reality Science, sometimes I call it Truth. But it is something we draw by pain and effort out of the heart of life, that we disentangle and make clear. Other men serve it, I know, in art, in literature, in social invention, and see it in a thousand different figures under a hundred names. I see it always as austerity, as beauty. This thing we make clear is the heart of life. It is the one enduring thing. Men and nations, epochs and civilizations pass, each making its contribution. I do not know what it is, this something, except that it is supreme. It is a something, a quality, an element, one may find now in colors, now in forms, now in sounds, now in thoughts. It emerges from life with each year one lives and feels, and generation by generation and age by age, but the how and the why of it are all beyond the compass of my mind. . . .[10]

In the great pageant of progress toward uncertainty which these novels represent, the apprentice theme quite naturally loses itself toward the end of the century in a maze of doctrines, social, political, religious, for which fiction formed a convenient vehicle. Religious uncertainty and the growing strength of scientific inquiry have given rise to a rich harvest of novels of religious controversy, or of the waning of faith before the discoveries of the new age. Edmund Gosse's *Father and Son*, Butler's *Way of All Flesh*, and Mrs. Humphry Ward's *Robert Elsmere*, with their large following, form the material of a separate study that might be based, perhaps, on the break between the two generations; the old order and the new sense of impermanence, the father who clings to the established orthodoxy and the son who struggles with doubt and finally adapts himself to some compromise—practical social Christianity, a settlement house in the slums, or other modification of the Gospel of Work. The members of the younger generation in these books may well be called apprentices too, but they are so preoccupied with religious matters that their apprenticeships have become highly specialized, and it has seemed expedient to pass them by.

Many other bypaths from the main course of development have not been pursued. *David Copperfield, Great Expectations, Pendennis*—to name only a few examples—have been omitted. They are autobiographical and they deal, it is true, with young men who learn from experience and who do grow up in the course of the story, but more by accident than design. David and Pip and Arthur Pendennis are, like Tom Jones, sadder and wiser young men in the last chapter than in the first, but their essential nature has not been modified. They have not developed through any inner realization of their own powers and the resolve to make their experience function. They have stumbled good-naturedly over their obstacles, righted themselves, and determined not to make that particular mistake again, but they are not imaginative or reflective enough to see the wider implications of what has happened to them. Their history leads back rather more distinctly to the eighteenth-century picaresque tradition of Fielding and Smollett than to the German form of the *Bildungsroman*, whose trail in England, however vague and perilous and full of pitfalls, we have chosen to follow.

CHAPTER II

APPRENTICESHIPS BEFORE *WILHELM MEISTER*

The end of man is the highest and most harmonious development
of his powers to a complete and consistent whole.
—Wilhelm von Humboldt, *The Sphere and Duties of Government*, 1804.

THE Renaissance had anticipated the eighteenth century in seeing the possibilities in the
Prodigal Son story which leads easily into the apprenticeship theme. The hero of Lyly's *Euphues* is
out for experience, scorns the advice of the mentor
Eubulus, but finally retires chastened to a scholar's
life at Silexsedra. The "prodigal child" of Greene's
Groatsworth of Wit Bought with a Million of Repentance
proclaims his origin in the very title. But certain
modes of eighteenth-century thought made the theme
a particularly congenial and appropriate one to that
period.

Goethe was ten years old when Rasselas remarked
that "To him that lives well, every form of life is
good," and Imlac observes, "While you are making
the choice of life, you neglect to live." Over the door
of Nathalie's castle Wilhelm sees the words, *Gedenke
zu leben!* Wilhelm was perhaps less in need of the
reminder than Rasselas; the eighteenth century in
Germany, for all its speculation and philosophizing,
remembered to get the most out of life. But it was

16

an intensely self-conscious period, especially for the creative artist whose *Genie* was much in the limelight. Before the seventies and eighties, Goethe says,[1] the poet only was credited with *Genie*. But because it soon became a common word, people began to think it was a common thing and all sorts of foolish extravagances were committed in its name. Klopstock had been the typical *Dichtergenie* many years before.[2] But although Goethe in the early part of his career got solid pleasure from the contemplation and apostrophizing of his own *Genie*, it never seemed to interfere with his work.

This idea of the artist as a separate and unique personality, divinely gifted because he is the creator, the maker, and not to be bound by rules, has been traced to nearly every thinker, from Leibniz and his monads to Rousseau. Perhaps it goes still further back to the Renaissance conception of the superman, the *Homo Universale*, the *Kraftmensch*, softened by eighteenth-century Pietism, the influence of English humanitarian thought, and Rousseau, into the more intuitional type of genius, at odds with the world, but in the manner of Werther rather than of Götz von Berlichingen. The *Genie* knows no boundaries, it strives into the infinite, it is expressible only by such German words as have no English equivalents, it is *ahnungsvoll*, given to a kind of *Dämmerungsstimmung*. Winckelmann had directed attention to harmonious development and to classic art, and the Germans cherished the notion that they and the ancient Greeks were the real *Genie-Völker*,[3] intimately connected with nature.   Only nature can form the real artist, is the thought that runs through *Werther*.   So in the work of such representative eighteenth-century thinkers as Lessing, Herder, and Diderot, discussions of the *Genie* are bound up with art and nature.

Lessing has much to say about the differences between the painter and the poet, and about the unity of art and nature.   Goethe writes of the immense effect that Lessing's *Laokoon* had on him and other young writers in 1766.   General rules of criticism were to be drawn from concrete observation.   "All previous criticism was thrown away like a worn-out coat."[4]   Lessing had that eighteenth-century urge to grasp and execute things thoroughly, in their entirety.   He believed in the direct approach to reality through the senses, not only through the *Verstand*. This directness of attack is the privilege and task of the *Genie* if it is not handicapped by poor technique. Vague as the *Genie* may sound, there is nothing slovenly about him at his best.

Herder's interest in primitive folk poetry, which affected Goethe's early work, and the idea that there is no scholarship in poetry, that it is something not done by rule, is another aspect of the *Genie-Cultus*. Herder was a great admirer of Ossian and his *Urkraft* and Goethe for a time shared his enthusiasm.   The critical faculty, Herder finds, is of a lower order than the creative; even when the latter goes astray it is superior—the *Schöpfer*, the maker.   Let judgment and the average taste be still before it.[5]   Nature is herself the greatest artist; her masterpiece is man, who must also be creative. How shall he become so? Through education. This is not always easy, but experience is the great teacher. "Also auch unter fehlgeschlagenen Versuchen, durch Mühe und Arbeit, erzog die Natur den Menschen; das grosse Gesetz war vor ihr: 'Nur was der Mensch versucht und erprobt, *kann* er! Nur was er sich erwarb, *hat* er!' "[6] On this principle enunciated by Herder, sound, thorough, and *echt-deutsch*, *Meister* was written. But by that time Goethe's idea of the *Genie* had come a long way from *Werther*, who was influenced by Goethe's reading of Rousseau in 1772 and 1773. Meister is no artist in any technical sense, but he discusses art with the Italian marchese as a serious calling;[7] the artist, even the greatest *Genie*, says the Italian to Wilhelm, must make infinite demands on his own powers. In these words the marchese is expressing Goethe's own conviction. Although Goethe never underrated the daemonic element in the artist's make-up,[8] he knew that industry and thoroughness were important too. His father had attended to that.[9]

For Diderot too, as for so many of these eighteenth-century thinkers, the man of genius is nature's masterpiece. He appears but rarely. Poets are born, Diderot believes, not made, and the philosopher must often marvel at the poet's quick grasp of the ideas over which he himself labors slowly.[10] Schiller, too, was conscious of this difference in mind and temper between the intuitional type of creative genius and the slower, more analytical mind of the philosopher.[11]

Diderot's definition of *génie* in the *Encyclopédie* is: "L'étendue de l'esprit, la force de l'imagination, et l'activité de l'âme, voilà le génie."[12]   He goes on to develop this on much the same lines that Wordsworth follows in his preface to the *Lyrical Ballads*. The poet, says Diderot, is a little more highly sensitized than other men; "il se rappelle des idées avec un sentiment plus vif qu'il ne les a reçues, parcequ'à ces idées milles autres se lient, plus propre à faire naître le sentiment. . . . Il ne se borne pas à voir, il est ému."[13]   Laws and rules, he adds, only shackle the genius. Genius observes, as indeed the philosopher does also, but the genius commands a wider field.

In his translation of Diderot's *Essais sur la Peinture* Goethe makes the point in his introduction that Diderot was too much inclined to confound and amalgamate nature and art, although he sees them in opposition to one another. But the two writers have in common Diderot's *Abrégé du Code de la Nature*, which rings the changes on Goethe's idea (and Shaftesbury's) that men must follow with childlike trust the just and benevolent *Allmutter* who is nature. However, Goethe had a more unified and dynamic idea of nature than Diderot. He had won it by consciously holding out against French influence. In his autobiography he tells us that Voltaire and Diderot and the other Encyclopedists were objects of aversion and scorn to the young men of the *Sturm und Drang*, who found them too mechanical.[14]   But a rather different construction can be put on this if we read

Goethe's later comment in 1830 to Eckermann: "You have no idea of the significance which Voltaire and his great contemporaries had during my youth, and of how they ruled the whole world of moral thought. My biography does not make clear what a great influence these men exercised over my early life, and what it cost me to defend myself against them and establish my own genuine relationship to the world of nature."[15] Although his debt to all the great French thinkers was a large one, it would seem that Diderot was a stronger influence on Goethe than Voltaire. We may judge from Goethe's expressed admiration for Diderot's novels, especially *Jacques le Fataliste*, and his translation of some of Diderot's essays, and of *Le Neveu de Rameau* in 1805. Even in the *Sturm und Drang* period Goethe felt Diderot's greatness and considered him in many respects more German than French.[16]

The contribution of his own countrymen, especially Lessing and Herder, to the ideas of the time and to Goethe's thinking is expressed in much fuller detail and with great eloquence in his own *Dichtung und Wahrheit*,[17] and needs no repetition here. All that he owed to the great Frenchmen may also be traced in much greater detail than has been attempted here, through Goethe's own writings and conversations. His connection with English thought is harder to determine, but his chief link with it, so far as *Wilhelm Meister* is concerned, seems to have been Shaftesbury, who came to him mainly through Wieland. Wieland, the perfect product of the *Aufklärung*, was a well-

balanced mixture of French, classical, and English
influences.   Although he never liked *Meister* (whose
relationship to his own *Agathon* will be discussed
later) Goethe was always for him the greatest among
human beings.   He was enthusiastic when Goethe
came to Weimar, admired *Götz von Berlichingen*
though not unaware of its weaknesses, and realized
that his own verse was far inferior to Goethe's, and
said so, which has generally been considered the perfect tribute.   Goethe apologized handsomely to him
for the devastating satire he had leveled at him in
1773, more in a spirit of *Übermut* than of malice, and
always thereafter expressed the greatest admiration
for Wieland's character and achievement.   Wieland's
attainment of spiritual balance and harmony seem
especially to have appealed to Goethe in his younger
days and after Wieland's death he writes on this
point to Reinhard.[18]   Goethe's memorial essay on
Wieland[19] points out the connections of his genial
and gifted friend with England, and especially his
spiritual kinship with Shaftesbury.   This philosopher,
Goethe reminds us, lived in a time of confusion, when
many standards were threatened, and he dealt effectively with his world through *Frohsinn*.   Both he and
Wieland showed how much *Geist*, *Witz*, *und Humor*
could accomplish, and what Shaftesbury taught by a
skillful appeal to reason, Wieland found means to
express artistically in verse and prose.

Besides this mental congeniality with Shaftesbury
which Goethe noticed, Wieland no doubt had other
English affiliations.   He probably knew the work of

Hutcheson, Reid, Cumberland, Ferguson, and other English moral philosophers. These men, as well as Shaftesbury, strove for the harmonious development of the whole man, the same idea that is implicit in *Meister*, and that Winckelmann, Herder, von Humboldt, Schiller, and Fichte expressed in various forms. Other English writers, Sterne, Fielding, Richardson, also had their effect on Wieland. But he found Shaftesbury particularly congenial because he combined the healthy philosophy of the ancients and the *Aufklärung* spirit of Wieland's own time. His study of Shaftesbury was most intensive during the period about 1766 when he was writing *Agathon*, the book which most affected *Meister*. Shaftesbury's conception of the "Virtuoso," the man who makes living an art, who "lives out to the fullest extent his whole personality and develops all his faculties"[20] is traceable in both *Agathon* and *Meister*, and is also a relation of Schiller's *Schöne Seele*. Shaftesbury further anticipates Goethe's ideal for Wilhelm when he stresses the need for art, science, and learning in developing character, and finds the perfection of grace and comeliness in action among people of a liberal education.[21] A similar conclusion that the *Bürger* is restricted in his opportunities of full self-development, made Goethe move Wilhelm up into the circles of the nobility.

If all these German, French, and English ideas on art and nature, the Genius and the Virtuoso, had their share in shaping the *Bildungsroman* and Goethe's contribution to it, then we might conclude that its origin was a highly international affair. And yet it was essentially German after all. To continue these dangerous generalizations about periods as a whole, the age that produced *Wilhelm Meister* was interested in education, in teaching; Rousseau's *Émile*, Goethe's friend Basedow, Pestalozzi, Fichte, Jean Paul Richter, they were all concerned with it in one form or another. But *Erziehung* is something a little different from *Bildung*. The emphasis in the former is more on training than on organic development according to inner capacity. It is the Germans, Lessing, Herder, Schiller, and Goethe himself, who have stressed *Bildung* particularly. Hoping for the future of the human spirit, much attention in the eighteenth century was focused on the younger generation and its adjustment to the world through experience. Not only objective experience, but individual spiritual development was involved.[22] The two together form the framework of the *Bildungsroman*, of any *Roman* for that matter, we should say today. But the long adventure-chronicles that preceded this genre in Germany had dwelt on external happenings almost exclusively, and people were ready for the *Seelengeschichte* even if it minimized action for a while.

The *Bildungsroman*, then, was in no sense a German invention, but a German reshaping of eighteenth-century ideas current in Europe but well steeped in German atmosphere, and growing gradually into a fiction form particularly congenial to German taste. Nor was it a form original with Goethe in Germany, as we shall see later, but with Goethe this idea of *Bildung* took an especially comprehensive sweep. He did everything on a little larger scale than other people, and it was a period of large, all-inclusive systems to begin with.   We can see why *Wilhelm Meister* became no mere *Erziehungsroman* and why the *Bildung* element is a peculiarly German contribution. An earnest, conscientious introspection which we do not meet with in England or France, enters into Goethe's ideas of *Meisterschaft:* "Let everyone ask himself for what he is best fitted, that he may develop himself zealously for this, and by means of it. He may regard himself as an apprentice, then as a journeyman, and finally, but only with great caution, as a master."[23] *Bildung* occurs again and again throughout Goethe's autobiography.[24] He is early concerned with an active life and strong feeling as the means toward *Bildung,* and finds Spinoza to be the philosopher who can best further his efforts in this direction.

This somewhat cursory examination of its background and origins may indicate why the nearest foreign equivalents of the *Bildungsroman* are still a long way removed from it. *Rasselas* is built on a smaller framework, with the moral and reflective strain so dominating the adventure element that it is hardly comparable with the great sweep of *Tom Jones* or *Meister*. And there is no intensity of purpose or of urge toward *Bildung* in *Rasselas* or in *Tom Jones.* Tom is a careless youth for the most part, far more human, coarser, and more robust than Wilhelm, and far less noble. But they are both good-humored and impressionable, the chief difference being that Tom is

out to try his luck in the world, not to adjust himself
to it or to master it in any serious way.   The picaresque series of adventures, the satirical detachment,
the morally didactic strain, the more or less typical
characters, all these are found in both *Jones* and
Meister, but one could not say that in *Meister* they
were due to Goethe's admiration for Fielding more
than to his reading of Scarron, Fénelon, or Voltaire,
or that the traces of the sentimental school in *Meister*
were due to Rousseau's *Héloise* or the work of Richardson, Sterne, or Goldsmith.   That Goethe admired
the great English writers is perfectly true.[25]   He used
the novel very much as Fielding did, and made it
not only a broad picture of contemporary life but a
catchall for many kinds of ideas.   He evolved from
the English novelists a kind of theory about the novel
that justifies this; it is discussed in *Meister*, when
Wilhelm and Serlo speak of the differences between
the novel and the drama.[26]

The French novel also was not without its effect on
Wilhelm Meister, though only in relatively unimportant details.   Certain similarities between Scarron's
Roman Comique (1651) and Goethe's *Meister* have
been shown.[27]   Both have companies of wandering
players subsidized by the nobility, somewhat parallel
characters, and long life-stories of unimportant persons interlarded.   Certain of the adventures, like the
robbers' attack on the traveling players, are found in
both books, and both have didactic and aesthetic
discussions breaking up the action of the story.
But the theater and travel themes can also be

found in *The Vicar of Wakefield*, in Wieland's *Don Sylvio*, and in Moritz' *Anton Reiser*, and they were part of the stock in trade of many of the sentimental English novels of the late eighteenth century. It is not even certain, though probable, that Goethe read Scarron before he wrote *Meister*, since his only mention of him is in a letter to Schiller of April 20, 1805. At any rate, Scarron's is no *Bildungsroman*, and the resemblances are purely external ones. The idea of the *Bildung* theme is traceable in Voltaire's *Candide* only so far as it fits in with the scheme of the satire, and any comparison of the book with *Meister* would be far-fetched. Voltaire was not trying to depict real life; he was attacking an idea. Candide himself bears little relation to any of the English or German *Bildung* heroes. To be sure, Voltaire does make him a German, a Westphalian in fact! He has a kind of simplicity of spirit, a naïve curiosity about the world, that may faintly suggest his contemporary brethren. He is easily "enraptured," slow to see through the fallacious optimism of his mentor, Pangloss, because he "has never been educated to judge for himself." After a series of tremendous adventures he arrives at something like Wilhelm's *Tätigkeit* by deciding to be useful in a small and humble sphere in the country. But he is given to short and pithy observations that present to us the fruit of his experience, such as the famous conclusion that is worlds removed from Wilhelm's more discursive modes of thought and expression: "All that is very well," he says to the philosopher who is still talking

about the best of all possible worlds, "but let us cultivate our garden."

Although Goethe owed much to French thought,
Wieland was closer to the French mind than Goethe.
Meister was, to be sure, the decisive book that laid
down a pattern for the modern German novel, but
Wieland's *Agathon* (1766–67) had foreshadowed it to
a certain extent. His hero, like Goethe's, achieves
his development not through deeds but simply through
his own strong impulse toward self-culture, which
leads him finally to a kind of balance between the
demands of heart and head.

Agathon is in exile after a political upheaval in
Athens, through which he has been cast from a prominent public position. He is captured by some Cilician
pirates and finds in the boat Psyche, his early love,
who was brought up with him in Delphi and conse-
crated in Apollo's temple to the god's service. Both
were devoted to moral purity and perfection, and had
formed an idealistic friendship. Pithia, a jealous
priestess in love with Agathon, had parted them.
Agathon is taken to Smyrna, parted again from Psyche, and sold by some slave-hunters to Hippias, the
Sophist, who tries in vain to divert Agathon to his
own sensuous and materialistic way of living. He
introduces the youth to a beautiful courtesan named
Danaë, with whom he has a long and intense love
affair. Hippias, whose mistress Danaë has formerly
been, finally becomes jealous and exposes Danaë's
checkered past to Agathon, who promptly flees from
Smyrna and becomes prime minister at the court of a

despot, Dionysius of Sicily. He is by this time a sadder and a wiser young man. He has learned through many disappointments not to expect much of people or to count on their coöperation, not to compromise and give in to circumstances, but to keep steadfastly to one's course in spite of enforced deviations.[28] He is forced to leave the court through the machinations of a dishonest official and his wife, whose advances Agathon has rejected. He now moves on to Tarentum, to a Pythagorean named Archytas. This man is the ideal rationalist, Wieland's own ideal, and has reached complete harmony between the sensual and the spiritual. He discourses at great length upon the attainment of moral goodness through Reason, which is to bring about a kind of universal golden age. Agathon's early love, Psyche, has married a son of this Archytas, and we learn that she is Agathon's sister, which accounts for their spiritual affinity from the beginning. Agathon has also meanwhile found his father, who has been unknown to him. The father at his death leaves him a large fortune, so that our hero is assured of a leisurely future in which to follow in Archytas' footsteps. Danaë also reappears, chastened by her misfortunes into renouncing Agathon, who wishes to marry her. She has become a *Schöne Seele* though not of so exalted a variety as Goethe pictures in *Meister*. All of Agathon's experience has led him to a prudent conclusion which faintly—but very faintly—recalls Candide's "But we must cultivate our garden."[29]

This is the book that Lessing so much admired that

he devoted a whole paragraph to it in his *Hamburg-ische Dramaturgie*.[30]   He complains that no notice is taken of it in Germany, while in England so important a book would have made a great stir.   He at least must express his admiration for it.   It is "the first and only novel for the thinking mind."

In his own introduction to the book, Wieland makes clear his view of the *Bildung* theme, as it is to be used in his novel.   He is not out to present a picture of complete moral perfection, but has chosen advisedly the Horatian motto: *Quid virtus et quid sapientia possit, utile proposuit nobis exemplum.*   Wieland thus announces at once a more definite and limited intention than Goethe's in *Meister*.[31]   Goethe adds the motif of a vague striving, stresses the same necessity of learning through experience,[32] but says nothing about learning through the good example of others.   Wilhelm's salvation lies within himself; one of his greatest mistakes is in thinking that he can profit by the experience of other people.   But both Wilhelm and Agathon arrive at a kind of golden mean, a healthful balance of feeling with intellect.

Both heroes are ingenuous, earnest youths, imaginative, sensitive, with an infinite capacity for reflection, and both are irresistibly attractive to women.   They have a way of letting things happen to them.   Like Tom Jones they are impressionable, and they learn, or try to learn, from certain representative types of people, such as the man of the world, the skeptic, and the philosopher.   Neither can "forget himself and live unreflectively and resolutely for the homely duties of the present,"[33] and each speaks for the life-experience of his author. But there are enormous differences also. One critic has called *Agathon* "an object lesson in rationalistic philosophy" whereas *Meister* is not an object lesson in anything except life. In spite of its discursiveness it is less didactic than Wieland's book and more modern in spirit if not in form. For Goethe is interested primarily in the process of Wilhelm's self-development, not in the end, while Wieland is bringing all of Agathon's experience neatly around to a definite conclusion on which his eye has been firmly fixed all the time. The state of individual perfection is what Wieland stresses, rather than a rich and varied experience for its own sake. Wilhelm stores up this experience better than Agathon, who goes from one stage of development to another, leaving a long trail of outgrown ideas behind him. Wilhelm, however misguided, manages to make his living somehow a cumulative affair, an organic whole.

Another forerunner of Goethe's in the *Bildungsroman*, though in a totally different style from Wieland, was Karl Philipp Moritz, a Lutheran clergyman, and Goethe's friend of the *Italienische Reise*. This tormented spirit produced *Anton Reiser*,[34] a novel in four parts, published 1785–90. It has at least two lines of connection with *Meister:* first, through the subject matter itself as indicated by the hero's name;[35] secondly, through Goethe's friendship with the author. Goethe read Moritz's novel during the Italian journey of 1786–88, and there is a possibility that this reading and his friendship with Moritz may have somewhat influenced Goethe's revision of *Wilhelm Meister* in 1793.

Karl Philipp Moritz, 1757–93, has left nothing untold about his life up to his nineteenth year. *Anton Reiser* is relentlessly autobiographical up to that point, and then breaks off unfinished. A fifth book of the novel was written by Moritz's friend Klischnig, carrying on the biography after Moritz's death by a collection of letters. In 1782 Moritz made a journey to England, of which he has left an interesting record,[36] and was *Prorektor* at the *Köllnische Gymnasium* in Berlin. In disgust with the Berlin *Aufklärer* circles he went to Italy in 1786, where he became acquainted with Goethe in Rome. He stayed there until 1788, visiting Goethe for two months on his way back through Weimar. He became professor of archaeology at the Berlin Academy of Arts, and died in 1793 at the age of thirty-six.[37]

By the time Goethe met Moritz he was sure of his poetic calling and had given up the idea of being a painter or a naturalist. It was one of his periods of great productivity; *Egmont, Tasso, Faust, Wilhelm Meister*, the poetic version of *Iphigenie*, all were occupying him at this time. He was losing interest in the theater, and developing, as his letters show, the idea of a many-sided *Tätigkeit*, and *allgemeine Ausbildung*. This may be the reason why the early version of *Meister*, dealing with the hero's education merely for the theatrical calling, was replaced by the broader theme of education for and by life itself. After Moritz arrived in Rome, a letter of Goethe's to Frau von Stein urges her to read *Anton Reiser*, "a psychological novel by Moritz; it is significant to me in many respects."[38] Whether Goethe had just then read it himself for the first time, we do not know. Only three of the four parts were then published, but he could have read part one at least a year before. The book may have seemed significant to him as showing the effect of his *Werther* on a suffering young supersoul of sixteen, or we may understand his admiration for it as being a purely literary and aesthetic one, or we may conclude that the book gave him some ideas for his later revision of the *Wilhelm Meister*. Part four of *Anton Reiser* bears unmistakable traces of Goethe's influence, both in its introduction on how far a young person is really competent to choose his calling for himself and in the announcement that this fourth book will present the many kinds of self-deception into which a mistaken zeal for poetry and acting can lead the inexperienced. There is an echo of Goethe too in the conflict set forth between truth and reality, dream and illusion.[39] It seems probable that this influence was stronger than any Moritz may have had on *Meister*. Goethe was the mentor and guide in this relationship; Moritz, the younger and more impressionable of the two. The points of resemblance in their books seem much more likely to be due to certain literary ideas current at the time, and to Goethe's influence on Moritz rather than to Moritz's influence on Goethe. That Moritz was much in Goethe's mind there is no doubt, and there are plenty of letters in which Moritz and *Meister* are

mentioned together explicitly.   But the whole tone of
Goethe's letters at this time shows his absorption in
the *Bildung* idea, quite independently of any association with Moritz.   He takes the tone of the educator,
of one who understands the lines on which others
should develop.   *Bildung* is becoming the great
theme in his mind, and his scheme for the revision of
Wilhelm Meister is built upon this change of attitude
and outlook.   Moritz and his novel may have aided
in the change but cannot be held responsible for it.

Anton Reiser has been generally recognized as an
important source of the *Genie Periode* in which the
artistic temperament came into its own as fiction
material, and as one of the first German followers,
after Sophie la Roche's *Fraülein von Sternheim* (1771)
and Jung-Stilling's *Autobiography* (1777), of Rousseau's *Confessions* and perhaps of the *Sentimental
Journey*, unless *Werther* in 1774 can be considered as
preceding *Reiser* in that field.   It has many typical
traits of this sensitive spirit school as well as of the
Bildungsroman.   The boy Anton (*i.e.*, Moritz) is
brought up by constantly quarreling parents whose
poverty, neglect, and misunderstanding embitter his
childhood and give him what can be called only a
most virulent and persistent inferiority complex
which lasts all his life.[40]   His father was a Separatist
or Quietist, addicted to the mystic writings of Madame Guion, and the permanently religious cast that
these books gave to Anton's thought made him even
more introspective and *empfindsam*,[41] with a "craving
for the infinite."[42]   After his unhappy early childhood

he is apprenticed at the age of twelve to a hatmaker
in Braunschweig, and this is the scene of all his emotional, would-be religious experiences. His father
cannot afford to send him to school and is not even
willing to have him work his way through. The
prince gives him a grant, arrangements are made for
him to "eat free" at various family tables, and he
goes to Hannover to school for five years. Here he
wins some interest and approval from the masters by
his zeal for Latin and his verse writing, but his companions persecute him and he comes to hate the city
with its four towers. Troupes of traveling players
and his own omnivorous reading arouse his interest
in the theater. He has a natural *Wanderlust*, so
he takes to the road, bound for Weimar and the Eck-
hoff company where he hopes to be engaged as an
actor. It is also in his mind to see the great author of
Werthers Leiden and to become a humble servant in his
household. But "Theater and travel had gradually
become the two ruling forces in his imagination"[43]
and these are two of the closest links of the book with
Wilhelm Meister. The author explains how general
this theater craze was among young people in the
seventies, because acting had reached its highest level
in Germany "and it was not surprising that the idea
of following such a glittering career as the theatrical
one should have struck sparks in the imagination of
many young people. . . . And for this [acting] one
did not need to have studied three years at a university."[44] After many rebuffs from managers and a
series of mischances and hardships on the road, even

the much-enduring Anton loses hope of becoming an actor, and stops at Erfurt where, as a last resort, he goes on with his university studies. He tries to write but cannot quite bring anything to completion. Finally he follows his old hankering for the theater, journeys on foot to Leipzig in search of a company which will surely give him work. He arrives at Leipzig to find the company scattered, and at this critical moment the book ends.

The most irritating thing about Anton is his complete self-absorption, his development of the *Kultus des Persönlichen* to an extreme degree. All sorts of large abstract ideas—God, world, life, death, *Dasein und Nichtsein*[45]—occupy his mind, and above all the burning question of "the whence and whither of his pilgrimage through life, which was made so hard for him without his knowing why."[46] It might fairly be objected that he made it hard for himself by a total lack of common sense, a great deal of false pride, and a certain spiritual hypocrisy, very subtly and yet frankly analyzed by the author, which made Anton always "aim to please" and draw attention to himself[47] in spite of an abnormal shyness. In fact, when we remember that this is the author's own story, these revelations become excruciating. Anton's revelings in the "joy of grief" (*Wonne der Thränen*), his self-pity, would be unbearable except for the fearful honesty and psychological skill with which they are set forth. Anton's fatal craving for the dramatically satisfying scene in which he shall find full self-expression is fostered early by his careful attention to the sermons he listens to only in order to invent lurid declamations of his own, while everyone believes him to be deeply and genuinely religious. This egotism is transferred later from religion to art; he does not really care about the thing he is writing or declaiming; "he was more interested in creating scenes from life *within himself* than in externalizing them. He wanted to keep for himself everything of which Art demands the sacrifice."[48] His vague, generalized enthusiasms and passions, his lack of power to grasp the objective and definite, thwarted the real creative ability which he did possess. His great difference from Wilhelm lies here. They were both sensitive, well-disposed young people, all but useless for real life, imaginative, purposeless, lacking in energy, easily led. But Wilhelm is unmistakably destined to "come out all right," while we cannot believe that anything but a dark destruction awaits the ill-fated Anton.

For no one need imagine that the story of this youth, vapid and foolish though it may sound in outline, is anything but heartrending. The effect of it in its own day, and on Goethe, was probably due in large measure to the cult of *Empfindsamkeit,* and to the fact that Anton's literary enthusiasms—Shakespeare, Homer, Young, Lessing, Klinger, *Werther, Tom Jones*—were close to the experience of many of his readers. Moritz boldly labeled the book "a psychological novel," and the effect of it today—if one can endure it at all—is powerful because of the uncanny skill and intensity with which states of mental anguish and despair are pictured, changes of mood brought about by changes of scene or association or reading. The repetition in Anton's mind of certain phrases that he associates with his worst moments of humiliation, the state of actual physical wretchedness due to cold and hunger, the immense force of small, accidental, outward things to bring about his most harrowing disappointments—all these are conveyed to us with an intensity far surpassing anything in *Wilhelm Meister*. Moritz had nothing to learn from Goethe in this field. To be sure, Goethe could never have let such an abjectly neurotic hero escape him; even *Werther* is sane and healthy and normal compared to the unfortunate Anton. Certainly Moritz's effects pall when the agony is piled too high. This may be a veracious narrative of his own career, but we are jaded with too many soul-crises. We scent from afar that any new enterprise of Anton's, undertaken in his usual heartbreaking spirit of golden hopefulness, can only lead to yet another disaster, and we cry out to be spared. To add to the general torture, we are not permitted to see this thwarted and unhappy young man reach any conclusion, if indeed Moritz ever intended him to do so. The book breaks off unfinished, as though' from sheer exhaustion, in Anton's nineteenth year.

The theater and travel themes, the idea of a life-pilgrimage, the *Irrwege* or false starts because of the hero's mistaken idea of his own capacities, the glorification of the artist spirit, the autobiographical element—all these point forward to *Wilhelm Meister*. But were they not a sort of current literary formula made of ideas and philosophies peculiar to the time, rather than a definite influence of one book or one man upon the other? Both books have a didactic and moralizing strain, Moritz's taking the form of a definite pedagogical intention to show educators how *not* to treat a sensitive boy. One of Goethe's utterances about *Meister* is very closely paralleled by Moritz's introduction to Part II (written *before* he knew Goethe):

He who looks attentively at his own past often thinks at first that he sees only a lack of purpose, torn threads, confusion, darkness . . . but the more he looks at it the more the darkness disappears, the purposelessness is gradually done away with, the torn threads knit themselves up again, the confusion clears, and the discord gives way imperceptibly to harmony.[49]

But in spite of these many obvious resemblances it seems as though Goethe scholars had been over-ready to construct from the many tempting masses of primary material their plausible but perilous theories in the fascinating realm of *Entstehungsgeschichte*.[50]

These predecessors of *Wilhelm Meister*, then, are not noteworthy in this connection for their resemblance to Goethe's great novel in general structure, or for any "influence" with which the reading of them may have slightly colored Goethe's mind. Their chief value lies rather in the evidence they furnish that certain ways of thinking about the form and purpose of the novel were prevalent in the eighteenth century before and during Goethe's time, not only in Germany but in France and England as well. Schlegel called *Wilhelm Meister* one of the three great

"signs of the times."   The other two were the French
Revolution and the Fichtean philosophy.   The full
complexity of the background—historical, social,
philosophical—out of which and against which the
ample structure of *Wilhelm Meister* arose, has been
no more than suggested in this chapter.

The following chapter reviews much material already familiar to readers and students of Goethe.   The
repetition may be justified, perhaps, in so far as the
curious story of Goethe's twenty years of intermittent
work on the book forms part of the history of the
apprentice novel in England.

CHAPTER III

THE ORIGINS AND COMPOSITION OF
WILHELM MEISTER

Or I will watch the ghost of Goethe move
Through its vast dream-world, where is still a place
For liberal human hope, and generous love,
And the slow-gathering wisdoms of the race—
And live his golden days, and feel his trust
That life is more than wind whirling the dust.
—Arthur Davison Ficke, *Selected Poems*.

SOONER or later, it would seem, almost every writer has to do one autobiographical novel, and —in recent years—the sooner the better. Sometimes it is a poet's first venture into prose; he is lured by the not too complete disguise which the form offers for subjective material colored by his moods. If he is any kind of poet, or even a pretty good journalist, he can evoke a certain amount of atmosphere in painting the impressions and experiences of his childhood, whether it was spent in a drab city of the Middle West, an English public school, or the Five Towns. Almost always this is the best part of the book. After this plunge into fiction, the author frequently disappears and is no more seen. He has used up all his reserve the first time. Or else he reappears on some later day, never quite recapturing the charm of those childhood "emotions recollected in tranquility," but equipped with the staying-power consequent upon experience and one or two ideas. "I do like," a

41

friend said not long ago, "a few *ideas* in my novels."
The words had a plaintive sound.

Too much of the modern "stream-of-consciousness"
novel might do worse than cause a reaction toward
Wilhelm Meister, although nowadays people tend to
take their Goethe, like their all-Wagner programs,
from the rear of the hall, on account of the brasses.
Goethe had got his great prose confession off his mind
in *Werther* (1774) but he was not through with the
novel.   He did not need now to use it as a confessional,
but he wanted perhaps to show how the author of
Werther had become a poet.   He was more concerned
now with depicting this process and its various
stages than with writing another novel like *Werther*,
which was what the public expected—a book all of a
piece and sustained by a single lyric mood.   Goethe
once spoke of *Wilhelm Meister* half scornfully, as a
"Pseudo-Confession," but in a sense everything he
ever wrote was autobiography, and if it were not, we
have been made to believe so.   Whether or not the
connection was really closer in Goethe's case than with
most authors, his experience has been so obstinately
and carefully tied up with his work, that there is no
use in trying to disentangle them.   If Goethe, returning among us, should take it amiss, we should have to
remind him that it was his own fault.   *Dichtung und
Wahrheit, Tagebücher*, letters, conversations, and an
overpowering sense of the significance of his own development—any one of these could have ruined a
lesser man.   And in *Wilhelm Meister* the temptation
to *Goethe-Forscher* has been too strong.   Even

without their equipment the ordinary layman can
work out careful parallels between Goethe's experience and Wilhelm's, from childhood up to 1796, and
earn the reward, not so much of illumination on
Goethe's life, which has been exposed to a brilliant
glare these many years, as of some light on a wide
panorama of German life and thought through half
a century. *Meister* is something for those who want
ideas in their novels. Sometimes these ideas are an
organic part of the structure, as, for instance, the
idea of individual culture consciously carried out by
Wilhelm, which forms the whole backbone of the book.
The indications of it are not oblique and allusive
either. There it is, and a multitude of more or less
extraneous ideas firmly attached to it, all of which are
roundly enunciated and soundly discussed pro and
con. But because of this, the book gives us some
notion of what the intellectual eighteenth-century
German was thinking about. It may be possible a
hundred and fifty years hence for earnest students to
reconstruct from fiction the intellectual background
of pre-war young Englishmen or Americans, Wilhelm's
descendants, almost all of them. Mr. Wells and Mr.
Galsworthy will be a help, but the indirect and glancing method of Mrs. Woolf and Katherine Mansfield
will make hard going for somebody. *Wilhelm Meister*,
on the other hand, seems to have all his cards on the
table. Here are Goethe and the eighteenth century
at one blow. We can scarcely credit Schiller's constant urging to make the *Leitmotiv* and purpose of the
book plainer.[1]

But here is one danger. Perhaps the very plainness is deceptive. Perhaps it was no wonder that many of Goethe's readers looked in vain for a *Mittelpunkt*. We can see Wilhelm now as the contemporary of the Declaration of Independence and the *Wealth of Nations*, of *Nathan der Weise* and the first steam engine, of Blake's *Songs*, Boswell's *Johnson*, and the Reign of Terror, of Paine's *Age of Reason* and Wordsworth's "Evening Walk." Strange company for one rather aimless young man. With many of them he had little to do, but he was created straight out of their time. Their echoes and shadows and reflections were all around him. For different reasons from those of 1795 we may well seek a *Mittelpunkt* ourselves, and not find it. We may be misled into thinking, because Wilhelm is ingenuous and *gesprächig* that he is also simple. Probably the safe course is, as usual, the middle one. We need not take him entirely at his face value, nor entirely as a product of his highly complex time.

From 1777 to 1785, that is, during the first Weimar years and prior to the Italian Journey, Goethe was working on *Wilhelm Meisters Theatralische Sendung*, the first version of what later became (1791–96) *Wilhelm Meisters Lehrjahre*. This first version, of which Goethe himself kept no copy, was believed to be lost until Gustav Billeter of Zürich chanced, in 1910, to get hold of a copy that had been made from Goethe's manuscript by Frau Barbara Schulthess. She was a devoted admirer and friend of Goethe's as early as 1775, having met him through their mutual friend Lavater when Goethe visited Switzerland. Her *Tagebuch* of 1783–85, as well as a letter of Goethe's to his mother[2] indicates that the manuscript of the *Theatralische Sendung* was sent to her from Weimar at Goethe's request, and that she and her daughter made a copy before returning it. This was found in the house of one of her descendants and brought to Billeter's attention. He does full justice to the drama of the occasion in the introduction to his edition of the find.

It has been ably argued[3] that plans for the *Theatralische Sendung* and materials for it, were in Goethe's mind before 1777—perhaps as early as 1773 in Frankfurt. The *Puppenspiel* and other recollections of his childhood, the love motif (possibly with Lili Schönemann in mind), his illness on the return from Leipzig, and later his activity in the theater—all these may have been stored up for the novel. At any rate they appear there. In 1776 the idea of the title is anticipated in the poem *Hans Sachsens poetische Sendung*, and the names Mariane and Wilhelm appear in *Die Geschwister*, also of 1776. Wilhelm in this play, as in the later novel, is a merchant, because, according to Berendt's opinion, Goethe had learned in Weimar to notice practical business life and its problems. In the *Geschwister*, too, the hero Wilhelm is represented as having won his prosperity through learning self-restraint and industry. In 1779 Goethe adopted the son of a friend of his who had died, and he left the boy with Frau von Stein's children for a while. This may have directed his attention to education, and from

1783 on he practically adopted Fritz von Stein, to be brought up on principles similar to those of Rousseau. Perhaps these children had something to do with Wilhelm's son Felix, who shames Wilhelm by asking questions that reveal his father's ignorance. We can merely indicate these things as possible influences, without trying to trace the connections between ideas that are too rapidly and mysteriously made in any mind to permit of analysis. Attempts at it are good exercise, and the results of it can be read in any quantity if one has the leisure, but the conclusions are shaky. One trouble is that Goethe's experience was so rich and varied that some part of it can be made to furnish the source of almost any of his works.

Goethe certainly composed the *Theatralische Sendung* with mixed feelings, and since it spread over the decade between his twenty-seventh and thirty-seventh years, that is natural enough. They were years of strenuous activity at the little Weimar court, as mentor to the young Herzog Karl August, and as minister. But his *Tagebuch* shows fairly steady work on it through 1777. By October 31 he has made *einen Salto Mortale über drei fatale Kapitel.*[4] As early as 1778 he knew it was to be distinctly a *Theaterroman.*[5] In 1779 we hear nothing of it, but according to a *Tagebuch* entry of August 7 he is thinking back over "die Verworrenheit, Betriebsamkeit, Wissbegierde der Jugend, wie sie überall herumschweift um etwas befriedigendes zu finden." By June 5, 1780, he has reached "meine Lieblings-Situation im *Wilhelm Meister*" (probably where Wilhelm looks over his keepsakes from Mariane or else the moving scene in which Mignon is accepted as his child.) "Ich liess den ganzen Detail in mir entstehen und fing zuletzt . . . bitterlich zu weinen an."[6] In 1782 he is "eben über meinem geliebten dramatischen Ebenbilde."[7] On August 10 he is getting solid pleasure out of it. One of the early chapters "machte mir eine gute Stunde. Eigentlich bin ich zum Schriftsteller geboren." This first version might really be labeled "Frau von Stein—her book." He is definitely writing it for her. "Wenn ich schreibe, denke ich, es sei auch dir zur Freude." "Meine grösste Freude dabei ist es Dir vorzulesen und Deinen Beifall zu haben."[8] But by 1783, when Weimar was wearing on him, he has moments of discontent with it. The work on the last part goes slowly and the end is not accompanied by any feeling of triumph.[9] A plan for six more books to complete the *Theatralische Sendung* was sketched by Goethe December 8, 1785, but very little was done on it, and the plan itself is not preserved. The first six books bring Wilhelm to the point where he definitely resolves to become an actor by profession. Goethe made a little progress on the seventh book, but inspiration was lacking.

The Italian journey, begun in September, 1786, made a break in Goethe's whole idea of *Wilhelm Meister*. As shown above Goethe realized that he was through with the theater, and the final version of the book has accordingly, so many critics think, an ironic, detached tone on this topic that is lacking in the earlier form. In the *Theatralische Sendung*

Goethe had still believed in his own and Wilhelm's mission to regenerate German life through a national theater.   Goethe knew also by this time that he was not destined to be a painter, and that he did not wish to be a statesman primarily.   He did no work on *Wilhelm Meister* in Italy—too many other works occupied him—but he was still "recapitulating"[10] his life thus far, and the idea of making his hero learn by his mistakes, as he himself had done, was growing in strength.   A many-sided harmonious activity was coming to be Goethe's ideal, and formed eventually the outcome of Wilhelm's development.   Goethe, like Wilhelm, had made the transition from the middle class to the nobility, thanks to Weimar and Frau von Stein.   As we have seen, *Bildung* was especially prominent in Goethe's mind, even more than in his earlier days, accentuated perhaps by his association with Moritz.   From him and from all sorts of other sources, of which no *Entstehungsgeschichte* can take adequate account, Goethe was picking up material and ideas for Wilhelm.   One of the main things was the conviction that goes back to Herder and Lessing and Shaftesbury: Art and life are one, and the greatest of the arts is the art of living.

After the return from Italy, *Meister* languished. The connection with Frau von Stein was broken; Christiane Vulpius, according to many opinions, was not adequate to share Goethe's ideas about his literary work.   In 1791 he begins a little half-hearted work on *Meister*.   But it lacks the push of friendly personal encouragement.   This, in 1794, was supplied by

Schiller, and continued in his voluminous letters and through the warm personal friendship of the two men long after the completion of the *Lehrjahre* in June, 1796.

The story of the *Lehrjahre*, the final form in which Goethe cast his idea, runs very briefly as follows: Wilhelm, the son of a prosperous merchant, is in love with Mariane, an actress whom he has met through his enthusiasm for the theater. This enthusiasm has flourished in spite of his father's disapproval, since the early days of his childish passion for the puppet play, and his own later experiments as a playwright. His father's business and the small *Bürgerkreis* in which he moves, do not satisfy Wilhelm. He wants to be an actor and has planned to run away with Mariane. She, however, apparently deceives him for a more prosperous suitor, and he is in a state of complete collapse for a time. Efforts to interest himself in business are unsuccessful, although in a fit of reaction against his former ambition, he burns almost everything he has written. He is sent on a journey to collect business debts for his father, and falls in with a troupe of wandering players, among whom he meets Laertes, the Melinas, Philine and Friedrich, and Mignon and the old Harper. His old affection for the theater flames up afresh, and he hopes again to be a great actor and producer. After Wilhelm has sojourned with the troupe in the castle of a nobleman, Shakespeare becomes his guiding star. His practical friend Werner, who has stayed at home and attended to business, tries to persuade him to return. But Wilhelm is now consciously bent on developing himself to the utmost. He thinks he can only do this in the theater, because no *Bürger* has a chance for complete self-culture, and only on the stage can he express himself fully and appear on the same footing as the nobility. He takes to the legitimate stage and plays *Hamlet* and the prince in *Emilia Galotti* with success. But the company with which he has been acting breaks up. One of the actresses, dying, begs Wilhelm to take a parting message from her to the nobleman Lothario, her faithless lover. In his castle Wilhelm meets the select company of wise and beneficent men, a kind of secret society which reflects the eighteenth-century interest in Free masonry—the *Gesellschaft vom Turm*. These men have watched over Wilhelm's development from the beginning. They show him that earnest, purposeful activity for others is life. Now he wishes to give up his dilettantism; he has been seeking culture where for him there was none. He has been pursuing the art of acting and found the art of living. Accompanying this story is the group of women in whom Wilhelm is successively interested or who are interested in him as he goes his way—some true to life, some more or less symbolic of the stages he has reached on his pilgrimage. The mystic, romantic figures of Mignon and the Harper finally bring it about that Wilhelm, at the close of the book, is turned—like Goethe—toward Italy.

The characters that move through this story are to a great extent abstractions. That Goethe first thought of them as such, we may gather from notes that he made for the book. Werner, Wilhelm's boyhood friend and the son of his father's partner, is an able practical merchant, with an enthusiasm for bookkeeping by double-entry, and for solid middle-class prosperity. He is "shown up" later in contrast to Wilhelm as the typical Philistine. Mariane, Wilhelm's first love, is a sprightly and charming actress, thoroughly experienced in the ways of the world but capable of being touched by Wilhelm's ingenuous nature and his boyish passion for her. Among the players whom Wilhelm meets when he is sent on his journey is Laertes, the average, competent, easy-going actor, a woman-hater because of an unfortunate early love affair. Philine, the gay, frivolous, kindly but "catty" little actress in the troupe, one of the many feminine hearts lost to Wilhelm, is perhaps Goethe's most successful creation in the whole book. He was always good at a certain type of commonplace girl, of the earth earthy, but genuine, whole-hearted, carefree, generous to those she likes, thoroughly independent, and able to "beat her way" anywhere. Goethe's notes mark her as representing *die reine Sinnlichkeit* but she fortunately turned out to be far more complex and interesting than that. Melina and his wife also belong to the company. Wilhelm lends him money to set the troupe on its feet again, and gets from him later his first bitter taste of ingratitude. He is cool-headed and calculating, and in comparison with the visionary Wilhelm, even mercenary, or, by ordinary standards, merely making the best of the bad busi-

ness of being an actor.   His wife is serious, stiff, hypo-
critical, jealous, clever enough to make flattery and
a kind of specious sympathy conceal the limitations of
her intelligence.   She has—need we say it?—a weakness for Wilhelm.   Friedrich, the impulsive, lawless
blond youth who pursues Philine and finally marries
her, is evidently meant to show what lack of self-
control and the untrammeled freedom of a superficial
cleverness and buoyancy will do.   Mignon, the mysterious Italian child, is rescued by Wilhelm from a
cruel oppressor, and is thenceforth bound to him by
ties of the most passionate gratitude, and finally goes
with him as his child.   She has been much written
of as the key to the Great Secret of the whole book,
the personification of Goethe's hankering for Italy.
But there is something theatrical about her laconic
and secretive speech, her boy's clothing, her obviously
suppressed emotion and intensity, her epileptic seiz-
ures.   Although for her songs we must needs forgive
her much, she can no longer be as impressive as she
seemed in the eighteenth century.   A companion figure
for her is the old Harper, oppressed by a sense of secret
and inexpiable guilt, singing melancholy or inspiring
songs, as Wilhelm's mood demands, and, like Mignon,
permanently attached to him by gratitude for his
kindness.   The cloud of the dark mystery surrounding Mignon and the old man is finally lifted only when
each meets a violent end toward the close of the story
—Mignon from unrequited love for Wilhelm, and the
Harper from an attack of insanity brought on by
remorse, in which he cuts his throat.   It is then dis-

closed that Mignon was the offspring of the Harper's incestuous marriage with his sister Sperata, which may account for some of her vagaries; *Wahnsinn des Missverhältnisses* was Goethe's note opposite her name.

At the castle of the nobleman, where the players are taken to entertain a visiting prince, Wilhelm is to learn how the upper classes live. He has an excessive admiration for them which his experience here does not justify. The nobleman himself is a pretentious and pedantic dilettant, his wife a somewhat colorless lady, emotional enough to work up the inevitable passion for Wilhelm against her better judgment. There is a sprightly and beguiling little baroness, an upper-class counterpart of Philine, and her husband the baron, who writes poor plays and has a roving eye. The only valuable person Wilhelm meets is Jarno, the drily cynical and sharply critical man of the world, a widely traveled realist, who introduces Wilhelm to Shakespeare and points out to him the folly of wasting his time any longer in this shoddy society, and the necessity of useful activity of some kind. He is, it develops later, a member of the omniscient Secret Society that has supervised Wilhelm's development all along.

The company to which Wilhelm then attaches himself as a full-fledged professional actor, is directed by his friend Serlo, a shrewd, competent dramatic expert, not without gifts, but not an artist by temperament and with no very high standards. A lively sense of the practical and expedient takes the place

of them. We cannot blame him for his exasperation
with his sister Aurelie, an excellent actress who plays
Ophelia in the company's production of *Hamlet*.
(Wilhelm's enthusiastic passion for Shakespeare insti-
gates and carries this performance through.)   Aurelie
is characterized by Goethe as *hartnäckiges, selbstquäl-
endes Festhalten*, but the modern diagnosis of hysteria
would go far toward explaining her. She enjoys her
feeling of being forsaken by her lover Lothario, and
the luxury of being emotional about it to a sympathetic listener.   She cannot stop acting even off the
stage.   She, like all the others, is devoted to Wilhelm,
and tries to set him right, noticing and pitying his
idealistic lack of real insight into human nature.   Her
death sends him on a mission to the lover who deserted
her, well-laden with suitable reproaches.   But her
physician (also a member of the watchful society) has
given Wilhelm a manuscript, the story of the *Schöne
Seele*, which he reads first.

This extraordinary interpolation in the middle of
the novel is the autobiographical account of a sensitive woman's spiritual development, which culminates
in a mystic exaltation and a kind of moral sainthood
achieved through self-abnegation and spiritual discipline.   Goethe based this on the journals of his
friend Susanna Katherina von Klettenberg, who was a
cousin of his mother's, and whose religious experience
and attachment to the cult of the *Herrenhuter* had
interested him as he was recovering at home after his
Leipzig illness. The *Schöne Seele*, as Schmidt points
out,[11] was part of the terminology of the ancient

mystics and of pietistic German hymn poetry. Wieland, Shaftesbury, Herder, Schiller, all dealt with
the phrase and its implication of Platonic spiritual
beauty. Rousseau's *Belle Âme* is akin to it. Phyllis,
the *Schöne Seele*, is advised by her uncle, who, so
Schiller thought, had more of Goethe in him than any
other character in the book. He is known simply as
der Oheim, and warns her against a too rarefied, introspective, one-sided development, and advocates de-
cisiveness and action—advice which Wilhelm might
well take to heart.

Proceeding on his way to Lothario, the dead Aurelie's heartless lover, Wilhelm finds no one to reproach,
but, on the contrary, an ideally developed, active,
altruistic, intelligent, practical man of the world—
heroisch aktiv as Goethe's notes labeled him. He has
been to fight in America's war for independence, but
has returned—something like Candide—to his own
orchard, with the famous words, *Hier oder nirgends
ist Amerika.* By his example Wilhelm is converted
to a useful, practical life for others.

Therese represents, among his many women friends,
pure activity—the opposite of the *Schöne Seele*. She
is the feminine equivalent of Lothario, to whom she
is betrothed. She is the intelligent, thrifty, friendly,
wholesome housekeeper and administrator of her
country estate. Wilhelm feels that she will make the
perfect mother for his Mignon and for Felix, the little
boy whom he has found to be his son by Mariane, his
early love. He proposes marriage to her, and since
there are obstacles to her marriage with Lothario, she

consents. But then Wilhelm meets Nathalie, the
perfect woman at last in the long and extraordinary
procession of womanhood that has come his way.
She is the feminine embodiment of Goethe's *Humani-
tätsideal*, a kind of prose Iphigenie, with all the spiritual quality of the *Schöne Seele* (who was, by the way,
her aunt) but with none of her detachment from the
world of real life, or her morbid and introspective
traits. She may have been partly modeled on Frau
von Stein, although she does not appear in the first
version, which was under that lady's influence. She
proves to be Wilhelm's permanent and final inspiration in his quest of the art of living.

In May 1794, Goethe plans to send the first book of
the revised version to Herder, and the change in his
attitude toward it since the days of the *Sendung* is
apparent. It has now been rewritten and still
needs touching up, according to the author's opinion.[12]
The youthful freshness of his interest in good autobiographical material is gone. What author today,
German or English, could withstand the temptation
offered by a childhood in Frankfurt with all its possibilities of local color and *Kindheitsstimmung?* In the
Theatralische Sendung Goethe had not withstood it
either, and for that reason the *Sendung* must always
appeal to some readers more than the final form,
especially the first part. For here Goethe cut relentlessly when he came to rewrite, and Wilhelm,
grown to young manhood, recounts his early history
to Mariane at great length and with some detriment
to the progress of the story; his ladylove goes quietly

to sleep in the process.   This difference in the two versions is but one example, perhaps, of how ideas predominate in the novel.   It is not going to aim primarily at creating atmosphere; it is to be no confessional, and in its final form it does not even make the most of autobiographical material.   If it parallels Goethe's life closely, it does so in a highly objective fashion, and only because he had come to consider his life so typical of much human experience that it was the only possible form a novel *could* take.   In a conversation with someone in Jena, January, 1795, he recognizes the change himself.[13]   Not only his distance in spirit from the first version made the rewriting difficult.   The technical difficulties were many.

Later in his life after the Italian journey Goethe was in the habit of regarding some of his earlier works as entirely foreign to him.   He seems to have had a strange capacity for utter detachment from them, almost unnatural in any author.   The fifteen years that had elapsed since the beginning of *Meister* had brought about some such change of heart.   When we read the two versions we cannot but regret it.   The early spontaneity is gone from the *Lehrjahre*, and it is always a question whether the more measured tone, the polished prose, and an attempt at a clearer form quite balance the loss.   Those splendid early scenes in the *Ur-Meister* in which Wilhelm's grandmother persuades his cross-grained father to take an interest in the puppets she is dressing for the children, and Wilhelm watches the puppet show on Christmas eve and wonders how David will manage to kill Goliath, while his brothers and sisters, less impressionable, remain *alle vergakelt*—there is nothing half so vigorous, concrete, and convincing as these in all the later version.

We need not go into the differences between the two versions too minutely, to indicate the chief changes that Goethe made. The *Sendung* was, in the first place, no *Bildungsroman*. It is only in the second version that Wilhelm gets the idea of self-development. There is the initial difference, before mentioned, in the way Wilhelm's childhood is presented. In the *Ur-Meister* we learn to know the hero gradually, from childhood up, through a straight, third-person narrative of his life from the days of the puppet play onward. In the *Lehrjahre* it is given us as recapitulated by Wilhelm for Mariane, thereby losing much of its direct appeal. Wilhelm's father appears at the outset in the *Ur-Meister* and in the *Lehrjahre* not until the story is well under way. He is not an appealing character in either version, but the second one is truer to life. For in the *Ur-Meister* he is represented as the victim of a marriage made unhappy by a faithless and shrewish wife, as unlike Goethe's own genial mother as possible. The grandmother, who does not appear at all in the *Lehrjahre*, takes her place in the early story as the children's particular friend. The gradual development of Wilhelm's and Mariane's feeling for each other is given us in the old version, while in the later one it is already at its height when the book begins—another sacrifice to Goethe's policy of condensation, since four books of the *Lehrjahre* were made from six of the older form. Wilhelm's sister, Amalie, (cf. Goethe's own sister Cornelia) appears prominently in the *Ur-Meister*, and is only mentioned in the *Lehrjahre*.   Only in the final version does the *Geheimbund* that guides Wilhelm appear as an accompaniment to the *Bildung* theme, probably the result of an effort to make this leading idea clearer, as well as a reflection of Goethe's own interest in secret societies.   The Abbé and Barbara, the old attendant of Mariane, are not in the first version, and only in the *Lehrjahre* does Friedrich emerge with any distinctness; Philine is elaborated into a vivid and racy little adventuress.   The Gräfin is not definitely in love with Wilhelm in the early form, nor is the Harper made Mignon's father.   In the *Ur-Meister* Wilhelm's early experiments in verse drama are shown us by extracts, which his sister recites admiringly to her husband; in the *Lehrjahre* we have to take them for granted.   The fine figure of the unscrupulous lady impresario, Madame de Retti, was deleted from the final version, along with some minor persons who are not missed.

The style of the later form has been held up as Goethe's best prose in his classical, more restrained, later manner.   It recalls, a little, Henry James's touching up of his earlier work and other revisions of that sort, which have never seemed altogether fortunate.   The didactic element, the excursions into general discussion, the conversation that seems inconsistent with character—all these weaknesses creep into the later version with the less dramatic and direct narrative, giving the book a curious air of unreality, considering the vitality of its thought. The character of Wilhelm himself has not changed materially between the two versions. He is a little more vigorous, enthusiastic, and simple in the first version, but in both he is impressionable, *bildungsfähig*, kindly and helpful but rather colorless, more imaginative than practical, wavering and indecisive, an always hopeful and earnest chaser of all sorts of chimeras, and in the second version definitely determined on only one thing—to develop himself to the utmost. But he is at the mercy of the world and outward circumstances, and led to his goal at last more by the author's forcible management of him than by any perceptible growth of his mental fiber. We feel inclined to sympathize with Jarno, the man of the world, who tells him, "It is well and good that you are vexed and bitter. It would be still better if you would become really enraged."

We have in these days become so accustomed to the commonplace hero, the mediocre young man and his experiences, as the basis of fiction, that we may wonder why his contemporaries, on the whole, found Wilhelm rather feeble. At any rate, he proved to be too vague and reflective to be popular. What people liked was the romantic and mysterious element supplied by Mignon and the Harper, and the unknown impersonator of the ghost at the *Hamlet* performance. They considered the purpose of the book mysterious. But the chief public outcry was that the book was different from *Werther*.[14] The older generation was on the whole not enthusiastic in its reception. Goethe was probably thinking of Herder and Jacobi when he defended the so-called bad company that Meister keeps, as a necessary artistic contrast to the ideal he wished to present.[15] Wieland disliked the book but infinitely preferred its first form. Others deplored its loose structure, its immoralism and sophistry. Jean Paul Richter considered that it defied all the canons of the novel. Friedrich Schlegel, however, gave a long aesthetic appreciation of it in the *Athenaeum*. Humboldt also was enthusiastic, and the romanticists, Tieck the chief among them, were loud in its praise. A long trail accordingly leads from *Wilhelm Meister* through the German romantic novels of the nineteenth century.[16] Schiller and Körner, of course, were a sympathetic audience even before publication, although the sixth book on the *Schöne Seele* was something of a stumblingblock. Körner praised especially the hero's aspiration toward the infinite, and what sounds like that side of Goethe's thought most nearly related to Shaftesbury's, the same sort of balance of harmony with freedom that we have seen Goethe most admired in Wieland. There was little criticism on aesthetic grounds in Germany, but in England, De Quincey and Jeffrey were both hard on it in 1825. The immoral tendency of the book, as English eyes saw it at the time, was its great drawback. Wordsworth could endure no more than the few opening chapters, and Carlyle's Puritan spirit fulminated, "When I read of players and libidinous actresses, and their sorry pasteboard apparatus for beautifying and enlivening the 'moral world,' I render it into grammatical English with a feeling mild and charitable as that of a starving hyena."[17] Emerson, however, admired it, and Matthew Arnold spoke of the "large liberal view of human life in it."[18]

But no tracing of the process by which Goethe gathered and welded his material, no discussion of plot or characters, no review of criticisms contemporary or modern, can give any idea of the singular atmosphere created by this book, which is not concerned with creating atmosphere, and by its very indifference achieves that difficult thing. It is a faintly preposterous book, and still arresting, not entirely as a literary landmark either. Surely it is the most tranquil and detached of autobiographical novels ever written, if we like to call it that—not so much a "portrait of the artist as a young man" as the portrait of an era. It is an era in which we may feel at home because we recognize the tendency to escape from a post-war world of social and mental chaos into—what? We call it self-expression, individual freedom; Wilhelm and his little group of intelligentsia called it *Bildung*, all-around personal development. But if we feel at home it is with the remote feeling of having-been-here-before peculiar to dreams. These characters with no last names, no pasts and no futures—where do they come from? We do not know, nor care. They come, and say their say, and cease, and we question them no more than we should question figures in a dream. Impossible, except in Wilhelm's case and perhaps Philine's, to imagine their childhood, their homes, their table manners, their appearance. But like dream characters they are oddly substantial and inevitable while they last. We take them for granted, feeling, until we wake, that probably things have always been like this, only no one has mentioned it. The shifting scene against which they move is never described. A small provincial town where trade is good, a mountain pass, an inn, a castle, a clearing in the woods—it is all as generalized and conventionalized as a back-drop in the opera before modern scenery came in. In its unhurried, ample way the story trundles on, passionless, reflective, as impersonal as the Fifth Symphony. Not quite everyone is noble, but we long for some of Fielding's cheerful vulgarians, someone or something that is *actual;* we shall not mind if reality becomes uproarious and shrieks in our faces, if only she will give us just a little plank to set our feet on. No matter how exalted the view, we grow tired of swinging them over space in an effort to hit something. But for a while we enjoy the feeling of spaciousness. The book is as roomy and comfortable, and its objective quality as exhilarating as the Prelude to *Die Meistersinger* or Siegfried's Rhine Journey.

And Wilhelm, the Alice of this eighteenth-century German Wonderland—what are we to think of him? Involuntarily we picture him as the Young Goethe, but wearing the wide-brimmed soft felt hat of the Italian Journey and the Tischbein portrait, the classical ruins of his beloved Rome in the background. But he is not Goethe distinctly enough to move us much, except in his childhood, and even then only in the *Theatralische Sendung.* Is he only a sublimation of what Goethe felt to be the weaknesses of the poetic side of his own character, a "working off" of these in another confession like *Werther*? Or is he simply the result of Goethe's habit of looking back upon periods of his own life and trying, as we all do, to justify them? Was Goethe more interested in a philosophy of living in a complicated world than he was in the young man who has to work one out to become properly adjusted to this world? Or did he wish primarily to give a picture of this world? Justification for any or all of these theories can be found in the book and in Goethe's letters and conversations about it. That is why Wilhelm is not so simple as he looks at first sight, and why it is well to remember his contemporaries in literature, history, and science. But perhaps we shall conclude that none of these theories matters, and decide to take him as he appears, only a little more real than the dreamlike company in which he moves, a very slightly dated and Germanized statue of Every Young Person. Only in this light can we be very much stirred by him. His enthusiasms and his confidence, his indecision and his errors, his spongelike way of absorbing every influence to which he is exposed without profiting visibly thereby, his lack of humor—all these are vaguely touching only as youth is always touching, when it is not maddening. We do not feel much anxiety over his occasional distresses; we know all will yet be well, and compared to Anton Reiser's tribulations, and the perplexities of certain nineteenth-century English followers, Wilhelm's sorrows are pallid things. By the time Goethe had finished with Wilhelm, he had forgotten what it felt like to be thoroughly miserable. He had achieved a classical restraint, and preached self-denial, objectivity, mastery of circumstances. And so it is one of the little ironies of literature that as far as their message is concerned, the last three books of the *Lehrjahre* might as well never have been written. For Wilhelm's successors, beginning with the German romantics, have almost all been passionate self-portraits of their authors, intensely personal and subjective, living dangerously and hearing not at all the measured words, *Hier oder nirgends ist Amerika.*

Goethe made his own attempt at interpreting the book later, when he was so far away from it that he could look at it almost as though it had been written by somebody else, and now, in retrospect, his idea seems to be worked out clearly enough. He thinks in 1819 that its beginnings arose from

an obscure premonition of the great truth that men often wish to attempt things for which nature has not fitted them. . . . An inward misgiving warns them to desist, but they cannot see themselves clearly enough, and are driven on the wrong road toward the wrong goal without realizing how it has all come about. . . . If from time to time they have flashes of insight, these give rise to a feeling that borders on despair, and yet they let themselves be swept on again by the wave of circumstance, only half resisting. Many people waste in this way the best part of their lives, and fall at last into a strange state of melancholy. And yet it is possible that all their apparently misguided steps may lead to some inestimable good. The suggestion of this develops gradually throughout *Wilhelm Meister*, grows clearer and more explicit, and finally finds expression in plain words, "You remind me of Saul the son of Kish, who went out to seek his father's asses, and found a kingdom."[19]

Later (in 1825) Goethe placidly expresses to Ecker-mann his own state of half-mystification over the book, but makes a plea for a simple interpretation of its message, as who should say, "Try this if you must have one."

This book [he says] is one of the most incalculable of my works, to which I myself scarcely hold the key. People keep looking for its chief message, and that is a difficult search and not a well-advised one. I should think that a rich and complex scene passing before the reader's eyes, might be something in itself without a specific purpose. . . . But if people insist upon it, let them fix upon the words of Frederick when he says at the end of the book to the hero: "You remind me of Saul the son of Kish who went out to seek his father's asses, and found a kingdom." Because fundamentally the whole book seems to have no other message than to say that men, in spite of all their follies and confusions, may at last be guided by a higher power to some fortunate goal.[20]

Some vague feeling of the future of the novel might have been at work in those words of Goethe's, though he had finished the book years before he uttered them; the mistakes, the false starts, the wavering will that cannot make them good, even though the intelligence sees what they are, the dilettantism and waste, all these have formed the substance of more finely psychological novels than his, and how many times since his day! But these heroes have not had Wilhelm's cheerful serenity and calm; they have been more like Moritz's Anton Reiser, tormented spirits, bound for destruction. We have not Goethe's optimistic belief in that *unschätzbarem Guten*, that beneficent if mysterious guidance that shall somehow make all right in the end. If our heroes are stupid and confused,

good intentions and an eager spirit will not save them
—the Russians and the war and the advance of
science have taught our novelists too much.   But a
long procession of Wilhelm's kindred were set march-
ing by that *Vorgefühl* of Goethe's, distant relatives
some of them, but his kind after all.   They are all
strugglers, learners, often bewildered and mistaken,
with so many more ways in which to be so than were
ever open to Wilhelm, all the myriad ways that the
complicated nineteenth century offered.   But they
speak his language and he would understand them,
even though they end in our deepest modern *Trübsinn*,
and never find a kingdom.

CHAPTER IV

MEISTER AMONG SOME EARLY CRITICS AND ENGLISH
ROMANTICISTS

Liebes Kind, ich will Ihnen etwas vertrauen . . . Meine Sachen
können nicht populär werden; wer daran denkt und dafür strebt,
ist in einem Irrtum.

— Goethe to Eckermann.

BEFORE Carlyle's translation of 1824, *Wilhelm
Meister* seems to have had an obscure existence
in England, known only to some of the romantic
poets and to rare critics especially interested in Germany—William Taylor of Norwich, and Henry Crabb
Robinson. The *Monthly Review* for 1798 contained
a notice of Goethe's *Clavigo* and *Stella* and added, "He
has also composed a comic novel entitled *The Apprenticeship of a Master* which gives the history of a young
poet who attaches himself to a company of players,
and becomes by means of the experiments which he
thus makes on the public mind and human manners,
a superlative dramatic artist."[1]   This remarkable utterance is revised at some length a few months later,
in the December issue. *Meister* is heralded as "a
Romance by the author of *The Sorrows of Werther*,
involving some of the most interesting questions in
English literature." The reviewer explains that the
book is entirely different from *Werther* in its hero and
in its narrative style and that "Goethe has now

68

chosen to rival himself in another department. . . .
We have here little flow of sentiment and scarcely
any swell of passion. All is light, airy, and comic,
but not ludicrous. In the latter part indeed the
writer's imagination has taken a bolder scope but
without deep pathos. . . . The incidents are very
numerous and minute and without surprising, they
sufficiently engage. . . . His stage achievements
are related at length but in a tone that bears no relation to Scarron. Afterward, the purposes of the
dramatic Quixote are changed; and here the author
departs from the familiar life, assumes a somewhat
graver tone, and pours out the treasures of his fancy."[2]
Long extracts translated into English are then given
from the passages relating to Wilhelm's enthusiasm
for Shakespeare, and the *Hamlet* interpretation is
quoted, since the reviewer will "not fear to be tedious
where Shakespeare is the text and Goethe the com-
mentator. . . . For the rest, we ought to observe
that the style of the romance before us is classical,
and that the coloring is chaste. The writer discovers none of that attachment to the extravagant
and the monstrous, which has so extensively infected
the modern literature of his country."[3] If the writer
of this review was William Taylor, as may be supposed, it is interesting to note that he did not take
exception to the book on moral grounds, as Wordsworth and Coleridge and even Carlyle did later. In
1812 the *Monthly Review* notices Goethe's *Wahlverwandschaften* which it considers superior to *Meister*
but inferior to *Werther*. With Jeffrey (who regarded

Meister as "an object of wonder rather than of contempt"), and De Quincey, we are encroaching on the criticism that followed Carlyle's translation, which could make a chapter by itself. William Taylor's *Historic Survey of German Poetry* (1828–30) also belongs with this later period of criticism, but he gives *Meister* short shrift. Indeed, Taylor consistently underestimated Goethe in comparison with the other German writers whom he discussed. In his book he says: "Four volumes (of Goethe's *Collected Works*) are filled with a tedious planless novel entitled *Wilhelm Meister's Apprenticeship;* it describes the education of a young dramatist who has attached himself to a band of strolling players. The character of a young Italian girl named Mignon, excites some interest, and a song she introduces has been imitated by Lord Byron and has made the tour of Europe. Here it is: [He then gives his own very respectable translation.] In general however this novel is written in a prose far inferior to that of *Werther's Sufferings*, in clearness, elegance, picturesque beauty or pathetic stimulation."[4] If Taylor was the author of the earlier criticism, his later antagonism toward Carlyle might go far to explain this change of tone.

Crabb Robinson's voluminous records of his German experiences and reading cannot even be summarized here.[5] So far as *Meister* was concerned, he knew Mignon's song, *Kennst du das Land*, as early as 1799 before he went to Germany, since it is found copied in one of his as yet unedited "pocketbooks," for 1799–1800.[6] In Frankfurt during the first four months of 1801 at the recommendation of his friends, the Brentanos, he was reading all of Goethe he could lay his hands on, and he read *Wilhelm Meister* among the rest. Among some of his letters from Germany is one of May 11, 1801 which says that some of the critics of the new school

have even asserted that the three great *"Tendencies"* of the late century are, the french revolution, the Fichtean Philosophy and Wilhelm Meisters Lehrjahre . . . a Novel certainly of first rate excellence, which I now speculate introducing to the Knowledge of English Readers—It has afforded me more delight than any German Work—It abounds with profound Criticism on the Drama—It was reviewed bet 2 & 3 years since in the Mon: Rev: with great praise And recommend[d] by them for translation—they extracted an original & curious Critique on Hamlet—Göthe is undisputedly the greatest living Genius in Germany—Wieland & Schiller & Herder bow with submission to him—[7]

Carré thinks that Robinson read it chiefly to "conform to the good taste of his friends. The book did not exercise over him, as over Carlyle later on, the irresistible attraction of a new gospel. He reread *Wilhelm Meister* with much more profit in 1818."[8] This was by way of preparation before going to Germany again, and this time he feels differently about it: "The disquisitions on human life and character are too delicate psychologically and too indelicate morally to please the many who hunger and thirst after gross incident, or the few who require rigid propriety. And for a tale in which there is so much sentimental thinking and disquisition, the incidents are too romantic. But its great fault in the eye of a common English reader would be that it preaches too much."[9] Carlyle, to be sure, did not fear this fault, but then, as M. Carré points out, he was not "the common English reader"!

Another estimate of the book, which is interesting because of its French origin, is given by Robinson's friend, Madame de Staël, in her *De l'Allemagne*, the philosophical sections of which, as well as the publication of the book in London through Murray, she owed largely to Robinson's kind assistance. Being a novelist herself she presumably did not have to consult him about *Meister, ouvrage très-admiré en Allemagne, mais ailleurs peu connu.* It is, she thinks, full of ingenious and spiritual discussions, it represents the life of certain classes of people more common in Germany than elsewhere, but its main interest lies in our knowing Goethe's opinion on every subject. The story is nothing. The hero is *un tiers importun, qu'il a mis, on ne sait pourquoi, entre son lecteur et lui.* Mignon she finds an impressive and touching figure. The chief difficulty of the book consists in Goethe's Homeric impartiality, his classic calm and detachment (Coleridge complained of this in him and in *Wilhelm Meister* later) in painting situations that are "romanesques." *Le résultat*, she concludes, *n'en saurait être très-attachant.*[10]

From these early criticisms it seems fair to conclude that, considering the general ignorance of Goethe's works except *Werther* that prevailed in England before Carlyle, *Meister* fared pretty well at the hands of his English critics, so far as they noticed him at all.

Werther was a towering predecessor to compete with, and almost no one knew enough about Goethe's life and mental development to account for the radical change in his outlook and style between 1774 and 1796, which *Wilhelm Meister* represented.

Coleridge's German connections and indebtedness have been too fully discussed elsewhere[11] to make a recapitulation necessary here. As far as *Wilhelm Meister* is concerned, we know from the ubiquitous Crabb Robinson that Coleridge read it in the original German. An entry in Robinson's unpublished journals[12] for March 20, 1813, says that Robinson found him "in raptures over *Wilhelm Meister* though he thought the conclusion bad, and Mignon's death and the scenes in the castle 'a sort of Ratcliffe scenes unworthy the exquisite earlier parts.' He repeated *Kennst du das Land* with tears in his eyes and he praised the Song of the Harper which Walter Scott told Coleridge was the original of his . . . Ministrel in the *Lay*." Coleridge may have read *Meister* in German before Robinson's 1813 record of it, since he went to Germany with Wordsworth and his sister in 1798 and probably[13] learned to read German fluently enough at Ratzeburg and Göttingen, where he collected vast stores of material for a proposed life of Lessing. He may have read Carlyle's translation, since Carlyle himself writes to his brother, June 24, 1824, that he had sent Coleridge "a copy of *Meister* about which we had some friendly talk."[14] His friend's appreciation of *Meister* must have pleased Robinson as much as Coleridge's blindness about

Goethe grieved him at other times.   Coleridge "denied to Goethe principle, and granted him the merit of exquisite taste only.   It requires great modification and great qualification to render this just.   There is something of truth in such assertions but they are more false than true,"[15] Robinson writes earnestly. Of earlier protests we have records.   Robinson praised Goethe to Coleridge and Wordsworth at a dinner at Morgan's.   Coleridge "denied merit to *Torquato Tasso* and talked of the impossibility of being a good poet without being a good man, adducing at the same time the immoral tendency of Goethe's works.   To this I demurred."[16]   What years of patient championship of an unpopular cause are summed up in those last words!   Again Coleridge "conceded to Goethe universal talent but felt a want of moral life to be the defect of his poetry.   Schiller he spoke more kindly of."[17]   Coleridge puts himself on record in his own *Table Talk* for February 16, 1833, as admiring Goethe's ballads and lighter lyrics, and says, "I like the *Wilhelm Meister* the best of his prose works."[18] He finds Wordsworth and Goethe alike in "utter non-sympathy with the subjects of their poetry. . . . Schiller is a thousand times more *hearty* than Goethe."

The results of this reading of Goethe's novel seem to be three—so far as direct influence on Coleridge's work is concerned: (1) a translation of *Kennst du das Land*, probably dating 1799 and therefore attributable to his reading the book in German (even before the date that Robinson gives), which may be one

reason why the translation is so good compared to
many English versions of the poem; (2) "The Historie
and Gests of Maxilian," a fragment printed in Black-
woods for January, 1822, which Campbell calls a
"fantastic piece of mental autobiography"[19] and
which partly liquidated an advance of fifty pounds
for some promised lectures on Shakespeare; (3) *The
Confessions of an Enquiring Spirit*, written in 1824,
but not published till 1840. This was directly inspired by the sixth book of *Meister*, which deals with
the life story of the *Schöne Seele*.

The prologue to "Maxilian" (which might have
come nearest of all Coleridge's writings to challenging
comparison with *Meister* if it had been more than a
fragment) begins in something like Jean Paul Richter's
style of forced humor. Maxilian is "agnominated
Cosmencephalus and a *cousin-German* of Satyrane,
the idoloclast—a very true novel founded on Acts,
aptly divided and diversely digested into Fyttes,
Flights, Stations, (or landing-places) Floors and Stories—complete in . . . Numeris, more or less."[20]

Maxilian is a Dublin student. He is first shown us
in the act of upsetting an old applewoman's basket,
and to recompense her he gives her his purse. But
she curses and yells after him so loudly and horribly
that every one is sorry for the young man. "The
females regarded the youth with increasing sympathy
and in his well-formed countenance . . . and his
àthletic growth, they found an apology, and for the
moment a compensation, for the awkwardness of his
gait, and the more than most unfashionable cut of his

clothes."[21] Maxilian is unable to celebrate the holi-
day (Whitsunday) because he has given away all his
money to the old woman. He had planned to "indulge his genius" with claret and olives and to talk
to the German professor of languages, Mr. Hunsh-
man, and his beautiful daughter Lusatia. The professor "had taught him to smoke and was teaching
him theosophy." But now this entertainment is impossible and Maxilian betakes himself to the banks of
the Liffey to smoke off his disappointment. He
loves his meerschaum, "for a thing was dear to Maxilian not for what it was but for that which it represented or recalled to him."[22] He soliloquizes to the
effect that he was "born to mishap and misery." He
has always been unlucky. His bread has always
fallen on the buttered side. "My shames are all
immortal, for I never get older." He cannot pardon
his persecuting Nemesis since she still makes him a
"whipping stock of Destiny, the laughing stock of
Fortune."[23] And there the fragment ends. Although
any comparison of this with *Meister* would be too
far-fetched and forced, there are a few points of
chance similarity in the autobiographical strain, the
young man's ability to arouse feminine sympathy, his
reflective and imaginative nature, and the reverses
which he meets with. Brandl finds "Maxilian" a
kind of connecting link between the "Tombless Epitaph" and *Sartor*. "He gave symbolic expression to
an individual experience, and in Carlyle's hands this
became an expression of the times," (*Ein Typus
der Zeit.*)[24]

The Confessions of an Enquiring Spirit were edited
after Coleridge's death by Henry Nelson Coleridge,
who calls them a key to most of the Biblical criticism
scattered throughout Coleridge's writings. They are
"an attempt to place the study of the written Word
on its only sure foundation—a deep sense of God's
holiness and truth. . . ." They consist of five
"Letters" in the first of which Coleridge says, "I em-
ployed the compelled and most unwelcome leisure of
severe indisposition in reading *The Confessions of a
Fair Saint* in Mr. Carlyle's recent translation of the
Wilhelm Meister, which might, I think, have been
better rendered literally *The Confessions of a Beautiful
Soul*. This, acting in conjunction with the conclud-
ing sentences of your letter, threw my thoughts inward on my own religious experience, and gave the
immediate occasion to the following Confessions of
one who is neither fair nor saintly, but who—groaning
under a deep sense of infirmity and manifold imper-
fection—feels the want, the necessity, of religious support."[25] From this introduction we can see that
these letters are to be no spiritual autobiography in
the sense that the sixth book of *Meister* was. They
have to do, in Coleridge's most ornate prose, with the
proper attitude toward the Bible, with various questions of dogma, and so on. Their point of departure
is their only connection with Goethe.

So far as I know, neither Byron nor Shelley read
the German or the English *Wilhelm Meister*.[26] Shelley knew German, but Byron did not. Both read
Meister's predecessor in the *Bildungsroman*, *i.e.*, Wie-

land's *Agathon* which was first translated into English as early as 1773. We should not expect Shelley to like it, and he did not.[27] Byron's "Bride of Abydos" begins with the well-known parallel to Mignon's song: "Knowst thou the land where the cypress and myrtle" which he got from a translation of the song in *Meister*[28] (although he never acknowledged the debt) and not from Madame de Staël, as she accused him of doing.

Although *Meister* had little to do with anything that Wordsworth wrote, he might have read it previous to Thomas Carlyle's translation; he understood more German than Coleridge when they went to Germany, after the publication of the *Lyrical Ballads* in 1798. For all the painstaking attempts made[29] to draw parallels between Wordsworth's and Goethe's experience and outlook—their pantheism, growing self-restraint, and conservatism—it seems plain enough from Wordsworth's own utterances that the two writers had little or nothing in common other than the vague general background provided by "the trend of the times." Wordsworth would have smiled dourly at Coleridge's and Robinson's idea that his mind had "a German bent."[30] His visit in Goslar while Coleridge was at Göttingen, seems to have given him little understanding of the German people or their ideas[31] although he and Dorothy read German busily and he might then have read *Meister* in the original; but there is no mention of it. He speaks only of the intense cold and how he managed to keep warm at night by wearing a dogskin cap. What he

wrote at Goslar might just as well have been written
at home.   He was homesick for England, and wrote
those parts of the "Prelude" that describe skating on
Esthwaite, the boy listening to the owls by Winder-
mere, and nutting near Hawkshead.   He also wrote
"Matthew," "Two April Mornings," "The Fountain,"
"Ruth," "A Poet's Epitaph" and the five "Lucy"
poems.[32]   Nevertheless, Robinson, who knew both
the poets well and was their defender when each had
least honor in England, seems to have been struck
with their similarities to each other.   He writes to
Dorothy Wordsworth:

Like the great poet of Germany with whom he has so many high
powers in common, he has a strange love of riddles.   Goethe carries
further the practice of not giving collateral information. . . .
Goethe says he had never an affliction which he did not turn into a
poem.   Mr. Wordsworth has shown how common occurrences are
transmuted into poetry.   Midas is the type of the true poet.[33]

And to Wordsworth himself, in the year of Goethe's
death: "Thinking of old age and writing to you, I
am, by a natural association of ideas, reminded of
the great poet lately dead in Germany.   As one of
his great admirers I wished but for one quality in
addition to his marvellous powers—that he had as
uniformly directed those powers in behalf of the best
interests of mankind, as you have done.   Deeply
interested in your welfare . . .   I have no other
desire than that you may retain your powers as he
did his.   . . .   When Ludwig Tieck was in England
some eight years ago (he is incomparably the greatest

living poet in Germany) I read to him the two sonnets, *On Twilight* and *On Sir George Beaumont's Picture*. He exclaimed, '*Das ist ein englischer Goethe!*'"[34] We cannot but wonder what Wordsworth thought of that! He expressed himself about Goethe and *Meister* in no uncertain terms. He did not consider Goethe a great poet in "either of the classes of poets. . . . I consider him a very artificial writer, aiming to be universal and yet constantly exposing his individuality, which his character was not of a kind to dignify. He had not sufficiently clear moral perceptions to make him anything but an artificial writer."[35] "I have tried to read Goethe. I never could succeed. Mr. ——— refers me to his *Iphigenia* but I there recognize none of the dignified simplicity, none of the health and vigor which the heroes and heroines of antiquity possess in the writings of Homer. . . . Again, there is a profligacy, an inhuman sensuality in his works which is utterly revolting. I am not intimately acquainted with them generally. But I take up my ground on the first canto (!) of *William Meister*, and, as the attorney-general of human nature, I there indict him for wantonly outraging the sympathies of humanity. . . . Yet man is essentially a moral agent, and there is that immortal and unextinguishable yearning for something pure and spiritual which will plead against these political sensualists as long as man remains what he is."[36] To Emerson, Wordsworth expressed himself even more strongly: "He proceeded to abuse Goethe's *Wilhelm Meister* heartily. It was full of all manner of fornication. It was like the crossing of flies in the air. He had never gone further than the first part; so disgusted was he that he threw the book across the room. I deprecated this wrath and said what I could for the better parts of the book; and he courteously promised to look at it again."[37] But something tells us that the elderly poet did nothing of the sort.

CHAPTER V

But the man put his fingers in his ears and ran on crying, "Life! Life! Eternal life!" . . . The neighbors also came out to see him run . . .
—John Bunyan, *Pilgrim's Progress.*

"MY GRANDFATHER has been particularly picturesque these two days," wrote Jane Welsh to Thomas Carlyle on the 3d of October, 1826. "On coming downstairs on Sunday evening, I found him poring over *Wilhelm Meister!* 'A strange choice,' I observed by way of taking the first word with him, 'for Sunday reading.' But he answered me quite sharply, 'Not at all Miss; the Book is a very *good* Book: it is all about David and Goliath!'"[1] Jane Welsh was a clever girl, and no doubt enjoyed her little joke at the expense of the old gentleman at Templand. Her correspondent, who had finished translating this "good Book" two years before, would smile over it too—not *too* indulgently, since that would mean giving way to the besetting sin of spiritual pride, which worried him a good deal. But without wishing to be too paradoxical, we may ask ourselves if Jane's grandfather was not essentially right. For Carlyle, all his life long, David and Goliath—the powers of light and the powers of darkness—were arrayed against one another. *Wilhelm Meister* ap-

82

pealed to him because it made him feel that he and Goethe in their different ways—how different Carlyle never knew—were standing on the same side in the conflict. Although he did not mean what his mother meant by "religion," surely no writer ever was less in need than Carlyle of his mother's exhortation "Do make religion your great study, Tom; if you repent it, I will bear the blame forever."[2]

He came upon this "good Book" of Goethe's while he was still in his apprenticeship—personally, and with regard to German literature. Although, as his latest biographer points out,[3] "German had been in fashion in Edinburgh for thirty years," it was only through his interest in mineralogy that Carlyle came actually in contact with it. Madame de Staël's *Germany* had given him something to think about, though later on her neat summaries of the German philosophers would have made him contemptuous enough. He read this most French of books about Germany in 1817, when "schoolmastering" in Kirkcaldy and, with a motley collection of other reading, it "suspended my operations these ten days."[4] In 1819, when he had given up his Kirkcaldy post and was taking private pupils in Edinburgh, he was sorry to hear of the illustrious lady's death. He had heard that she was "very ugly and very immoral—yet had fine eyes and was very kind to the poor people of Coppet and the environs. But she is gone; and with all her faults she possessed the loftiest soul of any female of her time."[5] Surely a handsome tribute, considering the source!

In order to get at what Werner, the German geologist, had to say about rocks, Carlyle stopped his private teaching, as he wrote to Mitchell in the same letter, February 15, 1819, to absorb "a slight tincture of the German language which I am receiving from one Robert Jardine of Göttingen (or rather Applegarth, a farm in Dumfries) in return for an equally slight tincture of the French, which I communicate."[6] In March he reports to his brother, "I am able to read books now, with a dictionary. At present I am reading a stupid play of Kotzebue's—but tonight I am to have the history of Frederick the Great from Irving. I will make an *awfu' struggle* to read a good deal of it and of the Italian in summer—when at home."[7] Irving looked with no friendly eye upon Carlyle's German pursuits[8] but seems to have been liberal enough to help him get books, and to listen to his enthusiasms. In May he is reading Klopstock's *Messias*, and also Rousseau's *Confessions*, a "remarkable tome" but, he thinks, obscene and possibly mad. It makes "a virtuous Briton content with the dull sobriety of his native country."[9] He had not met Jane Welsh as yet, or he might have been more lenient with the great Frenchman; for how Jane did love his *Héloise!* But Carlyle was still languishing a little for Margaret Gordon, and reading Kant and Fichte and *Faust*.[10] He dealt with these later in characteristic ways. Meanwhile he was straining his limited German to review a German book on magnetism for Brewster's *Philosophical Journal*, and for Longman's "a portion of Schiller's *History*

of the Thirty Years War."[11]   He had also made for
himself the discovery that "not only suffering but
acting" was necessary for him,[12] a discovery which he
was later inclined to attribute solely to the influence
of Goethe.   In any case we may feel with his biographer, "Pity he had to go so far to learn so little!"[13]
But common sense has never been conspicuous in
prophets, and though the New Evangel of Goethe
had not yet burst upon him, he was well on his way
to the light of the German Gospel, via the Everlasting No and the Center of Indifference.   During the
years 1821 and 1822 he was, at any rate, suffering
the tortures of the damned, partly from dyspepsia,
partly because of being separated from Jane Welsh,
and perhaps uncertain of her, and chiefly, we cannot
doubt, because of his faith and his soul—those two
preoccupations that haunted the nineteenth century
forever after.   We cannot blame Carlyle for that;
there were a thousand other causes.   But allowing
for differences in pitch, due to the variations of individual voices, the echoes of Carlyle's miseries and
agonies of spirit and self-exhortations fill the century,
giving it much of its peculiarly somber and poignant
character.   These plangent echoes of his individual
anguish have taken many forms, from the somewhat
shoddy novels of George Lewes and J. A. Froude and
Geraldine Jewsbury, to *In Memoriam* and *Robert Elsmere*—innumerable progresses from doubt to faith or
from faith to doubt, as the case may be—innumerable
cryings-out of "Life! Life! Eternal Life!" in the manner of Christian, innumerable despairs over immor-

tality and progress and the poor and the condition
of England—all full of the singular pathos that must
accompany insistence upon certainties in a day when
only Uncertainty is king.

The same spiritual strenuousness and heart-searching in all essentials is present in Carlyle in the pre-
Meister days. This state of mind, somewhat more
wavering because it had not yet emerged into the full
swing of prophecy and was still agonizing among
doubts, was what Carlyle brought to his first reading
of *Meister* in 1821—along with an excellent training
in mathematics, and a miscellaneous reading background which included on the German side some of
Schiller, at least the *Faust* of Goethe, and the modern
German philosophers. But as Carré points out he
had no wide acquaintance with German literature or
the German people, and in fact never went to Germany till he was sixty years old. All things considered it is surprising that he got from *Meister* as
much as he did. "I had at length," he says in the
Reminiscences,[14] "after some repulsions, got into the
heart of *Wilhelm Meister*, and eagerly read it through;
my sally out, after finishing, along the vacant streets
of Edinburgh, a windless, Scotch-misty Saturday
night, is still vivid to me. 'Grand, surely, harmoniously built together, far seeing, wise and true. When,
for many years, or almost in my whole life before,
have I read such a book?'" When indeed? And
when has a more incongruous picture of literary relations been presented to us than this of Carlyle, the
lean, poverty-stricken, harassed Scotch Presbyterian,

peasant, and Puritan, stalking the dark streets in his Dumfries homespun, and musing on that most tranquilly pagan of novels, the product of a ripe, successful, cosmopolitan life of deliberate, prosperous self-culture, balanced serenely in a careful harmony of sense and spirit, according to the classical eighteenth-century ideal of Wieland and Shaftesbury? What has a Scotch mystic, aghast before the crumbling in his mind of the old theology, and panting for moral certitudes, to do with the cheerful, casual Wilhelm, who, in spite of all vicissitudes, does after all enjoy this life with a placid Goethian *Heiterkeit*, and with little concern for a Christianity that would darken his love affairs and pleasant wanderings in search of *Bildung?*

The connection between them is only partly explained for us by Carlyle himself. He told a friend much later (1875) that he had been "plunged into miserable doubts and speculations" on finding the creeds incredible, and was delivered by German writings, and in particular Goethe's *Wilhelm Meister.* "I remember taking a long walk one evening from my lodgings near the College to Coates Crescent—there were no houses there then—when the full meaning of it burst upon me."[15] In 1877 he told William Allingham, "Goethe taught me that the true things in Christianity survived and were eternally true; pointed out to me the real nature of life and things—not that he did this directly, but incidentally; and let me see it rather than told me. This gave me peace and great satisfaction."[16]

The shorthand report of the 1838 *Lectures on the History of Literature* suggests some such experience as Rousseau had on the road to Vincennes:

To explain them [the German writers] best, I can only think of the revelation, for I call it no other, that these men made to me. It was to me like the rising of a light in the darkness which lay around and threatened to swallow me up. I was then in the very midst of Wertherism—the blackness and darkness of death. There was one thing in particular which struck me in Goethe. It is in his *Wilhelm Meister*. . . . It was the thing all the world was in error in. No man has the right to ask for a *recipe* of happiness: he can do without happiness. There is something better than that. . . . Spiritual clearness is a far better thing than happiness. . . . This higher thing was once named "the Cross of Christ"—not a happy thing *that*, surely—"the Worship of Sorrow," and it appears in all the heroic sufferings, all the heroic acts of men. It would be absurd to say that the whole creed of German literature can be reduced to this one thing. But that was the commencement of it.[17]

All of which goes to show that the message which Carlyle seized upon and wrenched out of Goethe's novel, is not Goethe's message at all—or only a very Carlylean version of it. We have seen that he knew from his own experience as early as 1819 the old truism about "acting as well as suffering." The gospel of *Meister's Apprenticeship* therefore—a life of purposeful activity for others—could only have reinforced his own conviction. But the main theme running through the book, the ideal of deliberate, harmonious self-culture (*Bildung*), which Emerson recognized so clearly,[18] Carlyle seems to have missed, or rejected as unimportant after he had used it in *Sartor*. It was the very most valuable thing that

Goethe could have given Carlyle—a sense of proportion, tolerance, serenity, a large cosmopolitan view of
men and things, or at least a detached and smiling
recognition of the fact that *Im Praktischen ist doch
kein Mensch tolerant.*[19]   But Carlyle used the mildly
pantheistic sage of Weimar to bolster up a shaky
Presbyterian Christianity, and fastened upon the
inferior second part of *Meister*—the *Wanderjahre*—
of much later date (1828) than the *Lehrjahre* (1795)—
culling from it one of its least characteristic and most
unimportant points, the "worship of sorrow" idea
(*Heiligtum des Schmerzes*).   In all his later utterances
about *Meister* it is this part that he reverts to—not
the *Apprenticeship*. And perhaps for this reason,
among others, the apprenticeships of most of the nineteenth-century novel heroes consist of a passing
through some sort of baptism of fire, coming out puri-
fied and ennobled by sorrow—whether in the manner
of Bulwer's and Disraeli's young poets and politi-
cians, or of the hero in Hugh Walpole's *Fortitude*.
But Goethe stresses happiness and the ideal of social
living, fully as much as the "sorrow" motif in his
scheme for the education of boys in the *Wanderjahre*,
a scheme which Carlyle admired so much that he
advocated its being reprinted separately to call the
public's attention to Goethe as an educator,[20] forgetting that by far the greatest educational contribution Goethe had made was in the long, careful
process of self-education which was his whole life.
   This part of the *Wanderjahre*—the *pedagogische
Provinz*—is an odd mixture of the ideas of Fichte,

Rousseau, Pestalozzi, and Goethe himself—the training for work by work being the underlying principle.
Carlyle has much to say about "reverence" but not in
the sense of Goethe's "three reverences"—for what
is above us, below us (the earth) and around us—
for our fellows.   Neither does Goethe hold any brief
for the Christian religion *per se*.   It is one of three
kinds, all of which are good, and the philosophical
religion includes it.   Carlyle perhaps missed the significance of the fact that in the *Wanderjahre* the last
gallery of religious pictures, that of the Christian
religion in the narrower sense, was only opened to the
students once a year, and then only to those who were
about to depart.   *Objectivity* is the great aim of this
educational scheme, as it was in all Goethe's ideas of
education and the conduct of his own life.   The
Schöne Seele in the *Apprenticeship* (Book VI) is a
failure in so far as she does not achieve it; that is why
they keep the children away from her.

It has of course become a commonplace that Carlyle misinterpreted Goethe's *Entsagen* or at least made
it fit his own needs and purposes.   Goethe meant it
as "self-control," a temperate restraint that should
help to strike the just balance between sense and spirit.
Carlyle takes it as "renunciation," a crucifying of his
pet sin, Pride, by humility and rigorous Puritan self-
denial; "Love not pleasure, love God."   Something
of this is in the curious idea he had of *Faust*,
when he wrote the 1822 essay that was afterward
incorporated, with changes, in the 1828 essay on
Goethe's *Helena*.   Mephistopheles' great mistake,

he thinks, is in "allowing his mind to wander, even in the search of truth, till it doubted the existence of a Providence and the foundations of moral distinctions" and so Goethe properly punished his Devil for this "pardonable transgression"![21] He later revised his ideas about *Faust*, but the fundamental mistake about *Entsagen* remained.

It is in many ways idle to complain of these misinterpretations or reinterpretations of Goethe by Carlyle. One might as well advocate the making-over of the peculiar temperament that gave rise to them and that made Carlyle and his work just what they were, and not otherwise. To quote his words about his own vain speculations, "Whither does all this lead? Unfortunately almost nowhither." These discrepancies have been pointed out often enough before, and their significance perhaps most adequately estimated by M. Carré,[22] who shows that Carlyle was the best disciple Goethe could have had in England. No one who did not reassure the British reading public of 1820–30 about the safety of its soul, could have hoped to make Goethe "go down" with the English in this period. Carlyle emphasized for them as for himself, Goethe's great *moral lesson* as he saw it, and if he saw it with a slightly distorted vision, perhaps Carlyle's Goethe was better for England than no Goethe at all. It remained for George Lewes to show in his *Life of Goethe* in 1855, that the great German was better understood as an artist and scholar than as a preacher of "moral certitudes."

It was not until the period of the Everlasting No

(1822) was safely past, and two years after Carlyle's first reading of *Meister*, that he began the translation of it at the instigation of the "fat bookseller," Boyd, of Edinburgh. The record of his reactions to it as the work progresses, is an amusing one—characteristically violent and contradictory. He always agonized over his work, and in this case he had good reason. The *Life of Schiller* was still on the stocks, and he was tutoring the Bullers, who could not be neglected. Schiller made him even more appreciative of Goethe, though he had no use for their "jargon" about art and aesthetics, querying, absurdly enough, in his notebook (March, 1823), "Did Shakespeare know aught of the aesthetic? Did Homer?" But Goethe is great because he understands Carlyle. "What *should* I think of Goethe? His *Wilhelm Meister* instructed, delighted, moved and charmed me. The man seems to understand many of my own aberrations still mysterious to myself. He is wise and great."[23]

Perhaps because of *Meister* the idea of an autobiographical novel was simmering in his mind, and he thinks of proposing to Jane that they should collaborate in writing it:[24]

We were to write a most eminent novel in concert: it was to proceed by way of letters, I to take the gentleman, you the lady. The poor fellow was to be a very excellent character of course; a man in the middle ranks of life gifted with good talents and a fervid enthusiastic turn of mind, learned in all sciences, practised in many virtues, but tired out—at the time I took him up, with the impediments of a world by much too prosaic for him, entirely sick of struggling along the sordid bustle of existence, where he could glean so little enjoyment but found so much acute suffering. He had in fact met with no object worthy of all his admiration, the bloom of novelty was worn off, and no more substantial charm of solid usefulness had called on him to mingle in the business of life: he was very wretched and very ill-natured; had determined at last to bid adieu to the hollow and contemptible progeny of Adam as far as possible—to immure himself in rustic solitude with a family of simple unaffected but polished and religious people who (by some means) were bound in gratitude to cherish him affectionately, and who like him had bid farewell to the world. Here the Hypochondriac was to wander about for a time over the hill-country, to muse and meditate upon the aspects of Nature and his own soul, to meet with persons and incidents which should call upon him to deliver his views upon many points of science, literature and morals. At length he must grow tired of science, and Nature and simplicity just as he had of towns, sickening by degrees till his heart was full of bitterness and ennui, he speaks forth his sufferings—not in the puling Lake-style—but with a tongue of fire—sharp, sarcastic, apparently unfeeling, yet all the while betokening to the quick-sighted a man of lofty thoughts and generous affections smarting under the torment of its own overnobleness and ready to break in pieces by the force of its own energies. Already all seems over with him, he has hinted about suicide and rejected it scornfully—but it is evident he cannot long exist in this to him most blasted, waste and lonely world,—when *you*—that is the heroine— come stepping in before him, with your tricksy ways and fervency, your "becks and wreathed smiles" and all your native loveliness. Why should I talk? The man immediately turns crazy about you. . . . The earth again grows green beneath his feet, his soul recovers all its fiery energies. . . . For a while you laugh at him and torment him, but at length take pity on the poor fellow; and grow serious as he is. . . . But alas! Fate etc., obstacles, etc., etc.,—You are both broken-hearted and die; and the whole closes with a mort-cloth, and Mr. Trotter and a company of undertakers.

I had fairly begun this thing, written two first letters. . . . But I could not get along: I found that we should require to see one another and consult together every day. . . . I threw it all into the fire. Yet I am almost persuaded that we might accomplish such a thing.

And he did, to some extent, in *Wotton Reinfred* and
the second book of *Sartor*, but without Jane's collabo-
ration except in moral support. He fancied himself
a good deal in this "fiery, sarcastic" rôle, but this
sketch is closer to the *Werther* mood, with a dash of
Faust and Rousseau, than the didactic stories of *Wotton* or Teufelsdröckh were destined to be.

Once he had got launched upon the *Meister* translation, June 15, 1823, life was hard. "Ten pages a
day is my task. . . . I seldom get begun till six
at night. Some parts of *Meister* are very stupid, and
it is all very difficult to translate. But 'let us not despise the day of small things.'"[25] He encourages
Jane in her struggles with the Germans. "You must
make another effort upon *Götz:* it is hardest at the
first. This Goethe has as much in him as any ten
of them: he is not a mere bacchanalian rhymester
. . . but a man of true culture and universal genius,
not less distinguished for the extent of his knowledge
and the profoundness of his ideas and the variety of
his feelings than for the vivid and graceful energy,
the inventive and deeply meditative sagacity, the
skill to temper enthusiasm with judgment which he
shows in exhibiting them. Wordsworth and Byron!
They are as the Christian Ensign and Capt. Bobadil
before the Duke of Marlborough."[26] Which was hard
on poor Wordsworth, who despised the "bacchanalian
rhymester" most heartily. As for Byron, Carlyle
might have been astonished at Goethe's honest admiration for him.

"You make a right distinction about Goethe," he

assures Jane a little later, when she had been reading his idol after a strong dose of Schiller. "He is a great genius and *does not make you cry*. His feelings are various as the hues of Earth and Sky, but his intellect is the Sun which illuminates and overrules them all. He does not yield himself to his emotions, but uses them rather as things for his judgment to scrutinize and apply to purpose. I think Goethe the only living model of a great writer. The Germans say there have been *three* geniuses in the world since it began—Homer, Shakespeare, and Goethe! This of course is shooting on the wing: but after all abatements, their countryman is a glorious fellow. It is one of my finest day-dreams to see him ere I die."[27]

Exasperation, however, mounts as time wears on.

Meanwhile I go on with Goethe's *Wilhelm Meister*, a book which I love not, which I am sure will never sell, but which I am determined to print and finish. There are touches of the very highest, most ethereal genius in it; but diluted with floods of insipidity, which even *I* would not have written for the world. I sit down to it every night at six, with the ferocity of a hyena. . . . Some of the poetry is very bad, some of it rather good. The following is mediocre—the worst kind.[28]

He then quotes his version of *Wer nie sein Brod mit Thränen ass*, which is indeed "mediocre." But poetry was never his forte, and he knew it; which does not tell us, however, why he should have been patronizing about Goethe's. To James Johnstone he writes:

There is poetry in the book, and prose, prose forever. When I read of players and libidinous actresses and their sorry pasteboard apparatus for beautifying and enlivening the "moral world" I render it into grammatical English—with a feeling mild and charitable as that of a starving hyena. The book is to be printed in winter or spring. No mortal will ever buy a copy of it. *N'importe!* . . . Goethe is the greatest genius that has lived for a century, and the greatest ass that has lived for three. I could sometimes fall down and worship him; at other times I could kick him out of the room.[29]

Jane is disposed to regard the translating as hack work, not befitting her intended: "I wish you were through with *Meister*. I would rather have you working the precious mines of your own heart and soul, than drudging for Goethe, though a princely master."[30]

Your letter [says Carlyle some months later] found me bending under the weight of *Meister* like an ass between two dust-panniers; . . . I fear, however, you will never read it. The romance, you see, is still dull as ever. There is not, properly speaking, the smallest particle of historical *interest* in it, except what is connected with Mignon, and her you cannot see fully till near the very end. Meister himself is perhaps one of the greatest 'ganaches' (milksops) that ever was created by quill or ink. I am going to write a fierce preface, disclaiming all concern with the literary or the moral merit of the work; grounding my claims to recompense or toleration on the fact that I have accurately copied a striking portrait of Goethe's mind, the strangest and in many points the greatest now extant. What a work! Bushels of dust and straw and feathers, with here and there a diamond of the purest water.[31]

But Jane enjoys reading it and, needless to say, he did not write the "fierce preface." "When shall I have more of *Meister?* I do not know yet what to think of it. I cannot separate your interest in it from Goethe's, or my own opinion of it from what is

likely to be the opinion of the public. I wish, however, that it had not been so—*queer.*"³² "You will
not like this second volume a jot better than you
did the first," he warns her. "I only tell you to pause
in your judgment till you have seen it all. There are
two leaves wanting at the end of Vol. I, but they
contain nothing save a *kiss* from the Countess to
Wilhelm, who, milksop as he was, deserved no treat
of that kind. It will keep me all April as busy as a
turnspit."³³

Whether he suppresses this passage of the book as
too indelicate for Jane's eyes, we shall never know.
The episode in the original is harmlessly sentimental
enough. But Jane had her suspicions. After de-
claring that "the money it will bring you in" is all that
reconciles her to this distasteful sight of "a mettled
racer set to draw in a dust-cart" (how Carlyle must
have loved that!) she takes up the matter of that kiss.

The unaccountable propensity to kissing which runs through all
your dramatis personae perplexes me sadly. I wish people may not
think *you* a terrible fellow for having any hand in such work. By
the way, what is the reason that you kept back the Countess' kiss?
The prelude to it gives promise of something extremely pretty. I
wish I had all of it. That poor little child with St. Vitus' dance! I
cannot possibly imagine what is to become of her. So far she seems
to play much the same part that the text does in the generality of
sermons: is perpetually recurring without having any visible connection with what goes before or after. How long will it be, for God's
sake, before she is done learning geography? Do tell me her end,
will you? I have a notion she is to die of eating sticks.³⁴

Carlyle playfully reproves her for this levity, and
goes on,

Seriously you are right about this book, it is worth next to nothing as a novel; except Mignon, who *will* touch you yet perhaps, there is no person in it one has any care about. But for its wisdom, its eloquence, its wit; and even for its folly and its dulness, it interests me much; far more the second time than it did the first. I have not got as many ideas from any book for six years. You will like Goethe better ten years hence than you do at present. It is pity the man were not known among us. The English have begun to speak about him of late years but no light has yet been thrown upon him, "no light but only darkness visible." The syllables "Goethe" excite an idea as vague and monstrous as the word "Gorgon" or "Chimera."[35]

He does not expect his brother Alexander to like it.

Did you get *Meister* and how do you *dis*like it? For really it is a most mixed performance, and though intellectually good, much of it is morally bad. It is making way here perhaps—but slowly. [This was after the translation had been published on the 19th of May, 1824.] A second edition seems a dubious matter.[36]

But from the proceeds of the first edition he bought himself "a suit of fine clothes for £6 and a good watch."

Contrary to all his predictions, the book sold. "*Meister* is growing a kind of small, very small *lion* in London: the newspapers puff him, the people read him, many venerate him very highly. The periodical Rhadamanthuses of Grub Street pat me on the head saying I am a clever fellow and must translate them much more. . . ."[37] Of all the reviews of the translation, De Quincey's in the *London Magazine* is the most notorious. It is called *Goethe as Reflected in his Novel of Wilhelm Meister* and appeared in the August-September number of 1824. It is a sad exposé of De Quincey at his worst, thoroughly cheap and nasty throughout, passing "Mr. Goethe" and "the ladies" of his novel in review. De Quincey's *Encyclopaedia Britannica* article on Goethe (1838–39) shows an uneven and limited appreciation of Goethe, featuring the "impiety" of his childish doubts of a beneficient providence occasioned by the Lisbon earthquake, and the immorality of his novels. *Wilhelm Meister* he maintains even at that late date, attracted no attention in England. De Quincey was always more sympathetic with Richter than with Goethe. Carlyle, an admirer of Richter, too, is full of a scornful pity for this

luckless wight of an opium-eater . . . who wrote a very vulgar and brutish review of *Meister*. . . . I read three pages of it one *sick* day in Birmingham and said, "Here is a man who writes of things which he does not rightly understand; I see clean over the top of *him*, and his vulgar spite and his commonplace philosophy . . . and if De Quincey, poor little fellow, *made* anything of his review he can put it in his waistcoat pocket. . . . The reviews of that book *Meister* must not go without their effect on me: I know it and believe it and feel it to be a book containing traces of a higher, far higher spirit, altogether more *genius*, than any book published in my day: and yet to see the Cockney animalcules rendering an account of it, praising it or blaming it! Sitting in judgment on Goethe with the light tolerance of a country-justice towards a suspected poacher! As the child says, "It is grand!"[38]

The reply to De Quincey by Hare, in the next number of the *London Magazine* was feeble enough. Jeffrey in the *Edinburgh* thought *Meister* "more deserving of wonder than contempt"—*Blackwood's* of course running counter to him with a favorable estimate. William Taylor, the veteran war horse, had

noticed the original in the *Monthly Review* twenty-five
years before (1798), as Goethe's "comic novel" and
now, 1824, came out his estimate of Carlyle's translation. "(Goethe's) *Wilhelm Meister* though full of
beautiful parts and patches, does not excite a grand,
sweeping continuous interest. It sketches a few
years of the life of a strolling player whose shifting
acquaintance and unimportant adventures offer some
variety of stimulant incidents, which have no other
coherence than the unity of the hero. Many eloquent critical dissertations on dramatic taste and
art are introduced: but they are expressed with
an oracular mysticism, not unusual in the lectures of
a German professor especially when tainted with
the Kantian philosophy, yet unworthy of a lumin-
ous reasoner or a precise thinker. If the text as
it now appears in English, does not always seem
intelligible, this is by no means the fault of the
translator, who renders skilfully both the prose and
the verses interspersed. . . . The whole novel turns
on the history of actors and of the stage in Germany," which was the view of the book most frequently taken in England, the development of the
hero seeming not to be worth remarking upon in spite
of Carlyle's preface. "Great praise is due to the
translator," Taylor goes on to say, "for fidelity and
eloquence and we exhort him to continue his task,
and to present us also with the *Peregrinations*. . . .
His admiration of Goethe transcends our own, and is
thus expressed in his preface."[39] From this he then
quotes the main ideas, to the effect that England is too

smug in its ignorance of such an international genius as Goethe, that German literature has been misrepresented in England because of the vogue of Kotzebue, and that in *Meister* the British public see the fruit of Goethe's matured genius, which has passed beyond the *Werther* stage.[40] Although he advised Carlyle to translate the *Wanderjahre,* the wise old Taylor shows himself under no misapprehension about them in his *Historic Survey of German Poetry,*[41] afterward (1831) so roughly dealt with by Carlyle. In this he has to say of the sequel to *Meister:* "Picturesque descriptions, sage reflections and poignant situations occur in all Goethe's writings; yet a senile garrulity creeps on him, his style is become more trailing, and those gushes of feeling which refresh the soul sparkle seldomer along the smoother but expanded current of his narrative."[42] Taylor seems to me to have put his finger on Goethe's greatest strength much more definitely and truly than Carlyle, even though he lacked Carlyle's fervency and religious zeal about Goethe: "Goethe has no moral monsters to delineate; he does not portray man as he should be, or could be, but as he is, the frequent victim of versatility, inconsistency, and folly. He has no lesson to teach but that such things are, and that the proper study of mankind is man."[43] The *Wanderjahre* have been overrated in the *Foreign Review,* thinks Taylor. (The review was by Carlyle.) "To me they do not appear to merit so unqualified a panegyric, such lofty praise, as is there given." He sees in them "a character of alloy . . . displaying more prate than thought,

more reminiscence than observation."[44]   Which looks
as though the shrewd old reviewer had almost an insight into the scrappy and amazing process which
the composition of the *Wanderjahre* really was.[45]
Carlyle seems to have had no inkling of what this
was, though his preface to the second edition of
Meister shows that he knew that Goethe had recon-
structed the book.   At any rate he hailed the *Wanderjahre* as a more significant, if obscure, part of the
Goethian Message than the *Apprenticeship*.

Anyone who has tried to translate German into
English knows the extreme difficulty of breaking up
the long, double-barreled sentences into shorter English ones that can be wielded comfortably, and of keep-
ing them, at the same time, close to the German.
One may manage the technical difficulties of this
pretty fairly, and produce a smooth-reading version
that is faithful enough, in all essentials, to the original.   And yet nine times out of ten it will be utterly
faithless by creating a false impression of simplicity;
a kind of ingenuous, childlike quality that is leagues
removed from the German.   In reading Carlyle's
translation of *Meister*, it seemed to me that he had
been so determined to avoid this mistake, that he
fell into the other pitfall, that of trying to convey
all the sonorous and profound effects of German prose
as Goethe uses it, and often, therefore, slipping of
necessity into blurred and confused English.   Part of
his irritation with his work arose from the baffled
sense of being trapped between these two dangers.
But on the whole it is an admirable translation, al-

ways excepting the verse! Crabb Robinson did not like it: His unpublished diary, under June 22, 1824, reads: "I called on Mr. Irving. Mr. Carlyle, the translator of *Wilhelm Meister*, was there. He had the appearance of a sensible man but his translation from what I have seen, appears bad. He renders the 'Confessions of einer schönen Seele' a 'fair saint'! And his version of Mignon's Song is as bad as possible."[46] In this last particular we must agree with Robinson, but the *Schöne Seele* was a phrase originating in the German pietistic hymn poetry of the early eighteenth century. The soul was symbolized as the bride of Christ, and must therefore be *schön* like any other maiden. The original of Goethe's *Schöne Seele* was a believer in a kind of mystic, pietistic cult, and so he uses this somewhat stereotyped phrase to denote her peculiar spiritual quality. If Carlyle had realized this, he would no doubt have rendered it "Beautiful Soul" quite literally.

Carlyle once told Espinasse that he thought he had only increased the general intellectual confusion by translating *Meister*, and trying to put Goethe before the English public.[47] However this may be, the book certainly clarified many things in his own mind. It strengthened his German and started him on his career among the German writers. It not only clinched his idea about the necessity for action, which goaded him all his life, but it seemed to present to him the only possible form in which a novel could be cast, and perhaps gave him the impulse to try writing one. It gave a great many other people the same impulse and the same form, and they were abler "fictioneers" than Carlyle.   It seems a little ironical that they should have so far surpassed him who, by his hard labor over Goethe's ideas, was in a sense the father of them all.

Thanks to *German Romance* (completed in 1826 but not published till 1827) Carlyle and Jane were finally married in 1826, and went to live at Comely Bank in Edinburgh where his "didactic" novel was one of the first of his labors.   His correspondence with Goethe has little to say about it; in fact, he does not talk about his work or his mental state in his letters to Goethe as much as one might expect.   For this reason, perhaps, the correspondence is a little disappointing—a little flat, considering what sort of people formed the two ends of it!   They never saw each other (though Carlyle was always talking about excursions to Weimar with Jane), and in comparison with his other letters, those to Goethe seem to labor under a kind of restraint, partly due to diffidence no doubt, and the difference in their ages and nationalities. Goethe was seventy-five when the exchange of letters began.   Carlyle's are overpoweringly respectful in tone, dealing with generalities as to the state of German literature in England, tributes to Goethe's genius and acknowledgments of Carlyle's debt to him, warming gradually into some description of Craigenputtock and their daily life there, and referring to their lively exchange of countless packages, containing German books, and English magazines with articles on Germany, a complete set of Goethe's works bound in silk, some medals with his picture, a Scotch bonnet that Jane made for Goethe's daughter-in-law Ottilie, and last but not least a lock of Jane's hair, for which she begs a lock of Goethe's in return. The Sage, alas, had by that time none to send her, and gallantly laments the sad deficiency.

Goethe was during this period chiefly interested in his idea of a *Weltliteratur*, and aside from considerable personal interest in Carlyle, regarded him as the strongest promoter of this view of literature in England. His letters are bland and fatherly, often full of the "simple patriarchal nothings" of his first one to Carlyle (1824) acknowledging a copy of Carlyle's *Wilhelm Meister*. His response to a request for a testimonial, when Carlyle was trying to get the post of professor of moral philosophy at St. Andrews, is as vague as such things may be, describing the Scotchman chiefly as possessing an excellent knowledge of German literature, and therefore an adherent of the Good, the True and the Beautiful, who would teach these generalities conscientiously to his pupils if appointed.

The famous seal that "Fifteen English Friends" sent to Goethe on his eighty-second birthday, August 28, 1831, was a project promoted by Carlyle, and the list included many eminent names, such as those of Scott, Lockhart, and Jeffrey. It evidently surprised and pleased the German "Master" not a little. He writes in a half-humorous vein to Zelter about the *merkwürdiges Geschenk das ich über den Canal erhalten habe,* remarking that the motto on it (*Ohne Rast doch ohne Hast*) very well expresses the British mode of procedure.[48]   Not without a certain pathos is his comment in the same letter: "The older I grow, the more fragmentary my life seems to me as I look back upon it, whereas other people treat it as a unified whole and delight in it." He enjoyed Carlyle's somewhat unfair review of William Taylor's *Historic Survey* because this book aired again a set of ideas about German literature that Goethe had found distasteful sixty years before.   But some of Goethe's letters suggest that if they had met, he and Carlyle might not have been so sympathetic in real acquaintance as they were on paper.   Goethe refers constantly to the large human view of life in German literature (of which his own work is an example), expressive not of an anxious and ascetic timidity but of a free and natural culture, a serene morality, a joyful submission to the law of the universe.   As Carré suggests, Carlyle could not have gone all the way with him there.   He defended *Meister's* morality to others but complained violently enough of its immorality himself, as his letters testify abundantly. He only half understood the Goethe of the *Italienische Reise* and afterward; he was all for "submission," but he did not mean the classically harmonious kind that filled Goethe's later life.

Carlyle was corresponding with Goethe but had not yet met Jeffrey, when he began his novel-fragment, *Wotton Reinfred* in January, 1827.   In March he writes to his brother Alexander: "I have not abandoned the *Book* which has long ago been christened

'Wotton Reinfred': only these Hunt people have knocked me sadly ajar ever since they started their scheme and poor Reinfred has been living not growing for the last three weeks. Nevertheless, I spend my forenoons till two o'clock over him; and Jane reads my writing when I have gone out to walk; and you will be happy to learn, *always* 'approves of the Essay.' If these Hunts do not give me their translation, I expect to have Wotton in print before quitting Edinburgh."[49] "Poor Wotton has prospered but indifferently," he writes in June, "though daily on the anvil; the metal is too unmalleable, often indeed quite cold, and the arm and the hammer have so little pith!"[50] Meantime he has met Jeffrey and is to do an article for him on Jean Paul, and Mrs. Carlyle writes a postscript lamenting the demise of Wotton: "Poor Wotton. Dear Wotton! He was growing such an angel of a Hero."[51] The book was never finished, and the MS consisting of seven chapters, was stolen after many years and was printed after Carlyle's death,[52] in the Centennial Memorial edition of his works, in the volume called *Last Words of Thomas Carlyle.* Wilson would have us believe that Carlyle was superior to fiction;

A mind awake enough to think of things as they are cannot grow backwards and play with events like a story-teller or a child with toys . . . and a very small share of such learning as Carlyle's handicaps a man of sense in fictioneering. Carlyle tried hard but could not do it.[53]

That last sentence by itself would seem to be the best explanation, not only of the ill-fated novel fragment itself, but also of Carlyle's attitude toward Bulwer-Lytton, Disraeli, and Scott. "Disesteem for fiction was the best of the Bible-religion now fading away," Wilson assures us[54] but after all his hero was human, and of course the grapes were sour.

The novel opens with a very Carlylean diatribe against happiness, put into the mouth of the equally Carlylean hero, Wotton Reinfred. He has come to despair of life at the age of twenty-two. He has, like his original, tried the law only to give it up in disgust, and the "tiger-ape" Edmund Walter, has done him out of his chance of marrying the lady of his heart, Jane Montagu. His friend tells him that all is not lost. "You have much to do and much to learn in this world; only nature must have her course, nay, she is teaching you even now."[55] These philosophical comforters to young heroes are seldom well-received. Wilhelm Meister did not pay much attention to Werner's admonitions either. Wotton bolsters up his skepticism and pessimism by his wide reading, which incidentally reflects the range and variety of Carlyle's own reading during his storm-and-stress period. His friend states the problem: "I care not for thy skepticism, Wotton: I tell thee it will grow to be belief, and all the sounder for thy once having doubted;"[56] which shows the direction Wotton's progress is to take, in common with so many nineteenth-century pilgrims in search of faith, primarily, and not *Bildung* unless it is thrown in as an extra. But education is to be part of the theme too: "Wotton was one of those natures which it is of most importance to educate rightly, but also of greatest difficulty, and which accordingly with a capricious contradiction we often find worse educated than any other."[57]   Like Wilhelm, Wotton is persuaded to travel, in order to take his mind off his troubles, and to gain experience, but not till he has voiced further views about "acting, not talking," and "be not solitary, be not idle," which have a familiar ring.

Wotton has been brought up by a stern father, and a simple and religious mother. He is imaginative and sensitive, and has been the object of persecution at school, where the boys called him "weeping Wotton." He is given to egotistical revery when driven back upon himself, and loves the Scotch countryside and the talk of the peasants at work. At the "Seminary" to which he is later sent, his spiritual snobbery becomes more marked. He consorts chiefly with his own countrymen. The speculations of the other students were "of far more earthly matters than his, and in their amusements, too often riotous and libertine, his principle forbade him to participate." He often felt as if "their impure influences were contaminating and seducing him. Contaminate him they did, but seduce him they could not."[58] At the "Seminary" this young Galahad reads science, metaphysics, and the skeptical French writers, and is plunged into the nightmare of Doubt with all its agonies. "What heart not of stone can endure to abide with them?" By degrees "a dreary stagnancy overspread his soul," something like the Center of Indifference, succeeding the fierce joy of Denial. "He was without fear

and without hope; in this world isolated, poor, and
helpless; had tasted little satisfaction, and expected
little, and in the next he had now no part or lot.
Among his fellow men he felt like a stranger and a
pilgrim, a pilgrim journeying without rest to a distant nowhere."[59]

Luckily he falls in with a congenial friend, Bernard
Swane, modeled in some respects on Edward Irving.
He is the perfect extravert, and a fortunate complement to the introspective Wotton, who is of the Hamlet type.   Bernard is less reflective and takes pleasure
in action; he has no doubts and is not given to mulling
over his soul.   At his house Wotton meets the beautiful Jane Montagu, for whom Jane Welsh and Margaret Gordon have both been proposed as originals,
though Jane seems the more likely.   Wotton, usually
tongue-tied in company, is as one inspired and "by
one or two Socratic questions in his happiest style contrived to silence for the night" a "vain, sophistical
young man" who was one of the party.[60]   This was
Carlyle's favorite form of indoor sport, if he exerted
himself at all in conversation.   He falls in love with
Jane and she reciprocates, but her hard-hearted aunt
interferes, and Jane is forced, for no explained reason,
to part from him.   Then he and Bernard start on the
journey discussed in the first chapter.

At an inn, Wotton comes across a mysterious locket
bearing his likeness, and in the wild hope that it perhaps belonged to Jane, he takes it with him.   They
meet a stranger, Maurice Herbert, in the mountains,
with whom they discuss philosophy and decry "view-

hunting" in the friendliest manner. "Your view-
hunter is the most irksome of all articulate-speaking
men."[61] Herbert takes them home with him to his
House in the Wold, which is a little on the order of
Lothario's castle in *Wilhelm Meister*. It is full of
free and fearless thinkers who do not seem unbelievers:
everyone is either artist, poet, scholar, statesman, or
something notable. These people engage in endless
conversations. Dalbrook, the Kantian, with many
ideas of Goethe's, is the most impressive figure, a
mystic and idealist, of the "transcendental kind."[62]
Something of Carlyle's idea about growing up is expressed by one of the characters: "And so when the
young gentleman goes forth into the world, and finds
that it is really and truly not made of wax, but of
stone and metal, and *will* keep its own shape, let the
young gentleman fume as he likes; bless us, what a
storm he gets into! What terrible elegies and pin-
darics and *Childe Harolds* and *Sorrows of Werter!*"
"All permanent enjoyment must be active, not passive," adds Bernard.[63] There is a satirical eulogium
of Cant, "good Cant" who reassures us about the
value of our pursuits, so that we do not hang or
drown ourselves, and with her one can live in surprising comfort.[64] The poet is the Seer, translating
the Divine Harmony to men, and "Fit audience he
will find, though few,"[65] which was the way Carlyle
reassured himself on many occasions. An echo of
Meister is in this discussion of the poet also: "Nature
in her bounty gives him much, but her most precious
gift is the wish and aptitude to cultivate himself to

become what he was capable of being."[66]   While Wotton is looking at pictures with his lovely hostess, who should suddenly appear but his deadly rival, Edmund Walter?   He is the type of *persifleur*, always most hateful to Carlyle, "alienating, oppressive, cool, indifferent, self-sufficient."[67]   Fleeing in rage and despair from the house, Wotton meets at sunset in the mountains, three riders—Jane, no less, and two gentlemen, her cousins.   This scene recalls the one where Wilhelm meets the beautiful Amazon in the clearing after the robbery.   He goes with them to an inn, and there has an interview with Jane.   She recounts to him the story of her life previous to their first meeting; like Jane Welsh she was brought up in Switzerland, and cultivated literary ambitions.   Her aunt wishes her to marry Walter for some mysterious and special reason, but Jane puts him off.   As in the case of Mignon, there is some mystery about Jane's parents, whom she has never known.   And here the story breaks off.

Certain parallels to *Meister* are noticeable in several episodes of this novel, which is more didactic than *Werther* but expresses the Werther mood rather than the calm optimism of *Meister*.   The only recognition of the self-culture theme of *Meister* is expressed incidentally, as in the discussion of the poet's function, and it is not an organic part of the hero's development. No doubt education would have played some part, as indicated in the first chapter, if the story had been completed.   Even as far as it goes, Wotton is shown absorbing new impressions and meeting new kinds of people, which ultimately would have helped to form his character. But the people are not individualized, and we leave them and the hero without regret, swimming in seas of conversation. The novel was not for Carlyle. He was strong for action, but he could not make his people *do* anything. Part of *Wotton* went into *Sartor*, but "doing" was no longer essential. Prophecy had begun.

After *Wotton* was abandoned, various German subjects occupied Carlyle for the next three years. *Richter* was published in 1827; the essay on Goethe, in 1828; the ill-fated *History of German Literature*, in 1829–30; and the review of Taylor's *Historic Survey*, in 1831. He was busy with English subjects also, such as *Signs of the Times* and *Burns*. It was during these years that his enthusiasm for the Germans was at its height, as was also the sense of his own "mission"— his call to prophecy. These were the first years of his friendship with Jeffrey, whose criticism was perhaps the frankest and most salutary that Carlyle ever received. "You have no mission upon earth, whatever you may fancy, half so important as to be innocently happy, and all that is good for you of poetic feeling, and sympathy with majestic nature, will come of its own accord, without your straining after it."[68] But Carlyle did not hold with happiness, and in his more disgruntled moments considered Jeffrey a fairly frivolous person. Carlyle's abnormally prolonged adolescence, or period of struggle for adjustment, was, as are all such struggles, fearfully earnest, and this earnestness irritated Jeffrey in a way that most of us can understand only too well.

You may talk as long as you like about a false principle of pride or honour, and the necessity of having a right creed as to your relations with the universe, but you will never persuade anybody that the regulation of life is such a mighty laborious business as you would make it, or that it is not better to go lightly through it, with the first creed that comes to hand, than to spend the better part of it in anxious verifications of its articles.[69]

He will never, Jeffrey insists, convert England to a worship of the Germans, who are connected in Jeffrey's mind with this unfortunate earnestness and self-conscious apostleship and "mysticism." But we cannot lay all the blame on the supposedly Teutonic lack of humor. "I have now almost done with the Germans," wrote Carlyle in his notebook in 1830 when he was still working on the history of their literature. "Having seized their opinions, I must turn me to enquire *how* true are they? That truth is in them, no lover of truth will doubt: but how much? And after all, one needs an intellectual Scheme—or ground plan of the Universe drawn with one's own instruments."[70]

This scheme he drew in *Sartor*, which does, nevertheless, rest heavily on the Germans, especially Fichte, whom he read avidly in 1827. Wilson does not think he accepted Fichte's "divine idea of the Universe" but he uses the Fichtean vocabulary and he was never "done with" Fichte, any more than the rest of his century was. On the ideas of this follower of Kantian metaphysics, almost any kind of superstructure can be built, from the writing of the Romantic school to the Puritan eloquence of Carlyle, or from German nationalism to the gospel of Marx or the philosophy of Emerson. But among the odd assortment of his disciples, our Scotchman was perhaps the oddest. The debt of *Sartor* to the Germans does not end with Fichte; it owes something to Richter's *Quintus Fixlein* and much to *Wilhelm Meister*. So perhaps it was as well that Carlyle, against Jeffrey's advice, held on to the Germans.

Wilson explains the beginning of *Sartor* by the metaphorical passage about clothes making the man, which Jeffrey cut out of the essay on Burns when Carlyle sent it to him, explaining that it was too trite. This was in September, 1830. By October it had grown into two articles for Fraser called "Thoughts on Clothes," which later made up practically the first book of *Sartor*.[71] This book, which was to "cause ears to tingle" and which he described to Goethe as "another curious enterprise of my own which is yet too amorphous to be prophesied of" he was working on with real pleasure through January, February, and March of 1831, finishing it in the summer more quickly than any of his long pieces of work. "I can devise some more biography for *Teufelsdreck*," he writes to his brother in January; "give a second deeper part, in the same vein, leading through Religion and the nature of Society, and Lord knows what." Other references to it reflect an unusually hopeful mood: "Teufelsdreck I '*hege und pflege*,' night and day. . . . It is not the *right* thing yet, but there is a kind of life in it, and I *will* finish it."[72] He thinks the "world will nowise be enraptured" with it, and

in fact Murray would not publish it, nor would anyone else, until Fraser brought it out serially in 1834.
In May 1833, he wrote his description of it to Fraser,
saying that it may best be read a few chapters at a
time.

It is put together in the fashion of a kind of Didactic Novel; but indeed properly like nothing extant: I used to characterize it briefly
as a kind of "Satirical Extravaganza on Things in General"; it contains more of my opinions on Art, Politics, Religion, Heaven, Earth,
and Air than all the things I have yet written.   The Creed . . . is
mine and firmly believed.[73]

He goes on to promise that it will at least "astonish"
and in this he was right.   Poor Fraser was distressed
at the outcries it caused.   John Sterling did not like
it, but the Americans did.

Something of the ponderous playfulness and half-
humorous, half-sentimental burlesque of Richter's
Quintus Fixlein can be found in *Sartor*.   A great point
has been made of the fact that the *style* is not Richter's, even though Carlyle admired him deeply, as his
essay on him shows, and translated his *Schmelzle* for
German Romance.   Carlyle even compared him favorably with the much-enduring Wordsworth.   It is perfectly true that the style of *Sartor* is no one's if not
Carlyle's and his exclusively.   If he had "borrowed"
some of its mannerisms from Richter, it would be no
great matter.   But there is rather a pervasive atmosphere of Richter than any direct borrowing.   The
humor of the two authors is similar.   Both books are
to some degree autobiography, apostrophizing Teufelsdröckh or the poor, romantic student, Fixlein, in

a strain half commiserating, half encouraging or exhorting. Teufelsdröckh's life-history is contained in the famous paper bags, Fixlein's in the *Zettelkästen*. There is emotional reminiscence of childhood scenes in both books, elaborate and tortuous historical and literary allusions and a habit of parenthesis and diminutive: "mankin," etc. The idyll of Fixlein and Thiennette ends happily in a village wedding scene, that of Blumine and Teufelsdröckh in the "basilisk-glance" of false friendship from the barouche that whirls his lady away with his rival. The fundamental nobility of soul, and a certain impression of rugged honesty and geniality, is the greatest bond between them, though Fixlein is more sentimental than Teufelsdröckh.

Nothing at all in common, on the other hand, has the tone of *Sartor* with the German book to which it owes the most in ideas—*Wilhelm Meister*. The meteoric, half-savage progress of Teufelsdröckh is more nearly akin to Wotton Reinfred's than Meister's. The keynote of Puritan restraint is sounded in the earliest accounts of Gneschen's Apprenticeship in the small remote village of Entepfuhl in which the training was too stoical, his instinct to experiment, too hemmed-in. "I was forbid much: wishes in any measure bold I had to renounce; everywhere a strait bond of Obedience inflexibly held me down."[74] In every way opposed to this was the pleasant, well-fed, agreeably stimulated childhood of Meister in the prosperous German trading town, where he amused himself with his puppets, learning to tinker with things freely, to declaim his theatrical pieces and puppet plays, and to direct the puppet theater and deal with other children. Omnivorous readers, indeed, they both were, but Wilhelm did not have to save up his pocket money to buy "stall-literature."[75] It is experience that is to teach them both, but from the beginning we are aware that it is bound to hit Teufelsdröckh harder than Wilhelm; he is begirt by that "ring of Necessity" that "dark ring of Care, as yet no thicker than a thread"[76] which all but ruined him later on, and bothered the more casual Wilhelm not a whit. Both autobiographers show that education was one of the watchwords of their times; there is much in both books about the importance of early impressions, and the unconscious process of learning by absorbing one's environment.[77] In spite of Wilhelm's early literary efforts, they seem to show him as a much less singular adolescent than Teufelsdröckh. He is fervent and fluent, but not so intense in his feeling: "I was like no other. . . . As in birth, so in action, speculation, and social position, my fellows are perhaps not numerous."[78] This idea of his singularity is fostered in Teufelsdröckh by his unfortunate experience at the university; not much education of a formal sort is dwelt on in Wilhelm's case. He works for his father's business in a desultory way, until he begins his travels. Both heroes have attendant friends, something like Bernard Swane in *Reinfred*—conveniently opposite in their dispositions to the hero with whom they associate. Towgood, or Toughgut, is "warmhearted, strongheaded and wrongheaded," talented, ignorant, humorous, and—in the end—faith-less. Werner is the quiet, prudent, philistine busi-ness man who seeks to divert Wilhelm from his scandalous love affair with an actress, tries to show him the beauty of bookkeeping by double-entry, and wants a footrule by which to measure the good and the bad in literature. Yet he encourages Wilhelm's creative efforts, and feels a tender concern for his health after Mariane's apparent infidelity has laid low his impressionable young friend.

One of the great themes of *Meister*—action and de-velopment according to natural gifts—is sounded in Book II of *Sartor*, in the chapter called "Getting Under Way."

Not what I have . . . but what I do is my kingdom. To each is given a certain inward talent, a certain outward environment of fortune; to each, by wisest combination of these two, a certain maxi-mum of Capability. But the hardest problem were ever this first: To find by study of youself, and of the ground you stand on, what your combined inward and outward Capability specially is. . . . And then how seldom will the outward Capability fit the Inward. Thus . . . we go stupidly groping about, to grope which is ours, and often clutch the wrong one: in this mad work must several years of our small term be spent, till the purblind youth, by practice, acquire notions of distance, and become a seeing man. Nay, many so spend their whole term, and in ever-new expectation, ever-new disappointment, shift from enterprise to enterprise, and from side to side: till at length, as exasperated striplings of threescore-and-ten, they shift into their last enterprise, that of getting buried.[79]

This is almost a paraphrase of Goethe's words in his *Tag und Jahreshefte*, quoted above, by which he ex-plained the main theme of *Meister*, and which Wil-

helm himself puts a little differently when he writes
to his friend Werner, "Mich selbst, ganz wie ich
da bin, auszubilden, das war dunkel von Jugend
auf mein Wunsch und meine Absicht."[80]   And the
Schöne Seele quotes the Abbé to this effect: "Wenn
man an der Erziehung des Menschen etwas tun wolle,
müsse man sehen, wohin seine Neigungen und Wün-
sche gehen."   One must give him a chance to work
out these capabilities as soon as possible, "damit der
Mensch, wenn er sich geirret habe, früh genug seinen
Irrtum gewahr werde."[81]   Both Carlyle and Goethe
hated dilettantism and the waste of human material
it involves, but Carlyle's answer to it was faith, action, renunciation of self and of all foolish claims to
personal happiness.   Goethe believed that his youth
could grow to manhood by learning the value of practical, unselfish living through understanding that it
was the only way to live harmoniously, *and* happily.

   Both heroes start off with unhappy love affairs,
which send them out on their wanderings.   Teufelsdröckh "loved once; not wisely but too well.   And
once only. . . . The First Love which is infinite,
can be followed by no second like unto it."[82]   Meister, on the other hand, has a whole series of educational love affairs following this first one with the
unfortunate Mariane.   They mark the stages in his
development.   The pilgrimage on which Teufelsdröckh sets forth is a "perambulation and circumambulation of the terraqueous Globe" into the highways
and byways of his author's spiritual experience.
Wilhelm travels in a quieter and more realistic coun-

try, but still a symbolic one that, simple as it looks, is not quite of this earth. Teufelsdröckh makes the mistake of not recognizing his literary bent early enough and so finding nothing to work at, and Wilhelm is led astray by thinking that the theater is his vocation, when he really has no great gift for it. Teufelsdröckh, in his "nameless unrest," journeys like the Wandering Jew and comes upon Doubt and the Everlasting No and the Infinite Nature of Duty. Wilhelm among his commonplace troupe of wandering players, at least is getting experience among other human beings and developing some gift of leadership and capacity to do things, although he has mistaken his field of action. Nothing like that huge, dead, mechanistic Universe (resembling the one pictured in a recent German film, *Metropolis*) which glared at Teufelsdröckh in the Rue St. Thomas de l'Enfer, ever confronted Wilhelm. He was not Puritan nor Presbyterian enough, and perhaps not so self-conscious and introspective as the Scotchman who "walked solitary . . . as the tiger in the jungle."[83] Wilhelm at least had company, even though it was inferior. After his fire-baptism, Teufelsdröckh begins to "clutch round him outwardly on the Not-Me for wholesomer food,"[84] just as Wilhelm's wounded spirit turns from contemplating the sorrows of unhappy love, to take an interest in the outside world again. Objectivity is one of the great lessons of *Meister*, and of Goethe's whole life, but it is to come from free, healthy, natural development, not from forcible and violent throttling of "Self," or one whole set of instincts that are human.

It would have been better for Teufelsdröckh had he let that "Satanic School" spout, instead of making himself forget it by pursuing knowledge, and reading in public libraries all over the world.[85]

He has reached the "Center of Indifference" through "Annihilation of Self" (*Selbsttödtung*) and views Nature in the words of Goethe and Fichte as the "Living Garment of God," with a new calmness.[86] Having taken hold of Goethe's *Entsagen* in his own interpretation of it, he enters the "Sanctuary of Sorrow," which he thought was the German's most profound holy of holies.   But all that Jarno tells Wilhelm about "Self annihilation" is that for true cultivation the individual must lose himself in action on behalf of the group.[87]   As for that Sanctuary of Sorrow, we have seen that Carlyle magnified it out of all proportion to its real place in the *Wanderjahre*.

Carlyle's scorn of money and position grew out of his upbringing and became part of his religion. Goethe, who had had both all his life, had no such inverted snobbery.   The eighteenth-century Germany that he is writing about in the *Lehrjahre* offered few chances to the middle class *Bürger* like Wilhelm to develop himself.   And so he makes Wilhelm aspire quite frankly to becoming one of the nobility, until he is disillusioned about their way of living after his sojourn in the castle.   He got a little more substantial nourishment from them than the "Aesthetic Tea" that exasperated the hungry Teufelsdröckh, and he is more willing to compromise and take what he can get, rejecting what is of no use to him.   Teufelsdröckh was not willing to sift his experience in this way; things were either true or false; he would not chaffer with the Devil.

Byron and pleasure, Goethe and God, are the antitheses to which the Everlasting Yea has led him. He is against Voltaire, now and always. In the words used so often today against that undergraduate God, Mencken, he was not a "constructive critic," and like Mencken, he was a *Persifleur*. He has "only a torch for burning, no hammer for building." Therefore away with him. Jarno has a little of the cynical worldling's coloring, and shocks Wilhelm now and then by unexplained laughter, but he turns out not to be a villain in the end. There is no devil in Goethe's piece, unless it is the patient Philister, Wilhelm's friend Werner, who appears at the end in the rôle of a harmless grotesque.

The faith of the nineteenth century speaks in Teufelsdröckh's conclusion that "the man is the spirit he worked in; not what he did, but what he became."[88] *Der Geist, aus dem wir handeln, ist das Höchste*, says Wilhelm's Lehrbrief at the end of his apprenticeship. And so says the whole book, in fact, by implication. It is concerned with "becoming" as all its followers in England were, Carlyle among the first of them. The process was viewed in different lights by Scotchman and German. Goethe made it, quite naturally, the process of learning a fine art, and attaining in the end to mastery—Carlyle used a different and sterner vocabulary. Art to him meant something not as earnest as he would have it. "For us in these days

Prophecy . . . not Poetry is the thing wanted; how can we sing and paint when we do not yet *Believe* and *See?* . . . Now what under such point of view is all existing Art and the study of Art? What was the great Goethe himself?"[89] We might answer, "An Artist," and not think we had done him an injustice. But Carlyle could not see it that way. To call Goethe the greatest master in the art of living, one who could believe and see and at the same time do creative work with constant joy in it and in life itself, was not enough. Nothing was good unless it was a little painful; if an agony and a struggle were involved, it was likely to be better still. And so Teufelsdröckh's "becoming" is quite a different thing from Wilhelm's —a kind of spiritual nightmare, leading at last to "Solitude and a life of meditation."[90] Wilhelm is no more smugly complete than his Scotch brother; he will go on growing. But he admits, *dass ich ein Glück erlangt habe, das ich nicht verdiene, und das ich mit nichts in der Welt vertauschen möchte.*[91] Like Saul, he has found an unexpected kingdom. For such as Teufelsdröckh there is no kindgom, and he would not know what to do with it if he had one. . . . He only wants to say his say, and perhaps it pleases him a little to have Jane read his book and give her verdict, "It is a work of genius, dear."

It is unfair, perhaps, to emphasize so much the differences between Carlyle and his German master, when the essentials were what mattered to both of them, and their differences in purpose were not so great as those in approach and method. For after all, the "shows of things" were what both of them sought to penetrate. "Thus everywhere do the shows of things oppress him, withstand him, threaten him with fearfullest destruction: only by victoriously penetrating into Things themselves can he find peace and a stronghold."[92] And so he proceeds to work out his Philosophy of Clothes, while Goethe used a less tortuous and more obvious method. Wilhelm is involved in the theater, which is only a mirror of life, not life itself. After he has been educated a little among these false appearances and "shows of things," he is ready for the things themselves—for active usefulness among real men, responsibility for those dependent on him, and a tolerant acceptance of human beings as they are.

CHAPTER VI

BULWER-LYTTON: THE DANDY'S PROGRESS

And Beelzebub, Apollyon, and Legion, with their companions, perceiving by the path that the Pilgrims made, that their way to the Celestial City lay through this town of Vanity, they contrived here to set up a fair.

—John Bunyan, *Pilgrim's Progress.*

THE span of Bulwer's earthly pilgrimage, 1803–73, covers threescore and ten troubled years, for him and for England. It is perhaps natural enough that none of the writers who reshaped Goethe's fiction pattern into English forms, should have led a peaceful or very happy life. Each was in the nature of things an experimenter in his art as in his personal life. So was the serene and Olympian German master from whom they borrowed, but he lived within the quiet, settled formalities of a small self-contained eighteenth-century German court, in the classic tranquility of that house on the Frauenplan, or in the solitude of the garden house in the Park. The English followers of his *Wilhelm Meister* lived in a struggling, changing England; Teufelsdröckh, Ernest Maltravers, Contarini Fleming, Beauchamp, have to make their adjustment to life in a stormier world than Wilhelm's; their pilgrimage, like Bulwer's, is fraught with perils of which neither Christian nor Wilhelm ever dreamed.

126

The very difficulties which beset them, however, explain, as much as such things can ever be explained, why the type of novel that deals with the hero's apprenticeship to life, took root so firmly in English soil. The French wars (Bulwer and Emerson were both born in the first year of war with France) brought confusion and poverty, but also that greater receptivity to foreign ideas, visible in so many of the romantic writers. Scott, Coleridge, Wordsworth, Byron, Shelley, and the romantic critics—in fact almost all the literary figures except Jane Austen who were eminent during the period of Bulwer's childhood, show an openness of mind to foreign influence and in most cases to German influence. The interest and faith in education, growing throughout the century and Bulwer's lifetime, made the theme of education by life an increasingly congenial one, and the rise of the great reviews brought discussion of the novel and its forms to a wide public; the criticisms of Bulwer's novels alone, from 1828 to the time of his death, furnish ample testimony on this point. Such diverse forces as Methodism, the writings of Carlyle, and the Oxford reformers, placed emphasis on the individual soul and its progress through a dangerous world. As for the colorful and varied background—the *Weltbild*—which forms such an essential part of the apprenticeship novel, no English novelist from Defoe to Kipling, has had far to seek for that.

During Bulwer's childhood the Napoleonic wars, the Luddite riots, the first passage of a steamer across the Atlantic, were only a few things among

many that enlivened the English scene. He was a
young aspirant for political honors and writing his
first successful novels when Britain abolished slavery,
passed the Factory Act and the Poor Law, began to
use the perfected telegraph, rejoiced at the coronation
of Victoria, and dealt in characteristic ways with the
Chartists and the Corn Laws. By the time Macaulay,
Wordsworth, and Dickens had died, Bulwer had
passed through the worst of his personal trials, and
was reading *The Mill on the Floss,* on which he writes
some curious comments to Forster, speaking of "some
admirable touches of human nature and character"
in the book but complaining of the "great want of fine
and delicate moral perception"![1] We may presume
that he read Meredith, Swinburne, and Ruskin too,
and that even Hardy, with one of his early novels,
Under the Greenwood Tree, may conceivably have
swum into his ken. So far as we know, he watched
without undue excitement the Crimean War, the
Indian Mutiny, the opening of the Suez Canal, and
other phenomena of an expanding England, nor has
he much to say about our Civil War or the Franco-
Prussian upheavals; the revolutions of '48 had interested him but mildly.[2] He and John Stuart Mill died
in the same year (1873); surely, two such significant
but for the most part unrelated signs of the times have
seldom passed at once from the British firmament!

Against some such background as this, along with
Bulwer himself (for autobiography is the very flesh
and blood of the apprentice novel) pass "all the sad
young men" of Bulwer's creation: *Falkland,* (1827),

Pelham (1828), Algernon Mordaunt (in *The Dis-owned*, 1829), *Percy Godolphin* (1833), *Ernest Mal-travers* and *Alice* (1837 and 1838), and *Kenelm Chil-lingly* (1873)—all eloquent of Bulwer's fine, florid taste in names, and of the setting in which they are to figure—"the Great World" as he loved to call it— of high life in the grand Victorian manner. The rooms of the wealthy are decorated in damask, with many mirrors and "girandoles of silver and mother of pearl," with masterpieces of Flemish and Italian art, with draperies and ormolu. There are buhl cab-inets and wardrobes, marquetrie and Sèvres china. In the ballrooms into which Bulwer's heroes glide and, if they are really irreproachable, disapprove of ladies who waltz, the conversation of cultivated in-tellectuals concerns "busts, statues, books," and the *élite* are given to snubbing the aspiring parvenus, who are generally summed up as "purse-proud roturiers" or "bankers and brewers and soap-boilers and other rich people—the Medici of the New Noblesse rising up amongst us." On the great country estates, where these young men "rise from sleepless couches" and indulge a tendency to "walk by the side of the brook . . . absorbed in thought," there is usually a set of picturesque ruins, a great many deer among the ferns in the park, and much riding to hounds on the part of the more robust masculine element, although the poetic hero sometimes figures here too, outstrip-ping everyone else on a small but incredibly swift Arabian horse.

In and out of such scenes these young men "of

luxuriant though dark imagination" take their way—
brilliant, imaginative, lonely—representing Bulwer
himself, in fact, and seeking, like him, the "Beautiful,
the Virtuous, and the Great." They are all guided,
or brought up short from time to time, by some more
practical, calm, well-adjusted friend or mentor, who
counsels action and preaches the gospel of work and
a return to useful living for others when the young
man has wandered too far afield in order to forget his
unhappy love affair by seeing the world. Sooner or
later he gets to Italy, even as Goethe and Wilhelm
Meister did, but often his friends at home have news
of his passing "from the haughty noblesse of Vienna,
to the gloomy shrines of Memphis," and he seems "to
tarry long in no place." He is almost always tall,
dark, slender, and eloquent, but, after Falkland, not
so Byronic as one expects, and with something oddly
touching in the persistence of his wistful search for
those capitalized abstractions so dear to Bulwer's
Platonism—the Good, the Beautiful and the True.
Despite the sentimentality, the gaudy writing that so
infuriated Thackeray, and the general absurdity that
must dog the footsteps of one so often innocent of all
humor as Bulwer, we cannot but follow that eternal
struggle of the dark young man toward some realization of his capacities, some adjustment to his time
and surroundings, partly because it was Bulwer's
own struggle, and perhaps too because it assumes
from much repetition a kind of epic grandeur, representing, after all, a conflict that is timeless.

Something of Shaftesbury's idea of the Virtuoso

and a tinge of the German eighteenth-century conception of *Bildung* or self-culture appears at the very outset of Bulwer's autobiography. "With strong tendencies to indolence, with vivid capacities of joy, I might have had little of that endurance or industry which has made my career one attempt to bring into culture all such faculties of my mind as gave the faintest promise of harvest."[3] A letter to Forster in 1849 speaks of the general European upheaval and adds: "More and more do we see that our only realm of liberty and improvement is in our own individual natures."[4] But he had a stormy youth to put behind him before any such notions took root. A boyish love tragedy reflected in *Falkland* and very much in the manner of *Werther* except for the suicide, sent him on the Grand Tour that all his heroes, and Disraeli's, make, in common with their German prototype, a journey which—in various forms—Christian and Tom Jones and Rasselas made before him. He falls in with gypsies in his wanderings over England, and after an affair with the sprightly Lady Caroline Lamb, he goes to Paris and sees society early in life, as Pelham does; begins writing *Falkland* and *Pelham* in 1825 while in Paris, as "experimental exercises in the two opposite kinds of fiction—the impassioned and sombre, the light and sportive,"[5] and admits in his autobiography that as a youth he was as arrogant and snobbish and spoiled as a fond mother, wealth, and a lack of public-school training could make him. Cambridge had not been very congenial to him, though he made good friends there and Alexander Cockburn whose father was minister at Stuttgart and who "knew intimately French and German"[6] perhaps gave him his first interest in foreign literature, though this is mere conjecture. His early industry in creative literature begins during his wanderings through the Lake Country, when, as he tells us in his artless way, "I sat down to form for myself a style. I found it exceedingly difficult."[7]

A list of subjects for projected essays shows the trend of his interests in 1826. It includes, among other things, "Perfectibility, The Proper Aim of Satire, *Wilhelm Meister*, and The Love of Improving our Fellow Creatures."[8] Bentham and Godwin and Goethe in strange fellowship evidently occupied his mind together, and this is the first mention of Goethe's novel by Bulwer. His first novel, *Falkland*, was published in 1827. It shocked the "Prudes and Canters" and Bulwer's mother, who lamented its lack of Christianity. Bulwer suppressed it after 1832, taking very seriously his duty to the rising "upper middle class" whose social virtues, intelligence, and courage he thought *Falkland* did not promote. But the Germans, who loved all his novels, never got over their affection for this early effort, perhaps because it is so redolent of *Werther*. The similarity to *Werther* in its main idea, in parallel characters, form, and emotional atmosphere is apparent enough and has been pointed out elsewhere with more than sufficient care.[9] Bulwer himself testifies that the writing of the book accomplished for him the same beneficial result that *Werther* did for Goethe: "I had rid my bosom of the perilous stuff. I had confessed my sins and was absolved. I could return to real life and its wholesome objects."[10] Like Carlyle and Goethe he has passed through the worst of his adolescence and is beginning to see light on the other side. The book contains, Byronic and theatrical as it is, some germs of the later "education" motif. Falkland is a fitful, tempestuous, and disillusioned young man. He gets "the education of life" but is disappointed in love and in knowledge. He goes back to nature for solitude and healing. Now he asks "only for action, but I can find no motive sufficient to excite it." In this dilettante stage he falls in love with Emily, the beautiful young matron with a child of three. He writes her passionate letters, with short, dramatic sentences all beginning with "I." Her proud, cold, rich husband, her love for her child, and a moralizing woman friend, who talks a great deal about the "irrevocable step" and "woman's virtue," almost prevent an elopement, and amid fearful convulsions of nature, storms, floods, lightning, and many italics, Falkland's anguish mounts to its highest pitch. The night before the elopement, against all advice, is to take place, Emily dies of a broken blood vessel *"the half-hour after midnight,"* and so the problem is solved. Falkland espouses the Spanish cause and is killed fighting the French.

His early essays, as well as certain elements of *Falkland*, show that the theme so dear to Goethe was revolving in his mind, taking on a somewhat Carlylean aspect in the process. The pieces called *On the De-*

parture of Youth and *The Knowledge of the World in Men and Books* speak much of the value of experience, and in one case Rasselas and his "Choice of Life" is mentioned. The essay *On Satiety* says: "When Pleasure palls, Philosophy begins. . . . Experience is not acquired by the spectator of life but by its actor."[11] And Bulwer adds, in good Carlylese, "(If) his centre of being is in the world and not in himself" egotism can be conquered. "Duty has pleasures which know no satiety." Shaftesbury comes up again in the essay on *Many Sidedness and Self-Completion:* "Self-completion unites all kinds of accomplishments;" it "pervades the whole disciplined culture of Athenian life" with "that yearning for universal accomplishment." "Goethe was a botanist as well as a poet and a philosopher." "Many-sidedness is manifold enjoyment." "It requires an eternity to develop all the elements of the soul!" In the *Conversations with an Ambitious Student in Ill Health* we have Bulwer's direct testimony, if it were needed, that *Wilhelm Meister* "had a very marked influence on my own mind."

After his disastrous marriage with Rosina Doyle Wheeler, Bulwer had to write at top speed to maintain an expensive ménage, and to keep his mind off his troubles, but *Pelham* appeared in 1828 before his domestic sufferings had become acute. There is a dash and an unforced gaiety about it that we do not find in his work again. This biography of the perfect dandy which Carlyle satirized in *Sartor* (Book III, Chap. X) in the "Dandiacal Body" and which poor

Bulwer later revised because of this attack, was itself meant to be a satire on the Byronic-Wertherian school of fashionable novels. It is perhaps only incidentally of the apprentice type. In his preface to the second edition Bulwer wrote: "We may glean no unimportant wisdom from folly itself, if we distinguish while we survey, and satirize while we share it." Pelham is, he says, a

Voluptuary and a moralist—a trifler in appearance, but rather one to whom trifles are instructive than one to whom they are natural—an Aristippus on a limited scale, accustomed to draw sage conclusions from the follies he adopts and while professing himself a votary of pleasure, in reality a disciple of wisdom.[12]

In the 1835 preface Bulwer announces that he will give a sketch of the book's history since he is now no longer a young author but "one who has served an apprenticeship as long as that of the ingenious *Wilhelm Meister.*" *Pelham* was meant to show how "a man of sense can subject the usages of the world to himself instead of being conquered by them and gradually grow wise by the very foibles of his youth." The theme of the book is certainly the story of how Pelham adapts himself morally to his world, but he is the gayest of all such moral pilgrims, and the jauntiest and most extravagant youth of all Bulwer's gallery. The biography of Bulwer by his son explains with what is probably good psychology, at least a part of the basis of dandyism as a cult.

The airs of indifference and frivolity assumed by him in his Pelham days were not merely literary artifices; they were partly the devices of a shy nature to protect from unsympathetic notice its own sensitive intensity.[13]

And Bulwer's private diary at a later date bears out the idea. Lady Osborne had remarked on his shyness and dandyism and he writes,

Both are natural. God gave my soul an exterior abode and the very fact that there is a soul within the shell, makes me think the shell not to be neglected. There is a poetry in dress.[14]

Pelham's family is poor but proud. At Eton he makes friends with a Byronically gloomy youth, Reginald Glanville, whose temperament is of "a deep and impassioned melancholy." After a rapid and flippant passage through Cambridge he follows the advice of his cynical and epigrammatic mother whose letters act as his social guide in life. "You may also pick up a little acquaintance with metaphysics," she tells him. "That sort of thing is a good deal talked about just at present." "Never talk much to young men —remember that it is the women who make a reputation in society." He goes to Paris to learn French and dancing, deliberately assuming a character— that of the coxcomb because it is "obnoxious to men and therefore pleasing to women," and he is "impertinent enough to become the rage." He has a successful duel with a Frenchman and notes carefully at his mother's request the differences between the French and the English character. He takes part in long digressive conversations, in the manner of *Wilhelm Meister*, on polite literature and the novel. His idea

of the novel as given here shows that Bulwer had
Goethe's story at least vaguely in mind:

Every good novel has one great end—the increasing of our knowledge
of the human heart. It is thus that a novel writer must be a philosopher. . . . It is in occasional dialogue, in desultory maxims, in
deductions from events, in analysis of character that [the novelist]
should benefit and instruct. . . . For my vehicles of instruction or
amusement I would have people as they are—neither worse nor better
—and the moral they should convey should be rather through jest or
irony than gravity and seriousness.[15]

Vincent, the perfect man of the world, shares the
honors with Lady Pelham of educating our hero. He
takes Pelham to *soirées*, assemblies, the opera, in
short with his aid Pelham "takes the greatest pains
to complete my education." Pelham achieves the
reputation of "a consummate puppy." He learns to
affect a fine carelessness; "the most consummate men
of the world are those who have considered the least
on it." The old Byronic acquaintance, Glanville,
turns up to form the subplot, and succeeds in ruining
an enemy, Tyrrel, in a gambling hell, whereupon he
disappears. Various type-characters appear inter-
mittently, such as the soured old wit, the glutton and
the henpecked husband, to show us that Pelham is
seeing all phases of human nature. On his return to
England to enter Parliament, his uncle, Lord Glen-
morris, finds that he has "already arrived at that
great epoch when vanity casts off its first skin and
ambition succeeds to pleasure."[16] His uncle makes
him read Bentham and Mill on *Government*, and Pelham now obtains "a clear knowledge of moral prin-

ciple." Formerly he has been ruled only by impulse and passion, but he says now, "I no longer divorced the interests of other men from my own."[17]   The first step in his moral apprenticeship has been achieved. Later on he will be an orator, a wit, or a scholar, he tells Vincent, but "It is *now* my object to be a dandy."[18] Realizing that he will not inherit his uncle's fortune, Pelham becomes "more thoughtfully and solidly ambitious."[19]   He will carve out his own career with a mind which is now "close, keen, enquiring."   He proceeds to see life still further by means of a drinking bout with some athletic young university men and an acquaintance with a "club" of ruffians about town, which brings in a bit of "low life."   He learns about political intrigue, and falls in love with his friend Glanville's sister, Ellen.   He finds Glanville's enemy, Tyrrel, murdered on a lonely road, and saves Glanville's life by a daring excursion into a den of rogues to get the testimony that will clear him.   Episodes of this kind are by far the most spirited and well-written parts of Bulwer's stories.   Pelham emerges as a pretty serious sort of hero after all.   "In this busy and restless world I have not been a vague speculator, nor an idle actor.   While all around me were vigilant, I have not laid me down to sleep—even for the luxury of a poet's dream.   Like the school-boy I have considered study as study, but action as delight."[20]   Bulwer apologizes for not having presented the conventional hero; he has allowed readers to laugh at his foibles.   "Forgive me if I have not wept over a 'blighted spirit' nor boasted of a 'British heart,' and allow that a man who in these days of alternate Werthers and Worthies, is neither the one nor the other, is, at least, a novelty in print, though, I fear, common enough in real life."[21]   Like Wilhelm, Pelham has come through an idle dilettantism to action for others.

Pelham had at first only three favorable reviews, those in the *Atlas*, the *Literary Gazette* and the *Examiner*, of which his friend, and Carlyle's acquaintance, Albany Fonblanque, was the editor, but after two or three months it attained a tremendous vogue.   Pelham's preference for black coats banished colored ones from London drawing rooms, and his gay affectations and witty philosophizings were translated into many languages, including German.   His point of view probably did as much to supplant Byronic melancholy and pseudo-Wertherian sentimentality as any of the polemics of Carlyle, pernicious as Carlyle thought any book that proclaimed so loudly that manners make the man.   It said quite as distinctly as *Sartor*, "Close thy Byron; open thy Goethe."   And if it did not say, "Love not pleasure, love God," it said at least that a man of pleasure need not be a total loss if he is also a man of action.   The early reviewers of the book, even when friendly, seem to have recognized no traces of a German prototype in *Pelham*.   Only the *New Monthly Magazine*, of which Bulwer was later to be editor, suggests something like it.

It is formed, [writes the reviewer],[22] on the old admirable but disused plan of Le Sage, Fielding, and Smollett—namely, the tracing the life of the hero from his boyhood upwards, and thus laying before the reader, as in a map, the whole history of the man, and of his opinions

and pursuits as modified by change of age and new connections.   Mr.
Hope in his *Anastasius* has practised this method of novel-writing,
but in his work, no less than in *Gil Blas, Tom Jones,* and *Roderick
Random,* the hero is a mere adventurer . . . and it seemed strange
that the same scheme of fiction had never, in any conspicuous instance, been adopted to delineate the life of any other class of persons.
The Adventures of a Gentleman [the sub-title of *Pelham*] are, it must
be acknowledged, something new in literature.

Bulwer fared so badly at the hands of Thackeray and
Maginn in *Fraser's,* that it is not surprising to find in
this magazine slurs cast on his early work, in the
general program of mud-slinging.[23]

With *The Disowned* (1829) Bulwer begins to
theorize about the novel.   As in the case of a great
many writers, his theory had little to do with his
actual practice, and was in the main not nearly so
good though much "neater."   A preface to the 1835
edition of *The Disowned* deals with *The Different Kinds
of Prose Fiction,* which he divides systematically,
under the heading of "The Narrative Novel" (as
opposed to the dramatic), into three categories: the
actual, the satiric, and the metaphysical.   His son
tells us that he tried hard to avoid repeating himself
by doing in turn one of each kind.[24]   Presumably he
thought *The Disowned* came under the "metaphysical"
classification, and this mysterious word, which he
uses often after 1829, is always more or less vaguely
connected in his mind with *Wilhelm Meister.*[25]   The
advertisement to the 1852 edition of the same novel,
The Disowned, says he was studying "metaphysics
and ethics" when he wrote it, and that he regarded
Wilhelm Meister as a successful example of the type.

"Metaphysics" meant German philosophy to most English readers of that period, though *Meister*, if Bulwer had not specifically referred to it, would no doubt have been far from their minds. But "metaphysical" meant to Bulwer something like what we mean by "psychological" today—one of those delightfully inclusive words that cover everything on which the lay mind is a little uncertain—and it was meant to include his somewhat limited and sentimental but very earnest researches into the springs of action, the hidden mental background of his characters. It meant a kind of personification of the abstract, a wavering between reality and allegory, between the shows of outward life and a pervasive, deeper meaning—all of which he found in *Wilhelm Meister*. The metaphysical novel, says his 1852 preface to *The Disowned*, is "not to be regarded as a mere portraiture of outward society. It often wanders from the exact probability of effects in order to bring more strikingly before us the truth of causes. . . . [It] often invests itself in a dim and shadowy allegory which it deserts or resumes at will, making its action but the incarnation of some peculiar and abstract qualities."[26] Of *The Disowned* he says: "The development of the Abstract was its principal object." His preface to the second edition says that he wanted "to personify certain dispositions influential upon conduct: For instance Vanity (Talbot), Ambition (Warner), Pride (Lord Borodaile), Selfishness and Sensuality (Crawford), Philanthropy (Mordaunt)." This sounds like one of the old Moralities, and in the guise of a novel, with the characters carefully balanced in groups of three as they are in *Meister*, it makes a somewhat stiff and dreary performance.

Clarence Linden, who at first glimpse appears to be the "apprentice" who is to make his way through the story of *The Disowned* scarcely qualifies for that rôle, except through the mere process of growing up. He is no learner with a purpose, who assimilates his experience or goes through the usual stages. Algernon Mordaunt, however, is the real apprentice. He has been to Germany and learned its "mysticism" and found "there can be no education in which the lessons of the world do not form a share. Experience, in expanding Algernon's powers, had ripened his virtues." His character is that of a philanthropic stoic, a "type of the heroism of Christian philosophy, an union of love and knowledge placed in the midst of sorrow, and laboring on through the midst of life, strong in the fortitude that comes from belief in heaven."[27] Here it seems as though Carlyle were beginning to take effect on Bulwer's use of the apprenticeship theme. There are traces of Carlyle in the early essays and they grow more distinct as Bulwer proceeds.

Mordaunt, bereft of his fortune, must carve out his own career, marries a poor girl, resists all temptations to evildoing which poverty presents, and lives in seclusion until he is foully murdered by Wolfe, the "republican" and villain of the piece, who also conveniently murders Lord Borodaile, brother of Clarence Linden, the "disowned," so that Clarence may inherit the family fortunes and settle down happily on one of those ancestral estates that Bulwer is so fond of, with the lady of his choice. Clarence has found a mentor during his troubles, in Lord Talbot, whose biography—"The Story of a Vain Man"—is inserted into the middle of the story in the manner of the incidental tales in many picaresque novels and also in *Meister*. Some of his advice to Clarence is presented in the form of a *Lehrbrief* like that with which Wilhelm's guides terminated his apprenticeship: "You are about to enter upon the great world," Talbot tells him, "and have within you the desire and power of success; let me flatter myself that you can profit by my experience. . . . Let me then call your attention to the hints and maxims which I have in this paper amused myself with drawing up for your instruction."[28]

The Westminster Review found *The Disowned* inferior to *Pelham* in "unity of design and felicity of execution."[29] The *Quarterly* complained of the confusion in the plot and of "Lord Byron's influence" which has "left unfortunate traces among others than the poetasters of his time. These recent novelists have all borrowed from him a vein of egotism which nothing but very high genius could ever render tolerable in any species of composition and which assuredly suits as ill with the novel as with any that could be named. Eternal rhapsodies about the personal feelings, opinions, circumstances and prospects of such a man as Lord Byron might be borne with even in such a piece as *Don Juan*—but things like this make one sorry for authors of less distinguished rank."[30]

It was in the same year as the publication of *The Disowned* that the friendship of Bulwer and Disraeli began.   In the spring of 1829 Disraeli sent Bulwer the manuscript of his novel *The Young Duke* for criticism.   Bulwer advised him to remove some of the more flippant passages, and Disraeli took this so to heart that for a while he gave up the idea of publishing the book at all.   Disraeli was contributing his novel *Alroy* to the *New Monthly* during Bulwer's editorship in 1831, and by 1832 they seem to be on intimate terms.   He goes to Bulwer's *soirées* and through him finds his way into "the charmed circle of Mayfair."[31]   He describes these parties of Bulwer's as being "very brilliant," and we get from him some idea of the people who passed through Bulwer's ornate drawing-rooms in the early thirties—the ill-fated Letitia Elizabeth Landon or "L.E.L.," gotten up in what Disraeli calls a "Graeco-Bromptonian" dress, mentioning also her snub nose and pink satin slippers; Lady Morgan, Mrs. Norton, Mrs. Gore, and other famous "Blues"; D'Orsay, the complete dandy; Fonblanque, Charles Villiers, and Henry Ellis. We may suppose that not the least gorgeous of these was Disraeli himself.   He speaks of another evening when "there were a great many dames there of distinction, but no Blues."   Bulwer comes to visit him at Bradenham, and Dizzy, evidently sympathizing with his domestic difficulties which were then becoming painful, warns his sister that Bulwer is coming for "absolute retirement really to write and all that.   He is to do what he likes and wander about the woods like a madman."[32]

In spite of Bulwer's help in the form of letters of recommendation from O'Connell and Hume, and his efforts to secure his friend from opposition Disraeli failed in his first stand for Parliament at High Wycombe in 1832. So perhaps it was with a slight tinge of jealousy that he wrote his sister of Bulwer's speech in the House: "He is physically disqualified for an orator and in spite of all his exertions never can succeed. He was heard with great attention and is evidently backed by a party."[33] Bulwer had by this time taken his seat on the Radical side as member for Lincoln. In 1833 we get Disraeli's picture of Bulwer's mother-in-law, "not so pleasant, something between Jeremy Bentham and Meg Merrilies, very clever but awfully revolutionary." While she advocated the rights of women during this particular evening, Disraeli defended himself as best he could and "Rosina [Bulwer's wife] played with her dog."[34] He and Bulwer came back from Bath together in September, 1833, and Disraeli confided to him a natural inclination to indolence. Bulwer answered that he was conscious of the same failing and the knowledge that "we are sacrificing our youth . . . but we are bound to go on! How our enemies would triumph were we to retire from the stage! And yet," he continued in a solemn voice, "I have more than once been tempted to throw it all up and quit even my country forever!"[35] Which goes to prove very little except that he was given to talking in private conversation in the same theatrical style that appears so often in his books. Evidently he had something to say, however, that Disraeli found valuable, for he continues:

I have not gained much in conversation with men. Bulwer is one of the few with whom my intellect comes into collision with benefit. He is full of thought and views at once original and just. The material of his conversation and many a hint from our colloquies he has poured into his *England and the English*, a fine series of philosophic dissertations.[36]

Paul Clifford (1830) though not in the apprentice-ship group, may be worthy of mention as having aroused much discussion as to the legitimate province of the novel and what constitutes fiction material. It dealt with prison discipline and the penal code, and in its sentimental way showed the criminal to be a human being like other men. The *Edinburgh* objected to all this portrayal of "low life," although the reviewer is obliged to admit that the book is "free, spirited, forcible."[37] The hostile *Fraser's* took occasion to express the opinion that Bulwer was at his best in depicting the "tap, the ken, the hedge-row pot-house" because these are his native element, but "finally, we dislike altogether this awakening sympathy with interesting criminals, and wasting sensibilities on the scaffold and the gaol. It is a modern, a depraved, a corrupting taste."[38] The *Edinburgh* maintains again that all objections to this school of fiction are not answered simply by proving that the scene or the characters have been taken from real life. Bulwer defended his realistic criminals by saying that even though punished by modern law, they were legitimate subject matter providing one could wind up with a good moral. But the *Edinburgh* explains that it "is not so much the moral tendency as the artistical fitness of such subjects that we differ about."[39] And so the battle was beginning to be waged that filled the minds of writers much later in the century. It is interesting to note in this connection much of the contemporary discussion over such books as *An American Tragedy* and the eternal question: "Is it Art?"

It was probably in the fateful year of the Reform bill and of Goethe's death and Scott's, that Carlyle and Bulwer first met. Carlyle was careless about following up possible jobs for editors, though he wanted work badly.

Thus when Proctor now (7/2/22) let him know that Bulwer Lytton had "some disposition" to employ him in the *New Monthly* and that it would be advisable to call, he answered nothing and did not call until, as he told his brother, "the mystagogue of the dandiacal body wrote to me a most bland and euphuistically flattering note soliciting an interview as my 'admirer.' "[40]

Which Bulwer no doubt sincerely was. He was not lacking in tact, and probably perceived how to get on Carlyle's right side, which he ultimately did. Carlyle wrote a paper on Goethe for his magazine and in the same year Bulwer, oddly enough, proposed a subject which Carlyle was not yet ready to consider; by the time he got around to it himself, he had no doubt long since forgotten this note of Bulwer's:

If you are disposed to undertake for the March number of the New Monthly the life of Frederick the Great, I beg to say that I would in no way tie you down as to quantity. . . . It is a fine subject.[41]

By 1840 Carlyle and Bulwer were meeting at dinners. In 1836 Carlyle had still spoken scathingly of him when he met him at a "rout" at the Bullers, as "Lytton Bulwer, whom I did not notice with the eye,"[42] but in 1840, "he is decidedly human, nay, has a kind of intellect faintly indicated about the eyebrows, perhaps too in the afflicted-looking large protrusive eyes: His appearance, adding the long nose and open mouth, the dandiacal apparel, weak padded figure, and adventitious renown, is *tragic-gawky*. Poor fellow, he has his own battle to fight, like us all. He and I agreed wonderfully well in the touch and go fashion; he seemed desirous to 'engrush' himself rather than otherwise."[43]

Carlyle had enjoyed *England and the English*, and had written to Mill:

Bulwer is an honest kind of creature, though none of the strongest; nay perhaps as you once said, "distinguished most for his tenuity."[44]

So Carlyle was already not unkindly disposed toward Bulwer. On *Richelieu* he makes the cryptic comment, "I have seen—Bulwer's Richelieu and Bulwer himself: Ach Gott im Himmel!" To Sterling in 1841 he writes that Forster is beginning to see through his friend Bulwer and to find that he is "no longer all gold to him . . . but . . . gives fatal symptoms here and there . . . of being mere scoured brass." In the same year as this discovery, both the Carlyles were interesting themselves in Bulwer's family difficulties, and Mrs. Carlyle was very much up in arms for Lady Lytton. They read her popular novel

Cheveley, which interested even Carlyle who did not think much of novels as a rule. "For Carlyle, the first Lord Lytton was 'a poor fribble' and Mrs. C. who had espoused the cause of the novelist's wife and championed her grievances, was still more plain-spoken, calling him 'a lanthorn-jawed quack.' She told me that Carlyle had refused I know not how many invitations to dine with him."[45] But, as Wilson reminds us, and Carlyle's letters too, he did not refuse all of them. He wrote Bulwer appreciative letters in 1842 about *Zanoni* and in 1844 about the translation of Schiller's *Poems and Ballads*. In the latter year they used to go for walks together, to talk about Schiller and Richter, Bulwer coming to Cheyne Row to call for Carlyle[46]—and a singular pair they must have made, if a friend's description of Bulwer about this time is accurate at all: Bulwer indulged a

fondness for personal metamorphoses, so to speak. One day he would appear in black from top to toe, with a dark-complexioned visage to match. Another day he would be all in brown, and on a third he would be all in white, with blonde hair and a fair complexion lighted up by rouge.[47]

Many years later we hear of Carlyle being "constituted chief mourner" at Forster's funeral, "next after Lord Lytton" (Bulwer's son), both of them "leading the mournful procession, which," adds Carlyle plaintively, "was at an hour much too early for me."[48] *Sic transit gloria!*

Amidst the Fraser attacks, a busy life in Parliament, domestic difficulties, and the publication of *Eugene*

Aram, as well as the editing of the *New Monthly*, Bulwer's interest in things German was still simmering in his mind.   It is impressive to see how it persists, though not very clearly, as a kind of undercurrent to all his vanities, platitudes and sentimentalities, to his very real griefs and to his earnest efforts to write good novels according to that semi-German idea of his about the "metaphysical" novel—efforts which finally by the grace of Goethe, were successful.   Something of the hold which "the massiveness of the German mind" supplemented by Carlyle's influence had on him, is explained in his notice of Goethe's death in the *New Monthly* of 1832, one of a series of papers called *Asmodeus at Large:*[49]

"Dead—the great spirit gone! and the Atlas newspaper says he was but a very poor creature after all." "What wonderful stores he has left behind him! every work illuminating a separate train of thought. *Werther, Wilhelm Meister, Faust.* How different, how mighty, each!" "Nevertheless," said Asmodeus, "the *Wilhelm Meister* is a wonderful stupid novel." "What an effect is produced on me! What a new world it opens! You read the book and you wonder why you admire it. When you have finished, you find yourself enriched: it is like a quiet stream that carries gold with it—the stream passes away insensibly, but the gold remains to tell where it has been. This is the great merit of the books of the German Masters —ineffective in parts, the effect as a whole is wonderfully deep. *Wilhelm Meister* is to the knowledge of thoughts what *Gil Blas* is to knowledge of the world. Peace to the ashes of a man that has left no equal!"

There is something reminiscent of Carlyle's impressions of *Wilhelm Meister* here, recorded nine years earlier in his letters to Jane and his brother.   Bulwer was less able to analyze his impressions than Carlyle was, and there is always a little confusion in his expressions about Goethe—a general vague sense of "depth" seems to have been the main thing he thought he got; perhaps the main thing he really got, was the framework for a series of novels.

Bulwer has more to say about *Meister* in a review of Disraeli's novel *Contarini Fleming*, published in this same year, 1832.[50] He much preferred it to *Vivian Grey* and *The Young Duke*, and his review shows that he took it to be, like *Wilhelm Meister*, a metaphysical novel such as he had discussed in his essays and novels. "The mass of readers will not perceive its object and therefore it seems to them bizarre, merely because its meaning is not on the surface." Here again it was depth (or was it vagueness?) that he admired:

In fact, *Contarini Fleming* is a delineation of abstract ideas, in which, as in *Wilhelm Meister*, the author is often allegorical and actual at the same time. Each character is a personification of certain traits of mind [as had been the case in his own novel *The Disowned*]; but in that personification the author now and then forgets himself and deals only with the external world which he designed at first merely as a covering to metaphysical creatures. I compare it, in this instance, to *Wilhelm Meister*. And I am quite certain that if *Wilhelm Meister* never had been written, *Contarini Fleming* would never have walked into the ideal world. Yet, for all that, there is no imitation in story, character, and least of all in style. The subdued calm of Goethe is as different as possible from the varying brilliancy of the author of *Contarini Fleming*. *Wilhelm Meister* is the mature produce of a very stupendous, brooding mind that worked out the block of nature with the most artificial and recondite tools. All in Goethe was the Artist—the great Artist—and all in *Wilhelm Meister* breathes of that Art, and of the time, thought, musing, which had been devoted to its cultivation.

This shows, five years before Bulwer's *Ernest Maltravers*, the same point he was to make in the preface to that novel—that *Art* was predominant in *Wilhelm Meister's* apprenticeship while Maltravers was to be the apprentice of "real life." Either he overlooked the qualities of Wilhelm's apprenticeship which were representative of the "real life" of the eighteenth-century Germany in which he lived, or he was so delighted with the conclusion, which contains a good deal about art and the projected journey to Italy after Mignon's death, that he overlooked the elements of realism in Wilhelm's progress to this conclusion. At any rate, whereas Carlyle saw Goethe primarily as a great moral teacher, the artist in him was what leapt to Bulwer's eye, as it did to Lewes in 1850.

Bulwer's next apprentice novel, *Godolphin*, was published in 1833, the same year as his journey to Italy and separation from his wife. It was published anonymously, which may explain why it got fewer reviews than some of his later work. *The New Monthly*, Bulwer's own magazine, thought it was written by a woman, since "certain passages betray a writhing consciousness of the social position of women" and ends up with a guess that the book was by Mrs. Norton! Bulwer always deals somehow with "the struggles of ill-regulated minds" as any apprentice novel inevitably does. This time he comes nearer to an actual parallel in treatment as well as in idea to *Wilhelm Meister*, than he has done before.

"Godolphin," his preface explains (what would Bulwer have done without his prefaces!), "is the man of poetical temperament, out of his place alike among the trifling idlers and the bustling actors of the world —wanting the stimulus of necessity—or the higher motive which springs from benevolence, to give energy to his powers, or definite purpose to his fluctuating desires; not strong enough to break the bonds that confine his genius, not supple enough to accommodate its movement to their purpose," the perfect dilettante, in fact, like Wilhelm in his earlier stages. "In evading the struggles of the world, he grows indifferent to its duties—he strives with no obstacles—he can triumph in no career." The book makes a conscious effort at something like the *Weltbild* or cross-section of contemporary life, in trying to show "certain phases of modern civilization and . . . some truths . . . worth considering in our examination of social influences on individual conduct."[51]

As is so often the case with Bulwer, his formulae and explanations are much clearer than his actual practice. Percy Godolphin, like most of Bulwer's heroes, is precocious. At sixteen he has the complete vocabulary of his kind—pseudo-Byronic, and every speech a paragraph. He slaps the face of the school-master who attempts to punish him (even as Bulwer did in his youth) and escapes from a miserly old father, to see the world. Like Wilhelm he meets the wandering actor and his troupe, and Fanny Millinger (a good deal like Philine in *Wilhelm Meister*) takes his eye. But in spite of his love for the brisk, hearty,

capable girl, he will not learn to act, partly because
he thinks it beneath him and partly because he has
"no propensity to imitation and a strong susceptibility to the ridiculous," qualities which in later life
"prevented his ever finding fit scope for his natural
powers."[52] He moves on to high life in London,
falling in with a middle-aged profligate and man of
the world, Saville, who had once been a suitor of
Godolphin's mother and been rejected.   While Godolphin is learning to be an accomplished gamester, his
father's elderly cousin, Harry Johnstone, sees and
likes him, and wants to make him his heir.   Fanny
Millinger meanwhile has become a famous actress, but
though Godolphin becomes stage-struck and the plays
he sees awaken romance in him as real life has not
yet done, Fanny is as unromantic as possible off the
stage.   Old Johnstone leaves Percy his fortune on
condition that he live at home or else out of London,
so the youth decides to go abroad.   We are given a
glimpse of overhanging fate in a reference to the "wayward and strange events" that "tinged Godolphin's
character with superstition.   He afterwards dealt
con amore with fatalities and influences."[53] Something of the secret society that presided over Wilhelm's fortunes is probably indicated here.   With "a
character half-formed and half-enervated" this accomplished youth leaves England at seventeen.

The proud and statuesque Constance who has lived
a life dedicated to revenge on her father's faithless
political friends (he had died of their neglect and injustice) and who has cultivated a mind with a natural

bent toward political affairs, sees Godolphin wandering among the picturesque ancestral ruins of his
country estate, and falls in love with him. Though
she admires Pope and Dryden, and he admires Wordsworth (this is highly significant with regard to their
futures) their acquaintance begun in the richly Victorian ballrooms and terraces of the country castle
owned by Constance's guardian and friend Lady
Erpingham, soon ripens into intimacy. It is apparent
from the start that Constance, strong-minded and
charming as she is, will not be able to make much
out of Percy. "Of a reflective and refining mind, he
had early learned to despise the common emotion of
men: glory touched him not and to ambition he had
shut his heart."[54] The vanity of all things is too
apparent to him, and though (or perhaps because)
brilliant and imaginative, he is also lonely. "Who
will not allow that he has met many such men? And
who will not follow this man to his end?" It is true
that the type has a melancholy fascination, from
Werther to *Moon-Calf*. We know they are bound to
go on the rocks, but we must follow them until we
discover just how they do it. Percy, however, is
more accurate in his self-analysis than some of these
young men.

I who have often vainly fancied I had the poetical temperament
[he tells Constance] have been so chilled and sickened by the
characteristics of the tribe that I have checked its impulses with a
sort of disdain; and thus the Ideal, having no vent in me, preys
within, creating a thousand undefined dreams . . . and dis-
satisfying me with the petty ambitions of the world.[55]

Bulwer laboriously brings in the allegory that belongs among the properties of the metaphysical novel. Percy again meets Fanny Millinger:

There was a sort of allegory of real life in the manner in which . . . our Idealist was brought into contact with the fair Actress of ideal creations. There was . . . something of a moral in the way these two streams of existence—the one belonging to the Actual, the other to the Imaginary, flowed on, crossing each other at stated times. Which was the more really imaginative—the life of the stage or that of the world's stage?[56]

Bulwer was thinking here, no doubt, of the mild irony of Goethe's novel, in which Wilhelm mistakenly busies himself in the sham world of the stage before having found what he must work at. Fortunately the versatile Fanny is also a great reader, so that Bulwer can get in his say about the kind of novel he thinks should be written, and evidently intends to write himself: "Sometimes," says Fanny, "I canter through a dozen novels in a morning," but there is no real knowledge of the world in them. They are too trite and superficial. There is more romance in real life, even when it is worldly.

The heart is a romance in itself. . . . Talking of books [Fanny continues], I want someone to write a novel which shall be a metaphysical *Gil Blas*; which shall deal more with the mind than Le Sage's book and less with the actions; which shall make its hero the creature of the world, but a different creation though equally true; which shall give a faithful picture in the character of one man of the aspect and the effects of our social system; making that man of a better sort of clay than the amusing lacquey was, and the product of a more artificial grade of society.[57]

Such a book, in fact, as Bulwer strove to make *Godolphin*, but only achieved in *Ernest Maltravers*. These discussions on literature and the stage, etc., are by way of corresponding to the digressions in *Wilhelm Meister* and in *Pelham* also, dealing with general "cultural topics." Like Goethe and Carlyle, Godolphin sees through shams: "The dialogue is gay, the actors know their parts, the lights are brilliant, but—the scene . . . cannot change for me! Call it what you will, I am not deceived."[58] But we are not convinced of any great penetration on Bulwer's part; he succeeds only in conveying a general idea of world-weariness.

The proud Constance, meanwhile, has married the son of her guardian, Lord Erpingham, and has set about gratifying her political ambitions by forming a select *salon* which discourses about "books, statues, busts." She hears of Godolphin wandering in foreign lands. He meets in Rome the Danish astrologer, Volktmann, and his beautiful child, Lucilla. This uncanny character is modeled in some respects on Goethe's Mignon. Her concealed love for the English stranger, "the play and lustre of expression that undulated in her features," her suppressed, elfin, prematurely passionate, mysterious nature, her tendency to burst into "a wild eldritch laugh"—all this makes her reminiscent of Mignon though much more disconcerting and less charming. Her father, the astrologer, acts as the purveyor of mysterious warnings to our hero, which smack again of Goethe and Carlyle: "It is from thine own self, thine own character, thine own

habits, that all evil, save that of death, will come. . . .
Search thyself, correct thyself, subdue thyself."[59]
They also discourse in the manner of Kant on reason
and imagination: Mankind has cultivated only reason
and banished imagination from life and philosophy.
This is perhaps one reason for Percy's downfall.
After a visit to his native land, Percy returns to
Italy, more cool and selfish from experience of life,
"indifferent but not sated." Lucilla, like Mignon,
wants only to follow her hero, and does; they live
happily enough together until he begins to discover
that she is not his intellectual equal. Constance
Erpingham, ill from boredom with society, comes to
Italy after her husband's death. The philosophical
friend, David Mandeville, a good Carlylean, reminds
her that happiness comes from within, if at all, and
"to be happy we must render ourselves independent
of others." "In Belief lies the secret of all true
action." Godolphin's character begins to show the
harmful results of genius without sufficient action.
He is becoming "the indolent sensualist or the solitary
dreamer," with "a speculative and Hamlet-like temper."[60] Lucilla discovers his attachment to Constance
and departs to a convent; but after his marriage to
Constance he decides to go in for pleasure, not action,
as she would like him to do. Fanny Millinger, the
actress, turns up again, and he decides to associate
with his fellows more than he has done. He has now,
Bulwer carefully points out to us, passed two eras of
his life, "the first of romance, the second, of contemplation." But he still thirsts insatiably for "the

Ideal, the Beautiful, and the Perfect" and fills the house with *objets d'art* while Constance supports him and continues her political machinations.[61] They grow apart; Constance discovers his remorse over Lucilla and finds her in London, earning her living as a soothsayer, but she disappears mysteriously, to die. Godolphin finally goes into Parliament as a Tory, and against the Reform Bill, which Constance favors. Godolphin's old friend and worldly mentor, Saville, dies, saying to his younger friend: "Life differs from the play only in this . . . it has no plot—all is vague, desultory, unconnected, till the curtain drops with the mystery unsolved."[62] How many modern novels have been built on that same assumption! Summoned to Lucilla's deathbed, Godolphin drowns in crossing the ford on his way back.

In spite of the many parallels to *Wilhelm Meister*, especially in the "life and the stage" idea, the book is obviously more the "rise and progress of the dilettante" than an advance toward a solution of the problem of finding what he can "work at." But Bulwer, according to his preface, was definitely out to show a character overcome by his world, not one who was going to be successful at setting himself to rights with it.

That Bulwer was much concerned with the moral purpose of "metaphysical" fiction in this same year, is shown in a review by him in the *New Monthly* of Harriet Martineau's *Illustrations*.[63] Fiction often instructs, he says, "not by the avowed moral but by the latent one. . . . A typical and pervading moral

will be borne more readily and can be admitted more
artfully into the metaphysical fiction than in any
plainer form of conveying morality. The Germans
have tried it—particularly Goethe, the greatest Artist
who ever lived—in *Wilhelm Meister* with prodigious
effect." The idea that fiction must *teach* is of course
implicit in all Bulwer's novels, though he was not so
skillful in concealing it as Goethe was. But one
reason that the *Wilhelm Meister* form appealed to him,
was that it gave him a good vehicle to set forth the
truths that he, like Carlyle, earnestly believed his
generation needed.

In 1834 his *Pilgrims of the Rhine* dedicated to the
German people, and *The Last Days of Pompeii* which
reminded Mrs. Hemans of Goethe (!) set Bulwer's
reputation forever on an unshakable eminence. Reviewers and detractors have always laughed at him
for his tendency to write about the "last" of everything—last days, the last of the tribunes (*Rienzi*), the
last of the barons—which indicated his choice of an
artificially melodramatic situation for his settings in
historical novels. But in *Pompeii* and *Rienzi* he
wrote two such stories as people will always read; he
probably set out to go Scott one better, and could not
really compete with Scott on his own ground. But
in his own grandiose way, and with a careful working-
up of his settings, he achieved immortality. It is one
of the little ironies of literature that he achieved it in
these stories, and not in that more difficult and obscure
field so dear to his ambition—the favorite "metaphysical" fiction. His novels of family life, *The Cax-*

tons and *My Novel,* (1849 and 1853) are excellent of
their kind, and reached great popularity in their day;
but his historical novels are the ones most read today,
perhaps because in them he was not interested in
studying "the influence of something upon something
else," the phrase by which one critic has summed up
the weakness of his work.

Bulwer's son tells us that *Ernest Maltravers* (1837) was
the most autobiographical of all his novels so far, though
Bulwer's preface to the 1840 edition expressly denies
any autobiographic tendency in it.   It is also the
strongest in its use of the apprentice theme, and he
acknowledges direct indebtedness to *Wilhelm Meister*
for the first time.   The other characters, as well as
Ernest himself, show some development, as was the
case in Goethe's novel, and they are not so allegorical
as to fly in the face of reality.   He does not talk any
longer about the "metaphysical" novel, and all its
worst features, visible in *The Disowned* and *Godolphin,*
have disappeared.   In *Pelham,* Bulwer writes in his
preface, he was trying to represent the surface of the
world distinctly, as youth sees it.   In *Godolphin,* he
was writing "a work devoted to a particular portion
of society and the development of a peculiar class of
character."   In *Maltravers* he finds "the most mature, and on the whole, the most comprehensive of all
that I have hitherto written."[64]

For the original idea which, with all humility, I will venture to
call the philosophical design, of a moral education or apprenticeship,
I have left it easy to be seen that I am indebted to Goethe's *Wilhelm
Meister*.   But in *Wilhelm Meister* the apprenticeship is rather that

of theoretical art.   In the more homely plan that I set before myself, the apprenticeship is rather that of practical life.[65]

He has therefore, he goes on to say, avoided distractions "lawful in romance" and concocted no "great scenes," but attempted to show us "life as it is."   He evidently did not think Goethe did this.

Ernest Maltravers at the beginning of his career, has a brighter, more active temperament, more extravert in fact, than any of Bulwer's other heroes. There is nothing even faintly Byronic about him.   He has studied in Germany at the University of Göttingen and read Plato and Kant and other idols of Bulwer's own, and is an excellent musician and poet at eighteen, with strongly "republican" sentiments.   He rescues the beautiful and simple rustic, Alice Darvil, from a murderous and ruffianly father, and falls in love with her.   During the sudden absence of Ernest, the father kidnaps her and she is lost to her lover for many years—until the end of a second volume, in fact.   Cleveland, the "Horace Walpole of his day," versed in the great world and liberal in his ideas about education, is Ernest's guardian and mentor.   He tells Ernest's father: "He must either go through action, and adventures and excitement in his own way, or he will be an idle dreamer or an impractical enthusiast all his life,"[66] (as Godolphin was).   Stricken by the loss of Alice, and foiled in his constant search for her, Ernest becomes a sadder and wiser young man, even as Wilhelm did through his unfortunate love affair.

Nine times out of ten it is over the Bridge of Sighs that we pass the narrow gulf from Youth to Manhood. . . . The intellect has been hardened by the fire through which it has passed. The mind profits by the wrecks of every passion and we may measure our road to wisdom by the sorrows we have undergone.[67]

Religion proves a temporary and superficial solace to Ernest, but he is roused from a kind of lethargy by Lumley Ferrers, a friend of a more practical, worldly type than himself (as Werner was more able to cope with the real world than Wilhelm).

I think it is Goethe who says somewhere that in reading the life of the greatest genius, we always find that he was acquainted with some man superior to himself, who yet never attained to general distinction. To the class of these mystical superior men, Lumley Ferrers might have belonged.[68]

He tells the melancholy Ernest that he should read less and live more: "Action . . . is the life for us." He and Ferrers go on their Grand Tour together, and where else but to Italy? In Rome Ernest meets the gay, cosmopolitan woman of the world, Valerie de Ventadour, who is, to Bulwer's Victorian eye, "that gay and unhappy thing—*a woman without a home!*" Ernest meets and learns from all types of women and is always attractive to them, as Wilhelm was. As yet Ernest has gained from experience only worldly wisdom—no definite purpose or plan of action. When he steals away from pleasure he is "ever and anon haunted by his old familiar aspirations for the Beautiful, the Virtuous, and the Great."[69] His mentor, Cleveland, reminds him that he must labor and not dawdle around in Italy too long:

If you do not fulfill what Nature intended for your fate, you will be a morbid misanthrope, or an indolent voluptuary. . . . But if you do fulfill your fate, you must enter soon into your apprenticeship. Let me see you labor and aspire—no matter what in—what to. Work, work, that is all I ask of you.[70]

Sartor had come out three years before, and the gospel of work, as such, had perhaps become more clearly defined in Bulwer's mind, especially since, as we have seen, he was not only an admirer but a social acquaintance of Carlyle's and probably followed his ideas and writings closely. Here we find the Carlylean gospel mentioned with Goethe's idea of apprenticeship and in close connection. They had always been more or less vaguely associated in Bulwer's mind, as the earlier apprentice novels show, but from this time on the connection is clear.

Valerie, though in love with him, renounces Ernest (since she is married) and through his struggle to accept this renunciation he finds "even an erring love, wrestled against with a noble spirit, leaves the heart more tolerant and tender and the mind more settled and enlarged. . . . Experience and wisdom must be wrought from the Philosophy of the Passions."[71] Ernest now resides on an island in Lake Como and meets M. and Mme de Montaigne, the philosophic Frenchman and his beautiful wife who is a singer. M. de Montaigne who represents "good sense" and poise is added to the list of Ernest's advisors and mentors. Mme de Montaigne's ambitious and morbid young brother, Cesarini, is the perfect Byronic hero run to seed. He desires above all things, fame in literature, with an almost insane intensity and jealousy. Ernest, who is beginning to write himself, learns from him the danger of sentimental second-rate writing and the self-deception that it may involve. Cleveland's illness calls Ernest back to England. De Montaigne warns him against lukewarmness and incites him to a career in public life, or, as Bulwer himself puts it, in his inimitable way, "Contend worthily in the world's wide Altis for a great prize."[72] Ernest has hitherto doubted the wisdom of effort, but now, like Carlyle, he looks on life "as a part of the eternity to which I *feel* we were born"; in short, we should work for others.[73] Bulwer reminds us that we have been following Ernest "along the noiseless progress of his mental education," but we should never be conscious of any connection between the various stages of his apprenticeship, or of any organic growth throughout the process unless we were thus abruptly reminded from time to time. Bulwer knew very well what he wanted to do, but was only able to do it by a forcible sort of literary mechanics.

Ernest's lost love, Alice, meanwhile, has escaped from her father and a "life of Sin," and with Ernest's child she takes to the road and begs from door to door. She is rescued by Mrs. Leslie and set up as a music teacher in a small cathedral town, where she is admired and protected by a solid and prosperous banker, Mr. Templeton, who later turns out to be Lumley Ferrer's rich uncle. Alice's father, who has been again molesting her, is pursued by this old gentleman, and caught and shot by the police. Then Templeton marries Alice. Her child and Ernest's has died.

Ernest has written two successful books, but the

second one receives abusive reviews and Ernest is as sensitive to these as Bulwer himself; something of his bitterness over the Fraser attacks goes into his description of Ernest's wounded pride when he becomes aware of "the sneer, the frown, the caustic irony, the biting review, the depreciating praise." De Montaigne comes to see him, and like Wieland in his *Agathon* (which Bulwer had certainly read) preaches "moral equilibrium" and "reason." But Ernest, a good Kantian, would rather assist reason with the "Imaginative Faculty" since he holds "all philosophy incomplete and unsatisfactory that bounds its enquiries to the limits of the Known and Certain."[74] There is a touch of Carlyle again in his Fichtean gospel that "from literature . . . had come all that makes nations enlightened and men humane."[75] He pays court to the wealthy, brilliant, and beautiful Florence Lascelles, who is also the idol of the passionate Italian poet, Cesarini. Florence turns out to be the composer of anonymous letters to Ernest (in the manner of the missives from the secret society in *Wilhelm Meister*) asking him,

Are you aware of your capacities? . . . Do you forget that action is the grand career for men who think as you do [*i.e.*, idealistically]? . . . You are too practical for the mere poet, and too poetical to sink into the dull tenor of a learned life. . . . Is it not worthier of you to *be* what you fancy or relate?[76]

which is a hint at Wilhelm Meister and his stage career again. Ernest enters Parliament, of course (that being always Bulwer's idea of "action") and so does the shrewd and selfish Ferrers, but with far different principles from Ernest's "high-wrought Platonism." Cleveland advises Ernest about his career and says:

The end of a scientific morality is not to serve others only, but also to perfect and accomplish our individual selves; . . . you are about to add to your experience of human motives and active men.[77]

This self-development idea is of course akin to Goethe's *Bildung* mentioned so many times before. Action to Ernest is now "the condition of his being." He has at least escaped dilettantism. "To keep the mind and body in perfect health it is necessary to mix habitually and betimes in the common affairs of men," as "one of his favorite German authors" said. Ernest is able and respected in his parliamentary work because of his "correct and well-considered views" but reaches no great eminence and goes "his haughty and lonesome way." Ferrers and Cesarini, both jealous of Ernest, unite against him, and separate him from Florence by the ruse of an altered letter. On his deathbed, Alice's husband and Ferrers' uncle, Mr. Templeton, binds Ferrers to marry Evelyn, his adopted child (not Ernest's child, be it remembered, since she had died), but Templeton's illegitimate child by another woman. Ferrers knows, however, that Alice is the lost sweetheart whom Ernest has been seeking. Poor Ernest, embittered by Florence's unjust rejection of him, is in the depths of misanthropy. The speed at which he, in common with all Bulwer's heroes, lives, is remarkable and startling: "At thirty years of age he had necessarily outlived the sanguine

elasticity of early youth." He is "always asking for
something too refined and too' exalted for human
life," and this is now the root of all his difficulties.
Florence, in a "decline" because of her loss of Ernest,
discovers the imposture that has been practised on
them by Ferrers and Cesarini, which the latter, in a
fit of remorse, also discloses to Ernest of his own
accord. Cesarini is by this time practically mad.
After Florence's death, in a fine melodramatic scene,
Ernest confronts him, denounces him, and concludes:
"Forgive the sinner, O God, as I do!" and departs,
bowed with grief and despair, to that refuge of all
hard-pressed Englishmen of fiction, the continent.

Alice, or The Mysteries, 1838, is the continuation of
Ernest Maltravers, and was destined to show his redemption by love, from his state of hardness and
resentment against the world. His experience, so
far, had taught him "the vanity of human life," but
Bulwer could not leave him there and have his
apprenticeship lead merely to so pernicious a conclusion. "Nothing really immoral is ever permanently
popular," was one of Bulwer's favorite maxims, and
a negative conclusion would have been immoral, with
Goethe and Carlyle and Bulwer's own idea of his
duty to the middle classes hard at his elbow. Goethe
is never far off. For instance, the "spectator-and-
actor" figure is used by De Montaigne, in his advice
to Ernest. "You . . . are passing . . . through
a state of transition. You have left forever the Ideal,
and you are carrying your cargo of experience over to
the Practical. When you reach that haven, you will

have completed the development of your forces."
"You mistake me," answers Ernest, "I am but a
spectator." "Yes, but you desire to go behind the
scenes. And he who once grows familiar with the
greenroom longs to be an actor."[78]

Something of the contemporary *Weltbild* is given in
the following passage on the middle class. De Montaigne says:

A new class is created, the Middle Class, the express creature of
civilization. Behold the burgher and the citizen, still struggling . .
. and therefore still discontented. . . . It is the discontent of
hope, not despair. . . . It makes the citizen an active and therefore
not an unhappy man. . . . Commerce, better than charity, feeds
the hungry.[79]

This was certainly the prevailing social idea of the
time in which Bulwer was writing.

Ernest has fallen in love with Evelyn, Templeton's
and Alice's adopted child, but gives her up to Legard,
a handsome younger man, and a dashing soldier, who
has already made up his mind to renounce her for
Ernest, thus achieving the renunciation that is necessary to complete his character. He lives on his ancestral estate and puts its affairs in order, thus learning
the practical activity and skill in husbandry that
Therese taught Wilhelm in *Wilhelm Meister*. First
honor, then justice, and then fortitude have successively been Ernest's favorite virtues, but he has been
too hard on people and too intolerant, and now he
learns the value of simple goodness. Templeton has
died, and he finds and marries Alice at last. His
apprenticeship is over.

Maltravers once more entered upon the career so long suspended. He entered with an energy more practical and steadfast than the fitful enthusiasm of former years . . . while the firmness of his mind was not impaired, the haughtiness of his temper was subdued. No longer despising Man as he is, and no longer exacting from all things the Ideal of a visionary standard, he was more fitted to mix in the living world and to minister usefully to the great objects that refine and elevate our race. His sentiments were perhaps less lofty but his actions were infinitely more excellent and his theories infinitely more wise. . . . Stage after stage we have proceeded with him through "The Mysteries of Life." The Eleusinia are closed, and the crowning libation poured.[80]

The book is less mechanical than the preceding apprentice novels, but it is still too evident that Bulwer is making Ernest's progress follow a set plan. He is to have all his intellectual mistakes corrected first, and then all his moral ones, such as pride. He must learn his duty and responsibility to the humble but virtuous and faithful girl, Alice, whom he finally marries, just as Wilhelm learned that he must care for his children, that *hier oder nirgends ist Amerika*, and that it is *vergebens in dieser Welt nach eigenem Willen zu streben.* But in spite of its shortcomings, we do get some sense of the development of a carefree and irresponsible and gifted young man, who is buffeted and beaten by experience into a more staid and ripened philosophy, even though we do not feel his experience very poignantly. It was left for the modern novel to make every day and hour of it so acutely actual to us, that many a reader has said, "Away with these young men!"

Between *Ernest Maltravers* and his final and most

successful effort to give Goethe's idea an English
form, many years of Bulwer's life intervened; he
wrote during this time his group of family novels,
among many others, and that extraordinary creation
intended to be a skit on Darwin and the superscientific
world, and radical politics, *The Coming Race* (1871).
He had also got into Parliament again in 1852 and
been elevated to the peerage in 1866. From 1870
to 1872 he was writing *Kenelm Chillingly*, his last
book, which was also a modified form of the apprentice novel, and artistically the most successful
one he did. It was not published until after his death
in 1873. He writes of it, "The hero is very strange-
humored, I think original, and there are more poetic
bits in it than in most of my later writings, but the
end of it is difficult and not yet approached."[81] The
hero is only original in the sense that he is a sort of
blend of Wilhelm and the melancholy Jaques.

After a Shandyan opening in the manner of the
Caxtons, about the question of naming the hero, we
see Kenelm developing into a precocious philosopher
who ponders at an early age over Locke and his in-
nate ideas. He is sent to school, after some family
councils about education, and makes a brilliant
record, especially in writing and in learning to box so
that he may get the better of his mortal enemy.
But he is peculiar, lacking "the faculty of amalgama-
tion," with a "melancholic and therefore unsocial
temperament." The headmaster says he must "see
more of real life and acquire a due sense of its practical
objects. My young friend is unlike other people and

with qualities that might do anything in life; I fear, unless you get him to be like other people, that he will do nothing."[82]   A middle aged relative says he must "seize the ideas that will influence his own generation" or he will not have "a start in the race with his contemporaries."   But in spite of so much good advice, Kenelm proves difficult.   He goes to Cambridge and does well, but develops no vanity and no ambition. He is dedicated to celibacy because of a book by Decimus Roach called *The Approach to the Angels*. He is a believer in tranquil indifference, and of a devastating honesty, unable to be amused like other people.   "It is a sham life that you wish me to study," he tells his father when that puzzled and anxious parent wants him to take notice of "real life."   There is in Kenelm something of the lighter and more spontaneous quality of *Pelham*, which was missing in the intervening books.

Kenelm resolves to wander on foot and encounters a traveling minstrel singing a German ballad and followed by his dog.   He is the poet who personifies nature, and Kenelm tries to point out to him this pathetic fallacy, and then passes on "in quest of adventure like Amadis of Gaul, like Don Quixote, like Gil Blas, like Roderick Random—like, in short, the only people seeking real life, the people who never existed except in books."[83]   He rescues a stage-struck girl whom he refuses to marry, and meets the Wandering Minstrel again, singing about love, which, Kenelm tries to convince him, is also a sham.   He works on a farm for hire, and beats the village bully, Tom

Bowles, whom he makes his devoted friend, and sets up the village coquette, Jessie Wiles, to a basket shop with the man she really loves and is going to marry. But in spite of all these good deeds, Kenelm is melancholy, "the solitary spectator with no part in the drama, and no interest in the vicissitudes of its plot . . . I am the one looker-on, the one by-stander and have no more concern with the active world than a stone has."[84]   Returning to civilization and the home of his father's friend, Squire Travers, he meets Cecilia Travers, who of course falls in love with him, but discreetly, since he feels no interest in her.   He meets the ubiquitous Minstrel again, who has written a poem about a little girl playing with a ball of flowers on the brow of a green hill, which he recites to Kenelm who is much pleased with it.   Seeing the Minstrel a little later, in danger of philandering, he murmurs the warning, "Remember the little child," and recalls him to the narrow path.   Realism, Kenelm discovers, is only a part of truth.   "I set out on my travels to escape from shams and begin to discover that I am a sham par excellence."[85]

There are many conversations in the houses where Kenelm stays, that deal with "business—that darling of the age," and with the idol of "progress" and the disappearance of the old aristocracy from the soil. The background of the age is woven in more skilfully than in most of Bulwer's books, and pictures of village life and scenery as well as life in the squire's house and in London, begin to make their appearance.   Cecilia tries to rouse ambition in him and an interest in litera-

ture and politics, but he lacks motive power, being
neither poor nor ambitious; the idea of duty will not
suffice; he wants happiness. To this extent has Bulwer traveled away from Carlyle into the modern
world. Kenelm is a misfit because, like so many of
his brother heroes, he has a "passionate longing to
find ideal truth in real life."[86] His cousin, Gordon
Chillingly, on the other hand, is the usual foil—the
cold, clear, practical, political mind, that goes with
the party, right or wrong. Kenelm is horrified at
political opportunism and chicanery, but this is "real
life." "Every day I live . . . still more confirms
my conviction that real life is a phantasmal sham."[87]
He inclines to indifferentism which sometimes "grows
out of earnestness baffled."[88] He finally meets Lily, a
fairylike "child of nature," and falls in love with her.
But she is promised to her guardian who has done
everything for her, and who is, in fact, the Wandering
Minstrel, really a painter of some note. Kenelm
recalls ironically his warning to him to "remember the
little child."

Kenelm has gradually learned "worth-while-ism"
from seeing that a man may do good merely by the
act of living, but one of his difficulties has been that
the "not-worth-while" idea was one of the governing
ideas of his generation—and a mistaken one. He has,
by falling in love, developed "heart" at last. "To
genius the first requisite is heart; it is no requisite at
all to talent."[89] All his realism has now become
idealism. Lily really loves him and not her guardian,
whom she plans to marry out of gratitude, but Kenelm,

thinking that she has no qualms about it, takes refuge in travel again, and goes to Italy. Revisiting Lily's home a year later, much crushed, but firm in his resignation, and expecting to find her married to the painter, he finds instead her grave, and learns that she died unmarried for love of him. Kenelm finally decides to go into a life of action in Parliament, like all his brother-heroes, "and so, into the crowded thoroughfares . . . passes the man of the Young Generation to fates beyond the verge of the horizon to which the eyes of *my* generation must limit their wistful gaze."[90]

It is the usual progress through one mistaken set of ideas after another, to something approaching peace in useful activity for others. Bulwer never got tired of preaching that lesson, sometimes by means of the hero who "goes under" like Godolphin, or one who learns his moral lessons lightly and easily and takes life gaily, as Pelham does, or one who, like Kenelm Chillingly, shows the temperament of the genius nearly broken against the rocks of "the age" before he finds himself in the end. While not one of these novels is a masterpiece, or in any way comparable with *Wilhelm Meister* in literary value, the accumulated effect of the novels with their incidental discussions which that scheme of fiction permits so freely, and the casual rambling of their heroes from place to place, forms a kind of composite picture of Victorian life which is not without historical value. Bulwer achieved this unconsciously, and so much of what he consciously set out to do he fell short in, that there is a kind of pathos in the spectacle of his effort and his laborious years of toil over the "metaphysical" novel.   But his final achievement, *Kenelm Chillingly*, has a dignity and a thoughtful grace beyond any of the others.   Here Bulwer did not try to stick too closely to Goethe's pattern, as he had done in *Maltravers*, but let the form adapt itself naturally to the English scene, and in adding much of the accumulated experience and thought of his own long and busy life, he was not straining for effect or forcing an artificially dramatic or humorous vein.   The shadow of Goethe, large, impressive, but dim, presides only from a great distance over this novel, and even the moral strenuousness of Carlyle, the companion deity, does not intrude overmuch.   The result is that we get the best of Bulwer's autobiographical material, which he used in part in all these novels, and his most artistic use of a transplanted theme.   It was to flourish sturdily on British soil for many long years after Bulwer, the pioneer in this field, had concluded his gallant pilgrimage across what we call the Victorian Era.

A brother novelist, Anthony Trollope, has in his *Autobiography* summarized as well as anyone the faults and virtues of Bulwer's novels:

He was always able to use his erudition, and he thus produced novels from which very much not only may be, but must be learned by his readers.   He thoroughly understood the political status of his own country, a subject on which, I think, Dickens was marvelously ignorant and which Thackeray had never studied.   He had read extensively and was always apt to give his readers the benefit of what he knew. . . . There is also a brightness about [the novels] the result rather of thought than of imagination, of study and of care than of mere intellect, which has made many of them excellent in their way. . . . But from all of them comes the same flavor of an effort to produce effect. The effects are produced, but it would have been better if the flavor had not been there. . . . I do not think he ever knew his own personages, nor do we know them. . . . In his plots he has generally been simple, facile, and successful. . . . The story comes naturally without calling for too much attention and is thus the proof of the completeness of the man's intellect. His language is clear, good, intelligible English, but it is defaced by mannerism. In all that he did, affectation was his fault.[91]

In spite of this, Bulwer's vogue in Germany was tremendous. No adequate study of his influence there has yet been made, but competent German critics have devoted much space to him and it was Goethe himself who said to Müller that Bulwer and Carlyle he regarded as the two most promising young English literary men of their time—an odd fellowship for these two characters to find themselves in! Both borrowed freely from the great German master, but it was Bulwer who went back into Germany to the widest number of readers, achieving there, as in England, immortality in the second rank, but still— immortality.

CHAPTER VII

ON THE SIDE OF THE ANGELS:

BENJAMIN DISRAELI

Time, which antiquates antiquities, and hath an art to make
dust of all things, hath yet spared these minor monuments.
—Sir Thomas Browne, *Urn-Burial.*

O READER dear! do pray look here, and you will spy the
curly hair, and forehead fair, and nose so high, and gleaming
eye, of Benjamin D'is-ra-e-li, the wondrous boy who wrote
Alroy in rhyme and prose, only to show how long ago victorious
Judah's lion-banner rose.   In an earlier day he wrote *Vivian Grey*—
a smart enough story we must say, until he took his hero abroad, and
trundled him over the German road; and taught him there not to
drink beer, and swallow schnapps, and pull mädchen's caps, and
smoke the cigar and the meerschaum true, in alehouse and lusthaus
all Father land through, until all was blue, but talk second-hand that
which at the first, was never many degrees from the worst—namely
German cant and High-Dutch sentimentality, maudlin metaphysics
and rubbishing reality.   But those who would find how Vivian wined
with the Marchioness of Puddledock, and other great grandees of the
kind, and how he talked aesthetic, and waxed eloquent and pathetic
and kissed his Italian puppies of the greyhound breed, they have
only to read—if the work be still alive—*Vivian Grey* in volumes five.
As for his tentative upon the *Representative*, which he and John
Murray got up in a very great hurry, we shall say nothing at all,
either great or small; and all the wars that thence ensued, and the
Moravian's deadly feud: nor much of that fine book, which is called
The Young Duke, with his slippers of velvet blue, with clasps of
snowy white hue, made out of the pearl's mother or some equally fine

thing or other; and *Fleming* (Contarini), which will cost ye but a guinea; and *Gallomania* (get through it, can you?) in which he made war on (assisted by a whiskered baron—his name was Von Haber, whose Germanical jabber Master Ben, with ready pen put into English smart and jinglish) King Louis Philippe and his court; and many other great works of the same sort—why we leave them to the reader to peruse, that is to say, if he should choose.

He lately stood for Wycombe, but there Colonel Grey did lick him, he being parcel Tory and parcel Radical—which is what in general mad we call—and the latest affair of his we chanced to see, is *What is He?* a question which, by this time we have somewhat answered in this our pedestrian rhyme. As for the rest—but writing rhyme is after all a pest; and therefore. . . . .

We shall finish what we have to say without any Alroy-izing, in plain prose. . . . The plain fact is then that Ben D'Israeli is a clever fellow, who has written some striking books, in which we think he has shown great indications of talent but nothing more. The books prove that the author is a man of abilities though they do not reach the mark at which he aims. Benjamin's politics are rather preposterous, but he is young and may improve. There is one good thing about him, viz., that he can never be a Whig; and while that can be said of any man, there is hope for him. Only, we beseech our friend not to write any more of that sounding fustian which infests the wondrous tale of *Alroy*. If we wished to Judaise, why does he not at once write us Tales of the Talmud, or Gestes of the Gemara, or Memorandums of the Mischna? *A Romance of Rag-Fair* or a *Heroine of Houndsditch* would be rather a novelty in these piping times. Scott, the novelographer of the border-thieves, is departed— why should not one of London breed attempt to occupy his place?

We have already expressed our favorable feelings toward Benjamin's father; and we must conclude this article by hoping that, in the end, he will indeed be old Isaac's 'son of his right hand' as his name imports in the original Hebraic. He could not follow a more honorable example in life or in letters than the old Curiosity of Literature: and we trust that as there is stuff, and good stuff, in Ben, he will speedily get rid of some ridiculous ideas that pursue him, and show those who think well of his talents that he can do what they wish to see him attempting.[1]

This facetious but comprehensive history of Disraeli by Maginn, supplemented by Maclise's well-known drawing, gives us the future Premier as some of his contemporaries saw him when he was twenty-nine years old.   If he read it, his reaction must have been similar to his hero's, Contarini Fleming: "I was ridiculous; it was time to die."

Yet Maginn's summary of his activities was better-natured than some others that had already fallen to Benjamin's lot, although there were those who *did* appreciate him and take him seriously—Bulwer, Lady Blessington and her circle, his faithful sister Sarah, and such American visitors as N. P. Willis.   The year of his first entrance into Parliament and of Victoria's accession was one of many social triumphs for "Dizzy."   He was evidently in fine form one evening (January 5, 1837) when Crabb Robinson saw him for the first time.   It was at Gore House, Lady Blessington's colorful mansion.

With her were D'Orsay, Dr Lardner, Trelawney, Edward Bulwer. A stranger, whose conversation interested and pleased me, I found to be young Disraeli. He talked with spirit of German literature. He spoke of Landor's "Satire" as having no satire in it. The chat was an amusing one.[2]

Knowing how Disraeli prided himself on his *bons mots*, we can imagine how airily he got off this one about Landor, and how tactfully he brought the conversation round to the older man's favorite topic —German literature. His ignorance might easily have betrayed him into an argument with one of the few specialists, besides Carlyle, in the field at this time. Many a young man would have avoided the subject altogether. But he skirted the pitfalls so adroitly that Robinson was probably flattered and amused, and never realized they were there. An able young man, surely, and one who deserved to get on!

Disraeli had, to be sure, been in Germany in 1824, in the course of his Grand Tour. He made the Rhine trip to Mannheim and Heidelberg. He saw Mainz, Cologne, Bonn, the Drachenfels, Ehrenbreitstein, Ems. At Frankfurt he went to the Opera and heard Cherubini and Mozart, and wrote home a good deal more glowingly about the food than about the German people.[3] In the course of his ill-fated venture with Murray's newspaper project, the *Representative*, he undertook to get foreign correspondents for the paper and established a German connection, among others. He wrote to Lockhart that he had been "very much assisted in the grand coup of Germany by Mrs. William Elliott, who, when devoid of humbug, is very clever."[4] Except for the fact that she was a lady of German birth who had married Murray's brother-in-law, Mrs. Elliott is shrouded in mystery, and we shall never know how much knowledge of her fatherland and its literature Disraeli owed to her. The sum total of that knowledge was not large. He uses his German travels in *Vivian Grey* rather than his more recent trips to Italy and Switzerland, "probably because the romantic genius of the Rhine was more in harmony with the mood in which he now found himself"[5] and not because Germany itself was more con-

genial to him.   Bulwer-Lytton's influence may have
turned his mind to German reading, but he never
became the devoted Goethe student that Bulwer was.
References to *Goetz von Berlichingen, Faust,* and to
the "great Goethe" himself, occur here and there in
the smart conversations of his early novels, especially
in *Vivian Grey,*[6] and he certainly modeled this novel,
Contarini Fleming, and *Lothair* more or less consciously on the apprenticeship pattern, as we shall
see later, but the theme did not fascinate Disraeli
throughout his life as it did Bulwer, much as he admired Goethe.   He probably read Carlyle's translation of *Meister* when it appeared in 1824, the same
year that he went to Germany, but it does not seem
to have occurred to him to make a pilgrimage to
Weimar, as various young literary men of his day had
done and were doing.   He may have talked to Crabb
Robinson during that memorable conversation, about
Wieland's *Agathon,* if he felt that it was not wise to
venture too much about Goethe.   At any rate, he
had read this notable predecessor of *Meister* three
years before their meeting at Lady Blessington's, and
it is to her that he writes about "that mad Byronic
novel."

I am delighted with *Agathon*.   It left me musing, which is a test
of a great work.   I invariably close one in a reverie.   Wieland indeed
always delights me.   I sympathize with him much.   There is a wild
Oriental fancy blended with his Western philosophy which is a charming union.   I like a moral to peep out of the wildest invention to
assure us that while we have been amused we have also all the time
been growing a little wiser.   The translation of the *Agathon* is very
clumsy.[7]

Considering Disraeli's temperament and his own novels, we can surmise that Wieland would be much more appealing to him than Goethe. Wieland's urbane wit and worldliness, his thoroughly eighteenth-century quality, his satirical, epigrammatic gifts, could not fail to charm one who had been nurtured on Voltaire and whose father was essentially an eighteenth-century man of letters.

For the same reasons, perhaps, the French court of the Second Empire was Disraeli's true spiritual home. He gloried in his visits there, later in his political life.[8] But he also got on famously with the old man of Blood and Iron after the Congress of Berlin (1878). Bismarck saw through him but appreciated him too.[9] *Der alte Jude, das ist der Mann!* he said. But by the time these two seasoned old campaigners were hobnobbing in the smoking room of the British Embassy at Berlin, the Germany of his youth must have been but a pale shadow in Lord Beaconsfield's memory, if it had ever left much impression there.

It is natural enough that Disraeli's two early apprenticeship novels should also be his most autobiographical ones. But in the case of so theatrical a writer, we shall not expect accurate reflections of his own experiences. *Vivian Grey* (1826) gives us the highly colored, active life of politics as the young Disraeli envisaged it, his own early ambition, a partial portrait of his own father in Horace Grey (Vivian's father), the conversation at John Murray's dinner table before Benjamin fell out of favor with that gentleman, Disraeli's taste for grandeur in dress, and his susceptibility to feminine influence which was characteristic of him all his life. Even as early as 1833 Disraeli himself came to regard the book as an indiscretion, not so much for the personal portraits in it that aroused such a furore among his friends and enemies as for its artistic faults "which even youth can scarcely excuse . . . the most unequal, imperfect, irregular thing that indiscretion ever published."[10] The preface to the 1853 edition strikes the same apologetic note: "Books written by boys which pretend to give a picture of manners and to deal in knowledge of human nature, must necessarily be founded on affectation." But in the "Mutilated Diary" for September 1, 1833, he testifies somewhat grandiloquently to the book's autobiographical significance and to the Goethe-Carlyle gospel of action which Bulwer's apprentice novels also preached:

My mind is a continental mind. It is a revolutionary mind. I am only truly great in action. . . . Poetry is the safety-valve of my passions, but I wish to act what I write. My works are the embodification of my feelings. In *Vivian Grey* I have portrayed my active and real ambition. In *Alroy* my ideal ambition. *The Psychological Romance* (*Contarini Fleming*) is a development of my poetic character. The trilogy is the secret history of my feelings. I shall write no more about myself.[11]

Vivian is a typical dandy, spoiled by his parents, like Bulwer's Pelham and so many other heroes of the fashionable novels. His school life, like Disraeli's own, is full of sudden ascents to power and popularity, owing to his gift for managing and fascinating his fellows, and as sudden descents due to his cold-blooded opportunism and trickiness. He reads for Oxford at home and develops a passion for the Neo-Platonists which is nipped in the bud by his wise father who sounds the note of the apprenticeship theme in his speech to Vivian about experience, and thereby saves him from "being all his life a dreaming scholar." "Try to ascertain," says this mentor, "what may be the chief objects of your existence in this world. . . . Human feelings tell me that we have some duties to perform; to our fellow-creatures, to our friends. . . ." He hopes Vivian is not "one of those who look with a glazed eye on the welfare of their fellowmen and who would dream away a useless life by idle puzzles of the brain."[12] In short, he is in danger of becoming, like Wilhelm Meister, a mere dilettante. He goes out in society and soon feels himself too mature for a university education. He "had all the desires of a matured mind, of an experienced man, but without maturity and without experience."[13] Experience, then, is to be his teacher, as it has been of so many apprentices before and since his time. But here Disraeli departs from the traditional pattern. Vivian is no passive recipient of the surrounding forces that mold him. His ambition to "get on" is the driving force in his education by life. He is more deliberate and calculating than his German brother or Bulwer's soft, sensitive heroes. "Mankind, then, is my great game," he says. There is a satanic, Byronic streak in his make-up. Whenever it is at all possible, he "laughs an answer of bitterest derision." His father's warnings reflect the effects of *laissez-faire* and British prosperity. It is an age "of unsettled opinions and contested principles" with many opportunities to the adventurous and the bold, but he warns his son against the prevailing greediness for great fortunes, exemplified by one of Disraeli's naïve allegorical characters, Mrs. Ormolu. Mr. Grey preaches also the golden mean in this age of great temptations for young men, who are naturally averse to "the only modes of acquiring property, fair trade and honorable professions" because these are not exciting enough.[14]

Vivian proceeds with his apprenticeship in success by allying himself with the disgruntled Marquis of Carabas and trying to put him back into political power. When this coup fails, owing to the intrigues of a mysterious German lady, Mrs. Felix Lorraine, Vivian fights a duel, kills his man, has a complete breakdown and goes to Germany to recuperate. Here we get the highly colored romantic descriptions of his own earlier travels, and after a year at Heidelberg he "wakes from his secret sorrow . . . with a new possession . . . he had gained Experience. . . . Experience is the child of Thought and Thought is the child of Action. We cannot learn men from books."[15] But he sets out again on mankind's "search for happiness" and thereby makes his second great mistake. *Sartor* had not yet been written, but no doubt Disraeli expected all readers to see at once that the search for happiness would be fatal. Vivian falls in with Baron von Königstein at Frankfurt and barely escapes being taken in by this gambler and imposter. He falls in love with the beautiful, if somewhat insipid,

Violet Fane, who dies just as he declares his undying passion for her. Plunged once more into grief, he wanders about the country with his faithful servant Essper George, meeting with all sorts of preposterous adventures. At the court of a petty German prince he encounters the great statesman, Beckendorff. This eccentric but powerful character, Disraeli's first portrait of a statesman, represents the Active Principle and gives Vivian some good advice in the manner of Wilhelm's unknown guardians:

Fate, Destiny, Chance, particular and special Providence—idle words. Dismiss them all, Sir! A man's fate is his own temper. . . . Man is not the creature of circumstances. Circumstances are the creatures of men. We are free agents and man is more powerful than matter.[16]

He advises Vivian to mix in the world and forget his disappointment and sorrow. He must struggle against adversity, not merely labor for advancement. But in spite of this excellent doctrine, our apprentice hero never makes much progress. After some entertaining descriptions of court pageants and parties, he sets off on his travels again, is caught in a flood and a landslide, and the book comes to a lame and hasty conclusion with this cryptic utterance: "The Disappointment of manhood succeeds to the delusion of Youth: let us hope that the heritage of Old Age is not Despair."

Aside from the slight impress of the apprenticeship pattern, which was more or less accidental—Disraeli was following the formula for the fashionable novel of the day, the novel of Mrs. Gore and Mrs. Ward, rather than any German model—the chief interest of the book is in its conscious and unconscious auto-biography. "The novel itself," said the *Edinburgh Review*, "will always remain an object of interest to the metaphysical enquirer as containing the germ, rude outline, and incomplete conception of the career which the author was even then meditating and in great measure has since contrived to run."[17]

The great Goethe himself enjoyed the book. While Disraeli was traveling in the Orient he wrote to his sister on May 28, 1831, "Goethe and *Vivian Grey* of course gratifying." Monypenny explains this as follows:

A friend of the Austens and Disraelis had just returned from Weimar and reported that "the old man himself and Madame Goethe, his son's wife, were among the warmest admirers of *Vivian Grey;* they had it on their own particular bookshelves and they spoke enthusiasti-cally of it as being after Scott the first of their English favorites. They could find but one fault, that the author had misconceived the German character in his youthful Princess!" Goethe according to his daughter-in-law, considered that there was more true originality in the work than in any he had seen for years.[18]

But Goethe is also said to have coupled Bulwer's name with Carlyle's as among the most promising of young Englishmen of the day. Either the Olympian judg-ment slumbered in this case as in that of *Vivian Grey*, or the old man was genuinely pleased by the use of German background for part of the book, and perhaps by the portrait of Beckendorff.

Vivian had another interested reader in foreign parts—no less a person than Emerson. He had a good deal to say, in his journals and essays for the *Dial*, about novels in general, and divided them into two classes: those of costume or circumstance, and those of character. He takes *Wilhelm Meister* to be the greatest example of this latter class, and his observations on this book and on Goethe, would fill a chapter by themselves. But he also followed the English output, even of the more ephemeral group, pretty closely:

The novels of Fashion, of D'Israeli, Mrs. Gore, Mr. Ward, belong to the class of novels of costume, because the aim is purely external success. Of the tales of fashionable life, by far the most agreeable and the most efficient was *Vivian Grey*. Young men were and still are the readers and victims. Byron ruled for a time, but Vivian, with no tithe of Byron's genius, rules longer. One can distinguish the Vivians in all companies. They would quiz their father and mother and lover and friend. They discuss sun and planets, liberty and fate, love and death, over the soup. They never sleep, go nowhere, stay nowhere, eat nothing and know nobody, but are up to anything, though it were the genesis of nature or the last cataclysm, —Festus-like, Faust-like, Jove-like, and could write an Iliad any rainy morning, if fame were not such a bore. Men, women, though the greatest and fairest, are stupid things; but a rifle, and a mild pleasant gunpower, a spaniel, and a cheroot, are themes for Olympus.[19]

And in his *Journal* he adds:

One would say of *Vivian Grey* that it was written by a person of lively talent who had rare opportunities of society and access to the best anecdotes of Europe. Beckendorff is a sketch after nature, and whoever was the model was a strong head, a strong humorist, who deserved his empire for a day over these college boys.[20]

Emerson and Margaret Fuller evidently first read the book together, with amusement:

Miss Fuller read *Vivian Grey* and made me very merry.   Beckendorff is a fine teaching that he who can conquer his own face can have no farther difficulty.[21]

Again he admits, a little shamefacedly, the power of novels over him:

Disraeli is well worth reading, quite a good student of his English world, and a very clever expounder of its wisdom and craft: never quite master.   Novels make us great gentlemen whilst we read them . . . Our novel-reading is a passion for results; we admire parks and the love of beauties, and the homage of parliaments.[22]

Later in life he found Disraeli vulgar[23] and mistrusted him politically,[24] though he always admitted his power as a romantic writer.   Of his actual meeting with him in London in 1848 at Lady Palmerston's, we unfortunately know little.   "I . . . had with him a little talk," Emerson tells us,[25] but that is all. Like the conversation with Crabb Robinson, it is one of those "talks" about which, for lack of definite information, the reader's creative imagination tends to run riot.

Contarini Fleming (1832) is at the same time more autobiographical than *Vivian* and closer to the apprenticeship plan.   It depicts the struggle, which was undoubtedly the author's own, between the poetic temperament and the thirst for action.   Judging from his own comments on the theme, Disraeli evidently considered it more original with him than it was.   He mentions *Meister* but considers his own book more profoundly "psychological," a word he was very fond of, and that plays in his vocabulary somewhat the same rôle that "metaphysical" does in Bulwer's. In his preface to the 1845 edition of *Contarini* he explains himself as follows:

The author proposed to himself, in writing this work, a subject that has ever been held one of the most difficult and refined, and which is virgin in the imaginative literature of every country—namely, the development and formation of the poetic character. It has indeed been sometimes incidentally treated and partially illustrated by writers of the highest class, as for instance Goethe in his "Wilhelm Meister" where are expounded, with so much felicity, the mysteries of predisposition; and the same illustrious author has, in his capricious memoirs, favored us with much of his individual experience of self-formation; in this resembling preceding poets, none more conspicuously than Count Alfieri. But an ideal and complete picture of the development of the poet had not been produced, nor had anyone entirely grappled with the thorough formation of that mysterious character with which, though unlike all of us, we all of us so strangely sympathize. When the author meditated over the entireness of the subject, it appeared to him that the auto-biographical form was a necessary condition of a successful fulfillment. It seemed the only instrument that could penetrate the innermost secrets of the brain and heart in a being whose thought and passion were so much cherished in loneliness, and revealed often only in solitude. In the earlier stages of the theme the self-discoverer seemed an indispensable agent. What narrative by a third person could sufficiently paint the melancholy and brooding childhood, the first indications of the predisposition, the growing consciousness of power, the reveries, the loneliness, the doubts, the moody misery, the ignorance of art, the failures, the despair? Having adopted this conclusion, the author then endeavored to conceive a character whose position in life should be at variance and, as it were, in constant conflict with his temperament; and the accidents of whose birth, nevertheless, tended to develop his psychology. The combination that connected in one being Scandinavia and the South, and made the image of a distant and most romantic city continually act upon a nervous temperament, surrounded by the snows and forests of the north, though novel, it is believed, in literature, was by no means an impossible or even improbable one. . . . This book, written with great care, after deep meditation, and in a beautiful and distant land favorable to composition . . . was published anonymously in the midst of a revolution (1831–2) and it seemed that it must die. But gradually it has gained the sympathy of the thoughtful and the refined, and it has had the rare fortune of being cherished by great men.[26] Now it is offered to a new generation, and bears the name of its author, because, on critically examining it, he finds that, though written in early youth, it has accomplished his idea. Were he equal to his subject, the book would last, for that subject is eternal.[27]

As far as England in 1832 was concerned, Disraeli was right about being the first to treat the theme. *Wotton Reinfred* had been written before this (1827) but had never seen the light, and Bulwer's *Maltravers* (1837) had not yet appeared. His *Pelham* (1828) had never been viewed as anything but the history of a Dandy of the most superficial sort. But the theme as Disraeli describes it here and uses it in *Contarini* is rather the progress of the Genius, the poetic temperament, which is indeed part of the apprentice novel, but not its root idea, which is *Bildung*, or "self-formation" as Disraeli says of Goethe's autobiography. Contarini is more closely akin to Werther than to Wilhelm, though his longing for the south may have been unconsciously influenced by Mignon and Goethe's own passion for Italy. He explains in the preface just quoted, what may be the natural reason for adopting the introspective, autobiographical method which all writers of such novels, except Goethe himself, have used.

Bulwer praised the book in his *New Monthly Magazine* and compared it favorably with *Wilhelm Meister*, saying that both were "allegorical and real" at the same time. He recognized its German coloring, which Milman also perceived vaguely, but no other English readers seem to have done so.[28] Heine and Beckford are among those "great men" who "cherished" the book, and to whom Disraeli refers in the preface quoted above. Heine wrote:

Modern English letters have given us no offspring equal to *Contarini Fleming*. Cast in our Teutonic mould, it is nevertheless one of the most original works ever written, profound, poignant, pathetic; its subject the most interesting, if not the noblest, imaginable—the development of a poet; truly psychological; passion and mockery; Gothic richness, the fantasy of the Saracens, and yet over all a classic, even a death-like repose.[29]

This high praise from a German reader makes one reflect that Heine and Disraeli had much in common and that it is a pity that politics occupied Disraeli so exclusively on his later trips to Germany that he never had the time to make literary acquaintances. Among all the spectacular and dramatic interviews of Disraeli's career, a meeting with Heine would perhaps have been the most congenial to him.

Contarini does pass through the stages of a kind of apprenticeship, but more by accident than design. He graduates from a tempestuous and misunderstood childhood into the approved Disraelian dandy group, and becomes an affected young man of the world.

Then he is an earnest and brilliant student at Cambridge, then an outlaw in the manner of Schiller's *Robbers*, in the romantic ruins of an old castle in the forest, then a successful but blasé and indifferent politician, since his father tries to force him against his temperament to become a practical man. He writes a novel, *Manstein*, which is much like Disraeli's own *Vivian Grey*, and causes the same public sensation by its youthful audacity. He determines to reeducate himself as a poet, and flees the unsympathetic North for climes more congenial to his exotic temper. He has meanwhile become a Catholic and met with various adventures with strolling players and travelers which vaguely recall the early parts of *Meister*. A "mentor" who appears to him from time to time is Baron Winter, a great painter in disguise, who gives him such cryptic advice as Vivian too had often received:

Be patient: cherish hope. Read more: ponder less. Nature is more powerful than education: time will develop everything. Trust not overmuch in the blessed Magdalen: learn to protect yourself.[30]

All this is as mysterious as Wilhelm's guides ever were, but it says nothing, as these did, and as many of Bulwer's "mentor" characters did too, about responsibility for others, or about action of a serviceable kind, though perhaps that is implied in "ponder less." In Venice, the city of his dreams, he meets Alcesté, his cousin of the house of Contarini, kidnaps and marries her. They lead an idyllic life in a villa in Crete till she suddenly dies in childbirth, and Contarini tries to commit suicide by jumping off Mount Ida.

From here on, the book becomes a series of rather monotonous "travelogues" describing his wanderings through Turkey, Syria, Jerusalem, Spain. Travel teaches toleration, he finds, but not happiness. Baron Winter opportunely turns up to counsel him for the last time. He tells him to live in the present.

"The period has arrived in your life when you must renounce meditation. Action is now your part. Meditation is culture. It is well to think until a man has discovered his genius, and developed his faculties, but then let him put his intelligence in motion. Act, act, act; act without ceasing, and you will no longer talk of the vanity of life." . . . "But how am I to act?" "Create. Man is made to create, from the poet to the potter."[31]

There is an unmistakable echo of Goethe here (*Die Tat ist alles*), and the derivation was probably direct from *Meister,* since in 1831–32 it was too early for Bulwer's apprentice novels to have been the medium. But still, the whole conception is different from that of *Meister;* creative activity receives the main emphasis in the end, not responsibility for others as the crown of self-development. The story is essentially that of the poet's youth, in a hostile and unsympathetic environment. His real apprenticeship in art is not shown us, and there is not much stress on apprenticeship in living.

Much later in his career (1870) and when he had already achieved his goal, Disraeli returned to the old theme in his novel *Lothair*. In this book it is subsidiary to the main theme of the struggle of the

Church of Rome against the Church of England for the allegiance of Lothair, the rich young nobleman. He is more closely related to Wilhelm in character than either of his two more ambitious, tempestuous, and headstrong predecessors, Vivian and Contarini. He is very impressionable, sensitive, wavering in temperament, but he discovers earlier than Wilhelm that "a sense of duty is natural to man, and that there can be no satisfaction in life without attempting to fulfill it."[32] He meets various mentors along his way, notably Mr. Phoebus, the artist, who warns him against book knowledge, and whose mania is "Aryan principles." He sees the world first in society and as the proprietor of a large estate—one of those typical Disraelian estates that surpass even Bulwer's in gorgeousness—and then in the field of military action. His guiding star, the mysterious Theodora, who has pointed out to him that possibly religion is merely a matter of conscience and not of orthodoxy, dies tragically, but not before making him promise that he will never join the Roman communion. She fears he is too impressionable: "I know your nature; it is gentle and brave, but perhaps too susceptible. I wished it to be susceptible only of the great and good."[33] After her death Lothair is a sadder and a wiser man. "He had become acquainted with sorrow; he had experienced calamities physical and moral. . . . It was that first great grief which makes a man acquainted with his deepest feelings. . . . But . . . the sternest and highest of all obligations, military duty, claimed him with an unfaltering grasp

. . ." and so he re-enters the world of action. But later he confides to Mr. Phoebus that he has "at length found out the truth," namely, that he (Lothair) is a "dreaming psychologist."[34] Mr. Phoebus admits that his fault is being too introspective and advises him, as Winter once advised Contarini, to give up reading and to "profit by the vast though calamitous experience which you have gained in a short time."[35] Another friend, too, advised him to "give up dreams. . . . Action may not always be happiness but there is no happiness without action. . . . I would return home and plunge into affairs."[36] He does so, and finally wins the hand of the young lady who represents the Church of England. His pilgrimage is over. "I know the world now. I have committed many mistakes, doubtless many follies, have formed many opinions, and have changed many opinions."[37] He has been throughout a thoroughly colorless and insignificant young noble whose difficulties never are representative enough of his age or *milieu* to be at all interesting. The political history of the period has indeed been vaguely reflected in such episodes as the Fenian disturbances and the Oecumenical Council at Rome, but, as in all Disraeli's novels, the action and characters seem suspended in mid-air in a hectic atmosphere of heightened and unnatural brilliance. We watch their gyrations but we can never invest them with reality. Even Bulwer-Lytton's earnest moral allegories and theatrical heroes can better endure the sober light of day than Disraeli's.

Disraeli's partial use of the apprentice theme seems,

on the whole, to be due to the "fashionable novel" formula, which he may have borrowed from Ward,[38] and to possible discussions with Bulwer, rather than to *Wilhelm Meister* itself, though he certainly read and admired it. The "action" motif may be due to vague echoes of Goethe, and probably not to the Carlyle influence which did color his friend Bulwer's work. A brother-novelist, Anthony Trollope, was even harder on Disraeli's efforts in fiction than he was on Bulwer Lytton's,[39] and Carlyle's dislike of him and his work is well-known, though it seems to have been mitigated later in life.

The similarity between Carlyle's ideas and Disraeli's has often been pointed out[40] and certain parallels between *Past and Present* and *Chartism* and Disraeli's "Tory Democracy," especially as expressed in *Sybil*, are very marked. Millbank in *Coningsby* expresses ideas about a "natural aristocracy" which sound a good deal like some of those in *Chartism*. It seems to have been noted at the time that *Past and Present* "furnished material for thought to be wrought up into fresh forms as speeches, leading articles, reviews, etc., by the 'clever men' and the 'rising men' of the day—who in Parliament and elsewhere are, to an extent that is quite amusing, gaining a reputation for themselves by expounding Carlylism into the 'vulgar tongue.' Disraeli and Tennyson were examples of this."[41] We may believe, then, that if Carlyle had got over his prejudice early enough, the two might have had a good deal in common. Both were essentially religious minded

men, and opposed to the utilitarian and evolutionary
tendencies of their time.

But after reading Disraeli's detractors (who were
many and sharp and bitterly personal) and his friends
(whose praise is too often mere flattery, as theatrical
as his own novels, and almost never disinterested and
impersonal), we return to that earnest young New
Englander whose comments on him are all the more
interesting because so often made in connection with
comments on the novel in general and *Wilhelm Meister*
in particular. It seems as though Emerson had some
shrewd foreknowledge of the trend that novel-writing
was to take, and he expresses it most often when his
reaction against Disraelian theatricality is at its
height: In writing of *Meister*, his ideal novel of character, he says,

> Yet a novel may teach one thing as well as my choosings at the
> corner of the street which way to go,—whether to my errand or
> whether to the woods,—this, namely, that action inspires respect;
> action makes character, power, man, God.
>
> These novels will give way, by and by, to diaries or autobiogra-
> phies:—captivating books, if only a man knew how to choose among
> what he calls his experiences that which is really his experience, and
> how to record truth truly![42]

And seven years later:

> I still feel a little uneasiness about these novels. Why should these
> sorceries have a monopoly of our delicious emotions?—The novel
> still weakly uses the cheap resource of property married away instead
> of earned, and that is the chief conjuring-stick it has; for the instincts
> of man always attach to property as he knows what accumulations of
> spiritual force go to the creation of that, and sobs and heart-beats and

sudden self-sacrifice very easily result from the dealing with it.   But the novel will find the way to our interiors one day, and will not always be novel of costume merely.   These stories are to stories of real life what the figures which represent the fashions of the month on the front page of the magazine are to portraits and inspired pictures.

Are you fond of drama? say the Gods.   Said you so my fine fellow?   Verily?   Speak the truth a little, and truth on truth, to every man and woman; try that a few hours, and you shall have dramatic situations, assaults and batteries, and heroic alternatives to your heart's content.[43]

He might almost be prophesying the stream-of-consciousness novel which is so plentiful today, and in speaking of new fields for drama he might be referring to *Strange Interlude* itself!   In reflecting on Harriet Martineau's novel *Deerbrook*, he mentions a danger to which many people feel the modern novel is subject:

Yet the author is of that class who mistake a private for an universal experience and venture to record it.   A perfectly sound nature may accept all his own experience for the uniform experience of mankind, and so record it.   But a man partially sick may not.   If he record his morbid passages they will be accepted only by the sick for general truths.   To the well they will be offensive.

It is a delicate matter—this offering to stand deputy for the human race, and writing all one's secret history colossally out as philosophy. [He may have been thinking of *Vivian* and *Contarini* here.]   Very agreeable it is in those who succeed: Odious in all others.[44]

Goethe, in short, could do what Disraeli could not. And yet we should not judge Disraeli's novels too severely, especially these three that show some tinge of Goethe's great theme.   *Sybil* and *Coningsby* were far more successful.   Here he was not trying to be what he would have called "psychological," or what

Bulwer called "metaphysical," and what critics like Milman called "German." His very much diluted versions of Goethe's idea are significant only in showing the transition stage between Bulwer, who borrowed it directly and consciously from its source (with a slight admixture of Carlyle), and the authors of the later nineteenth century who transformed it entirely and hardly realized where it came from, so completely had it dissolved in and become a part of Victorian thinking.

CHAPTER VIII

CANDIDATES FOR TRUTH,[1] 1833–1850

Zarathustra was fond of all such as make distant voyages and
like not to live without danger.
— Nietzsche, *Thus Spake Zarathustra.*

CONTEMPORARY with Bulwer-Lytton's and
Disraeli's apprentice heroes, another and far
different group of young men travels on its way
through Victorian England. Ernest Maltravers and
Kenelm Chillingly, Contarini Fleming and Lothair
would scarcely acknowledge them as traveling companions, not from any feeling of antagonism so much
as a lordly forgetfulness of their existence. They
have whirled past them, perhaps, on some of those
sudden, melodramatic journeys they are always taking
from London to their country estates, during which
they are so often "a prey to the gloomiest thoughts,"
occasioned by some earl's daughter of statuesque
proportions and stately conversation, who has given
them the cold shoulder; by the possibility of a lost
seat in Parliament; or by an impending journey to
Italy or Egypt on some dark errand connected with
their birth and the inheritance of vast estates covering whole English counties, to which they will one day
return chastened, to welcoming bonfires, and the
cheers of the loyal peasantry, and rule with firm
benevolence for ever after. But sitting far back in

the upholstered corner of his traveling carriage, lost in sad philosophic reveries of a German cast, "his chin sunk upon his breast" as like as not, our young hero of the dandy school will not even look out of the window at his plainer, poorer brethren who travel afoot, "a very good sort of people" no doubt (Disraeli was conscious for a moment of some of them in *Sybil*), but not the sort who would be welcome at Gore House or eligible for invitations to Bradenham or Hughenden or Knebworth. The dandy apprentice may be ardent, thoughtful, intrepid in facing the heights and depths of his experience, but his is an apprenticeship *de luxe* after all; it has the comfortable background of inherited wealth and position, with leisure enough not only to taste life and find, sooner or later, that it is dust and ashes, but also to muse and philosophize in ample paragraphs upon this phenomenon. He may, like Kenelm Chillingly, travel on foot from eccentricity, but he can always send home for a "portmanteau" of clean clothes. He has time to develop a fine taste in waistcoats, and to carry his pilgrim's staff and scrip with a difference.

So unlike this is the tone prevailing among his fellows, that we find it hard to realize that the same steep, perilous roads of England in the 1830's and 40's formed the setting for the life journeys of them all. Not one of them runs the whole gamut of English nineteenth-century society, as Wilhelm Meister does in eighteenth-century Germany; but taken together, and not leaving the Dandies out of the picture, these novels form an impressive panorama of

English life during the first twenty years of the Great Queen's reign—its squalor and its heavy magnificence; its worldliness and its mysticism; its hypocrisy and its desperate heart-searchings and wrestlings with the Devil; its painful, puzzled clutching at the old truths that crumbled in its grasp, and the supreme gesture of its slow, faltering, stoical turning to front a new age. Many gestures in the drama of human history have been clearer, swifter, more decisive, and satisfying to our modern eyes than this of the Victorians. But the spectacle of the human spirit sorely tried, proving again its limitless power to survive and grow through long, dark, unwritten days of transition and to readjust itself to an alien world, has a dramatic value of its own. The agony has been too long, perhaps, for aesthetic effect, and too profound. But if we have watched it at all, we have felt the almost intolerable heaviness of the struggle which the Victorians made, and heard the rush of the dark waters that went over them, and sensed the full weariness of their victory, that must have seemed to so many of them like defeat—their final tragic acceptance of uncertainty. It was the thing they feared and hated most, and they accepted it. Most of them were too battered by the conflict, or too lost in some small corner of it, to realize that they had met the ultimate test of valor. But if we who look back can be stirred at all by human courage, we shall find it here, and feel our hearts moved "as with a trumpet."

In a sense, the whole long line of English apprentice heroes illustrates the gradual progress toward this acceptance of the Unknown and the Uncertain, and none more clearly than this group created by authors who were preoccupied with religious changes, with new professions like journalism, with the question of social reform, and the changing position of women. That is why these pilgrim heroes of theirs speak a different language from Bulwer's and Disraeli's. Their roads run far from the beaten highways, where the aristocratic carriages roll, and out across uncharted country. They live more dangerously, because they are closer to reality. Accordingly, the problem of individual adjustment to the world is more acute, and because that world is constantly growing more complex, the possible failure to make any adjustment at all begins to form the tragic ending in defeat and futility, in such books as Froude's, for example. The gospel of work that solaced Carlyle, and that carried over into Bulwer's and Disraeli's books, where the young hero usually goes into Parliament or settles down into altruistic management of his estates, will not solve the problem for everyone.

But the influence of Carlyle looms large in almost all of these novels. Their authors were personal friends or disciples of his; Sterling, Froude, Geraldine Jewsbury, and Kingsley were very ardent ones. Almost all of them, too, were readers of Goethe and German literature in general; Lewes and Sterling were well-known as enthusiasts and experts in this field. Besides having Carlyle and the Germans in common, this little group was connected within itself by various relationships and bonds of friendship, or at least acquaintance. Froude and Kingsley were brothers-in-law; Kingsley and Lewes were both friends of Arthur Helps and met at his house; Lewes was a member of Miss Jewsbury's Manchester circle where he was a fellow guest of Froude and helped Geraldine to publish her articles; Miss Jewsbury reviewed *Alton Locke* and *The Nemesis of Faith* in 1849, and went out to meet the author of the latter, "a very nice, natural young man, though rather like a 'lost sheep' at present.. He has only been used to the Oxford part of the world, so that sectarians and unbelievers are strange to him."[2] All of them had moved along parallel paths which ran near enough together to have come under the eye of one quiet, thoughtful Quaker lady in her lifetime, though chiefly in the 1840's. Caroline Fox noted all the good things said by them or about them, and has much to report of those friends whom they all had in common—the Carlyles—as well.[3]

Given the relationship to Carlyle and the familiarity with his ideas, especially his version of the Goethian "work" gospel, and also their exchange of ideas among themselves or in circles of people thinking along similar lines, it is not surprising that when it came to writing novels, the apprenticeship pattern proved a natural one to slip into, almost unconsciously. They may have borrowed slightly from each other; almost all the novels date from the 1840's. But the pattern has lost many of the characteristics of *Wilhelm Meister*. There is less of Goethe and his self-culture ideal than in Bulwer's and Disraeli's stories, and more of Carlyle and his passion for setting himself right with the universe. The life-journey in search of *truth*—religious, social, moral—takes the place, more and more, of the effort to make oneself an artist in living, or developing one's powers to their full extent. The Oxford movement and Evangelicism together stressed the importance of the individual soul, and the apprentice form lent itself admirably to chronicling Odysseys of religious experience. The growth of the historical attitude of mind, at once a cause and a result of the great Victorian conflict, may have given fiction a tendency to dwell on and analyze shifting points of view more carefully and vitally than the dandy school was taking the time or thought to do, even though they lived during the same decades as these more earnest doctrinaire novelists. As Morley says, "The marked progress of criticism and interpretation of life has been the substitution of *becoming* for *being*, the relative for the absolute, dynamic movement for dogmatic immobility."[4] Even fiction of the "society novel" type that Disraeli and Bulwer wrote, followed the tendency of the age in emphasizing the *process* by which the hero achieves his destiny. If we care to attribute this emphasis to Carlyle rather than to "the spirit of the age," that may also be possible. Certainly no one ever stressed more than Carlyle, the spiritual guide and literary father of all the novelists in question, the importance of *inward* growth toward moral strength. The outer "shows of things" were unimportant to him always.

As far as any possible German influence goes, it seems only secondary in most of these novels. Not only, as we have said, does the self-culture theme of *Wilhelm Meister* tend to disappear, but much of the machinery of the typical apprenticeship pattern goes with it. The reason may be in part suggested by Morley when he says:

Carlyle and others had given a certain vogue to the great names of Goethe, Schiller, Ranke, Niebuhr, but their effect on general opinion was not effective, and even so late as 1854 serious men spoke of Goethe's work in England as at an end. The European movement since 1830 was little studied in England by even the leading men, much less by the average.[5]

The authors in question in this chapter were indeed zealous readers of German; they could scarcely be faithful Carlyleans and not be. But it is doubtful whether Goethe's fiction made much impression upon them, even though the *Wahlverwandschaften* and *Wilhelm Meister* are alluded to here and there by most of them. But Goethe's ideas had become so much a part of educated thinking, and the life-journey pattern for novels so much a matter of course, that in this sense his work in England may indeed be called at an end. These novelists took the pattern and adapted it to their own purposes, without even thinking of its origin. No one of them found it a revelation in novel technique as Bulwer did, writing with the specific idea of an English apprentice (Ernest Maltravers) in view, who should closely parallel Goethe's hero. Some of these more serious authors may have read Bulwer, and so freshened-up in their minds the idea of using the theme themselves. But it becomes one of those questions of vague influences too complex to trace. Perhaps Carlyle, Goethe, and Bulwer all had a share in it.

Among the parts of the *Wilhelm Meister* machinery that are dropped during this phase of English novel development is the series of light love affairs, or "mistaken choices," we might call them, which is one side of Wilhelm's apprenticeship. The quality of his love affairs marks the stages in his development. This may be a survival of the picaresque tradition in Goethe's novel, but it is missing in most of these English ones. Only *Pendennis* shows some traces of it. This light-hearted hero of Thackeray's novel is the only worldling in the whole group if, indeed, he belongs in the group at all; he alone has any of Wilhelm's gayety and careless, adaptable amiability. There is a mentor or guiding power in all these novels, as in Goethe's. This device is too valuable for purposes of plot and character-contrast for any of these authors to let it go. Experience as the greatest teacher is the important part of the *Meister* theme that still comes out clearly in these books. But these English heroes take their chances with it. There is no secret guiding force, such as Wilhelm benefits by, to shape their destinies. To be sure they, like Wilhelm (and Parsifal and Christian before him) are dedicated spirits, destined to attain their goal, or at least (in the case of Froude's heroes) to fail in a superior way, going to destruction, like religious Werthers as they are, after such struggle as only the supersensitive may know. But most of them are like the heroes of the old moral allegories; they are to be sorely tempted, but we are in no doubt about the outcome. The process alone holds our interest.

With these deviations from, and modifications of, an old theme, and against the stormy background of mid-Victorian England, these desperately earnest young people—descendants of Carlyle and the Germans—set forth on their life-pilgrimages. Their chief claim to interest is that they illustrate to the full the wide variety of forms that the struggle for adjustment could take while England was in the throes of transition.

1. JOHN STERLING

The man who most clearly *lived*, as well as wrote, a story of apprenticeship, was John Sterling. Carlyle's biography of him emphasizes this, and Wilson surmises that this was what interested Carlyle in him in the first place.

The only thing interesting about him was his moral evolution. Handicapped by having money enough to be idle when he liked, Sterling avoided common frivolity and grew into harmonious activity, which is the best human happiness, by dint of doing daily the duties at hand and finding guidance in the voice within. By a happy marriage he emancipated himself from sexual sentimentalities, as a disciple of Carlyle should; but he suffered all the other current ailments of intellectual adolescence, including political measles and religious mumps, and recovered perfectly from them all,—decidedly an interesting "case."[6]

It is significant of Carlyle's influence, perhaps, that John Mill, who was a good friend of Sterling's and introduced him to Carlyle, speaks of him in terms of a kind of apprenticeship, or it may merely mean that the simile was a convenient one. Caroline Fox reports that in 1840 Mill gave her his

version of John Sterling's history. In early life he had all the beautiful peculiarities and delicacies of a woman's mind. It at length dawned upon him that he had a work of his own to accomplish; and earnestly and long unsuccessfully, did he strive to ascertain its nature. All this time he was restless and unhappy, under the sense that doing it he was not. This lasted until his returning voyage from the West Indies, where his patience and perseverance, his earnestness and sincerity, received their reward; he saw the use he might be to others, in establishing and propagating sound principles of action, and since that time he has known quietness and satisfaction.[7]

This sounds more like *Sartor* than Goethe, but when Mill dwells on this idea in other connections, he shows that it is one he has turned over in his mind a good deal, probably not because of his German reading so much as from ruminating about his own early education or perhaps because the idea was "in the air" among his friends. Caroline Fox writes of a conversation with Mill:

There is also a guide to the path you should take in the intellectual and active world. Carlyle says, "Try and you'll find it." Mill says: "Avoid all that you prove by experience or intuition to be wrong, and you are safe; especially avoid the servile imitation of any other, be true to yourselves, find out your individuality, and live and act in the circle around it. Follow with earnestness the path into which it impels you, taking reason for your safety lamp and perpetually warring with inclination; then you will attain to that freedom which results only from obedience to light and reason, and that happiness which proves to be such, on retrospection. Everyone has a part to perform whilst here, and he must strive with enthusiasm to perform it."[8]

Carlyle did not set out to make his biography of Sterling the story of an apprenticeship. He plans in 1848 to write "some picture of a gifted soul whom I knew and who was my friend. Might not many things withal be *taught* in the course of such a delineation?"[9] And his primary incentive was certainly his affection: ". . . for I love this man; a radiant, lambent, all-hoping brotherly being,—one of those you call 'too good to live.' " But it is true that many passages in the *Life* lend themselves to the apprenticeship idea, some of them in the vocabulary reminiscent of *Sartor:*

Here then is a young soul, brought to the years of legal majority, furnished from his training-schools with such and such shining capabilities, and ushered on the scene of things, to inquire practically, What he will do there? Piety is in the man, noble human valor, bright intelligence, ardent proud veracity . . . a kingly kind of man;—whose "kingdom" however, in this bewildered place and epoch of the world will probably be difficult to find and conquer![10]

Carlyle dwells on the representative value of Sterling's pilgrimage:

[Sterling] more than others . . . took intensely into him such tint and shape of feature as the world had to offer there and then . . . participating ardently in the world's battle, and suffering deeply in its bewilderments;—whose Life-Pilgrimage accordingly is an emblem, unusually significant, of the world's own during those years of his. . . .[11]

It is this representative quality which the whole gallery of apprentice heroes has, that makes the books in which they figure significant to us. Often the novels themselves are vapid enough—as Sterling's own book was, in many ways—but their pilgrimages, like Sterling's, stand for many others of their time. In Sterling's case, his own life, rather than his book, is the record of such an emblematic struggle with, and journey through, the world.

Having found that radicalism and the priesthood will not do for him, he inquires once more where the way lies. Carlyle moralizes here on the struggle for adjustment:

The roads are many; the authentic finger-posts are few,—never fewer than in this era, when in so many senses the waters are out. . . . Illusions, in his chase of the summum bonum, were not likely to be wanting, aberrations, and wasteful changes of course were likely to be many! It is in the history of such vehement, trenchant, far-shining, and yet intrinsically light and volatile souls, missioned into this epoch to seek their way there, that we best see what a confused epoch it is.[12]

Sterling finally settles on literature as his true career, and gradually becomes, under Carlyle's guidance, familiar with German literature and gets over his prejudices about Goethe's "want of feeling," and some other misunderstandings which had horrified Carlyle. This German reading, however, and his trip to Germany in 1833, did not affect his novel, which was written earlier in his life, in 1830, and reflects his Radical-Democratic interests rather than his later literary ones. He was not given long to follow his true bent, once he had found it. Carlyle, the mentor of this, in some ways, tragic apprenticeship, dwells in grim pity on the apparent futility of it all:

Poor Sterling, he was by nature appointed for a Poet, then,—a Poet after his sort, or recognizer and delineator of the Beautiful; and not for a Priest at all. . . . He had strange aberrations appointed him, and painful wanderings amid the miserable gas-lights, bog-fires, dancing meteors and putrid phosphorescences which form the guidance of a young human soul at present! Not till after trying all manner of sublimely illuminated places . . . did he, when his strength was all gone, discover his true sacred hill, and passionately climb thither while life was fast ebbing. . . . Many a high-striving, too-hasty soul . . . will recognize his own history in this image of a fellow-pilgrim's. . . . And so he played his part among us, and has now ended it: in this first half of the Nineteenth Century such was the shape of human destinies the world and he made out between them.[13]

Sterling's *Essays and Tales*, especially the essays on Carlyle[14] and on *The Characteristics of German Genius*[15] show the great importance he attached to the German civilization, and its literature. Caroline Fox's journal, too, bears eloquent testimony to Sterling's rhapsodies on this theme; her reports of his conversation—in fact, all the entries in her journal that refer to him—come as close to having a faint tinge of the romantic as anything this sober-minded, conscientious young Quakeress ever wrote. His whole personality was evidently a romantic one to her, as to many others who knew him. Perhaps it was this element in his character which gave him his early Shelleyan enthusiasm for revolutions (which is reflected in his novel) and led him to admire in the German writers the "freedom" which he thought the English lacked. But his definition of freedom is a very German one:

The willing choice of those conditions which enable our best, most laborious powers to exert themselves for the fittest ends. . . . This victorious effort it is, which glorifies more or less every truly great man; and above all in modern times, those of Germany.[16]

We should expect, then, to find the novel that Sterling wrote on a general apprentice pattern to be strongly flavored with Carlyle's and Goethe's gospel of work, and perhaps with echoes of the transcendental German philosophers, although his reading of them came later. But it is the earlier period of Sterling's apprenticeship that reflects itself in *Arthur Coningsby.* Arthur is an enthusiast for the Rights of Man and the French Revolution. He recapitulates for his beautiful young cousin (Isabel Barrington, who loves him), the story of his early life, much as Wilhelm does for Mariane on that memorable night when she drops off to sleep in the middle of his recital. Isabel listens more attentively than the little actress, but there is nothing very arresting in the story that Arthur tells her. He has passed through the usual doubts and struggles of early manhood, and is unable to attain the steady resolution and humility of his more practical friend—Wilmot; (there is always one of these on hand as a foil for the poetic hero.) His mind is "confused and pained" by obstinate suggestions "on a thousand points." The world does not spread out plainly and simply before him. He is "always longing to enlarge the plan" of any undertaking, "and to attempt what was impracticable." He is imaginative, and enters in as hero of all his own imaginary stories of chivalry. He feels the spell of the theater for a while, goes to Oxford but proves a poor mixer, and joins a small group of congenial spirits who are also interested in the Rights of Man. "The dreamy uselessness and selfish activity of boyhood" give way to "the sunny realities of manhood,"[17] for he feels at last that a field of activity opens before him. He is offered and accepts a secret ambassadorship from England to Paris, in the cause of the Revolution for which he has been working. Isabel pleads with him for the simple, pious life of love and domestic duty in England, but he breaks away, feeling that he must not let her restrain him from his work and the world. He gets to London, and his comrade Osborne betrays him and some friends who are having a secret meeting, to the soldiers, who raid their meeting-place. Arthur escapes but is bitterly disillusioned about human nature.

Before leaving for France, he visits his old friend Harry Wilmot who is now married and a clergyman. He is warned to "distrust his understanding and cherish his conscience" and to have hope for the world. He is shaken in his enthusiasm for the cause, but the struggle has cleared his mind.

He began to perceive more accurately the difference between mingling with mankind and looking at them. His activity became readier and more ingenious. Saddened by misfortune and unconsciously governed by the necessity of his circumstances, he comprehended others better; and thought of himself less constantly than before.[18]

In France he rescues Agatha, the French nun in disguise, from robbers on the road, but the gendarmes catch them. Arthur is dismissed, and the nun imprisoned. On his way to Paris he falls in with the mad girl, Louise, who has been crazed by the horrors of the Revolution. She is a vague mixture of Ophelia and Mignon, and, as might be surmised, not particularly effective. In Paris at the salon of the beautiful and noble Victoria de Valence he meets all the celebrities of the Revolution, conveniently assembled there for our survey, and is warned against taking active part in the Revolution. Victoria before long confesses her love for him, (like all his brother-heroes he has a fatal attraction for women), but after viewing, in some scenes appropriately dripping with gore, all the horrors of the conflict that is convulsing France, he breaks away from her and resolves to die. He remembers his past life and is now guilty and shame-stricken. He has made "a vague and loud philanthropy a pretext for the neglect of his individual duties."[19] He has been fleeing from the inward spirit that he should have followed. Now it has seized him, and he will work against the Revolution. The lurid assembly at the house of the sinister Mme Carfours inspires him with further bitterness and disillusion. She represents the senseless extreme of radicalism and the Revolution as Sterling evidently saw it.

Louise, the mad girl, helps Arthur to escape from Mme Carfours' house. She stabs Corvet, one of the Revolutionary leaders who has dishonored her, and Arthur is implicated and imprisoned with her, but Mme de Valence rescues him, and he goes to live with her at her chateau, far from the madding crowd. He broods over the past, but to no effect. "For sharp as was the impression of all his past life, and vivid as was his self-consciousness, his reflections did not shape themselves into any moral system, nor lead him to measure himself severely by any practical standard of duty."[20] Mme de Valence admires what he tells her of the simple, benevolent, disciplined life of England, but he, the incurable romantic, yearns for "the vague, strange, and distant." Their reading and discussions include *Hamlet* and Goethe, death, religion, and immortality. But "his will is insufficient to create a visible and active life, corresponding with the purport of his meditations," and hence he is tortured with self-questionings. Mme de Valence is gradually fading away from illness and a conviction of sin, and leaves him a packet containing the story of her life, the conclusion of which is that "we seek in vain to construct for ourselves a binding and supporting law out of our own tastes, impulses, notions while we turn from that which exists without us, based eternally in the Being of God, and reflected in every human heart."[21] She dies, and Arthur, after some travels on the continent which convince him that all is vain and transitory, and that man cannot struggle with fate, returns to England.

Isabel will have nothing to do with him, though more in sorrow than in anger. She writes him that he has shown "so much selfishness with regard to others, such hopeless abandonment to every impulse, and such indifference to what he might have known as the truth,"[22] that he can have no influence over her any longer. She prays that "your self-delusions may in time be dispelled, and your terrific pride subdued by Christian faith."

He considers his future and finds it blank.

The great only in action I have intellect enough to consider as my inferiors. The great in thought have built their superiority upon a moral foundation to which I find no counterpart in myself. That sympathy with mankind by which they have come to be its leaders, champions, and teachers, has been rooted up in me, like a dead stump, by the pickaxe of worldly experience.[23]

He despises both worlds, the outer and the inner. There is no hope for English society either, since all classes are worthless, and religion, poetry, philosophy are vain shows. He would, however, still apply himself to the things of the mind, "mean and barren as it may be." In reviewing his travels he remembers that in Germany he has found "that all-pervading intellect" but on the whole he prefers America. In a rhapsody reminiscent of *The Revolt of Islam* and also of some passages of Chateaubriand, he hails the new world. He will seek the primeval Indian and the "broad and green savannahs." "Some future wanderer in the western forests will perhaps stumble or pause at a low mound in some dark thicket, but there will be no inscription nor emblem to inform him that the bones of an English outcast were there laid in earth by the hands of red warriors."[24]

So ends this melancholy pilgrimage, with echoes of Werther and Byron, not of Carlyle and Goethe, who later gave the young Sterling himself a far more positive and hopeful philosophy than his hero has voiced. The confusion and indecision the novel pictures, was what Carlyle found noteworthy in it, as we can see from his *Life of Sterling*. He says of it:

The hero, an ardent youth, representing Sterling himself, plunges into life as we now have it in these anarchic times . . . finds, by various courses, utter shipwreck in this; lies broken, very wretched: this is the tragic nodus, or apogee of his life-course.

Carlyle deprecates his clutching at the church for help, and continues:

Some of the delineations are highly pictorial, flooded with a deep, ruddy effulgence, betokening much wealth, in the crude or the ripe state. . . . *Arthur Coningsby*, struggling imperfectly in a sphere high above circulating library novels, gained no notice whatever in that quarter, gained, I suppose, in a few scattered heads, some such recognition as the above, and there rested. Sterling never mentioned the name of it in my hearing, or would hear it mentioned.[25]

2. George Henry Lewes

A more fruitful and complete understanding of Goethe and Germany than John Sterling's, influenced two singular novels by George Eliot's "miniature Mirabeau," the little Bohemian journalist, poet, playwright, novelist, and editor, whom all his friends who have left reminiscences of him unite in praising for his versatility. We cannot wonder at this when we realize that in addition to his literary activities he was no mean philosopher, an intelligent promoter of Positivisim, a good linguist, and an able scientist. His friend William Bell Scott, the artist, describes him as being able to achieve what no mere dilettante could do:

No sooner did he possess himself of a science or a language than he used his knowledge in such a manner that the men who had been all their lives occupied with that single subject, acknowledged him their comrade.[26]

This same friend, Mr. Scott, may be partly responsible for the fact that both the novels of Lewes which take the apprenticeship form, *Ranthorpe* (1842), and *The Apprenticeship of Life* (1850) follow the life-journey idea. Lewes met Scott in 1837, through the kind offices of their mutual friend Leigh Hunt.

I was at that moment [says Scott] brooding over a series of designs in outline to represent the stages in life of the self-seeking man of ordinary powers and unscrupulous ability, the man of the world who becomes a judge, bishop, or Court doctor, to be called *Chorea Sancti Viti*, or *The Steps in the Journey of Prince Legion*. . . . Lewes proposed to write to these designs, but I found his notion was to appropriate the idea in question . . . as his own, and to relegate me to the position of an illustrator. So I brushed away his offer.[27]

Twelve of these designs were published later, in 1851, and Lewes in the *Leader* wrote some recollections of Scott which his friend regarded as fantastic but amusing. In the same article Lewes writes:

I left England and solaced many long nights by the composition of my "Life Journey of Prince Legion." I have the fragment still and read it not long ago. It is detestable! The boy starts on his career resolved to be crowned in the Capitol; midway he discovers that he is bald, commonplace, and gouty. He meant to be a hero; he finds himself Mr. Smith.[28]

Lewes may or may not have read *Wilhelm Meister* at the time of this acquaintance with Scott, but as he went to Germany for two years soon after (1838–40) we may surmise that he read it there, if the account of Ranthorpe's life in Germany be taken as substantially Lewes's own.

Ranthorpe remained two years in Berlin, supporting himself by giving English lessons to the young ladies of the upper classes and devoting all his leisure to hard study. He lived a solitary life, but on the whole a happy one. He knew that he was preparing himself for the great combat with the world. . . . Many were his delicious reveries while rambling through the wild Thiergarten which in winter, when covered with snow, looks so poetically desolate, and which in summer forms a shady retreat. There, amidst its "leafy solitudes" he meditated on the vexed problems of philosophy or scrutinized the mysteries of art. There he was supremely happy.[29]

Before he saw Germany again (in company with George Eliot, many years later), Lewes had evidently read and studied Goethe carefully. His essay on Goethe in the *British and Foreign Review* for 1843,[30] which Arthur Helps called "one of the best specimens of biography I have ever read, or rather it showed the way in which biography should be written,"[31] contains the germ of the later *Life and Works of Goethe*. Carlyle thought the essay "wide of the mark"[32] perhaps because it showed that Lewes saw Goethe primarily as the artist and poet, not as a great moral teacher. Lewes in 1843 as well as later, saw him "devoting his life with all its brilliant prospects to the complete evolution of his own being . . . living the life of an artist."[33] *Wilhelm Meister* is not often mentioned in the article except to prove the justice of this point of view about Goethe. "Renounce all, endure all, but develop yourself to the utmost limit.

This is his exhortation."[34] *Meister* is mentioned along with *Faust*, *Werther*, and *Tasso* as a picture "of various phases of the artistic idea" and in this light Lewes sees Wilhelm's weakness of character not only as justified but as artistically necessary. He makes this point again in the chapter on *Wilhelm Meister* in the *Life of Goethe*.[35] This earlier article may show that his reading of Goethe gave Lewes his interest in the struggle of the young person for adjustment to the world, which he dramatized in *Ranthorpe* (written about this time) and *The Apprenticeship of Life* later, but the interest may have been aroused still earlier, if we take his "detestable" poem inspired by Scott's *Prince Legion* designs, to be valid evidence. Of course, as a student of philosophy, Lewes would meet the *Bildung* idea again and again, though this does not dominate either of the novels. In the article on Goethe he mentions its recurrence: "This dogma of self-culture is common indeed in all ethical systems; the difference lies in the *latitude* given."[36] Altogether, the article shows a wider and more sympathetic appreciation of Goethe by means of the historical method than had been achieved by any English writer up to that time. Perhaps Crabb Robinson was the only other English Goethe disciple who was capable of it, and he could not bring himself to write about it; conversation was his forte.

The remarkable thing about Lewes's versatility was that his interests were tenacious in spite of their wide range. His interest in fiction, though a minor one, was lasting. His *Fortnightly Review* articles on *Criti-*

cism in Relation to Novels[37] and on *The Principles of Success in Literature*[38] as well as the penetrating one on Dickens, quoted by Espinasse[39] and his letters to Charlotte Bronte[40] prove a keen critical insight into the novel form, which he loved to experiment with himself. He took a naïve pleasure in the results of these experiments, which may strike us as a little crude. But there is a freshness and animation in these novels which is disarming.

Lewes wrote *Ranthorpe* when he was twenty-five, in 1842. Espinasse calls it "a crude performance, but, so far as I know . . . one of the first, if not the very first, of those novels, since so plentiful, which are mainly pictures of modern literary life in London: its struggles, failures, and triumphs."[41]

It depicts the seamy, Bohemian side of journalism in London as Lewes undoubtedly experienced it, but the progress of the genius, or the poetic temperament, through reverses, to the power to come to terms with life, is the main theme of the book. That this was not usual among novels of the day, the reviews of *Ranthorpe* testify:

Ranthorpe, [said the *New Monthly Magazine*] is, curious to say, the picture of those severe struggles, those fearful "pantings on the thorns of life" which belong to the career of the novelist . . . and depicts with earnestness and sincerity what he who undertakes to combat misery with his pen may have to undergo.[42]

This ancestor of a long line of young literary aspirants in London, Dublin, New York, and Chicago, is a young man without much humor and with some poetic gifts. His pilgrimage is roughly indicated by the headings of the five books into which the novel is divided: "The Poet's First Struggles," "The Lion," "The Unsuccessful Author," "Struggles with Circumstance," "Isola" (this being the name of his ladylove). The life-journey of this Prince Legion of Lewes's literary morality play is punctuated also by the mottoes to the various chapters, many of them quotations from Goethe, and some from *Meister*, reiterating the self-development and life-journey themes in various ways.

Percy Ranthorpe is a weak, impressionable young man, with a clerk's job which he despises, and deep blue eyes "shaded with the sweetest fringe imaginable." His practical father forbids him to give up his job for poetry, but Isola, large, gentle, and practical in a less philistine way than his unsympathetic father, sustains him in his choice and helps him through all his subsequent struggles. He becomes a hack journalist, and his experiences reflect some of the log-rolling and throat-cutting tactics incident to the pursuit of what was then not a firmly established profession. His father dies; Isola, who had been his ward and lived with them, takes a position as governess, and Percy succeeds in publishing his poems and gives up journalism. He becomes a literary lion, in a small way, and it goes to his head. He leads an extravagant life and falls in love with Florence Wilmington, a heartless flirt. He tries to write a successful play, and partly breaks with the faithful Isola. The value of experience is dwelt upon by

Lewes again and again, in the course of this Prodigal's Progress, and is reminiscent of *Meister* and all the other novels in this tradition. "A knowledge of life is the result of abundant experience drawn by a reflective mind. . . . The student of mankind can only learn from his own experience, not the results of experience written down by others."[43]   From a series of failures and hard knocks, our hero does learn, like Sartor, "the feeling of majestic self-reliance,"[44] but this throws him back upon himself through hatred of mankind.

The book of life had lain open before him, and on its fair pages he had scrawled the characters of folly and misery; were it not better at once to throw that book into the flames, than tear those blotted pages out? . . . The truth is, he was unfitted for the work,[45]

and Lewes goes on to explain that an author's life must be calm. *Past* experience forms the material for his work; present agitation only hinders him for the moment.

He should know the *real* world—he should have suffered in it, and experienced all its phases . . . but this experience which is to be the fountain of his inspiration, must not mingle with the current. The stream flows bright and limpid over the sandy bed; but if you disturb that bed, the sand mixes with the water.[46]

Percy has mistaken aspiration for inspiration, and decides to commit suicide. He is saved by Mr. Thornton, a brusque old playgoer who has attended the fiasco of Percy's first play in London, and who "had lived at Weimar and had known Goethe of whom he loved to speak." He restores Percy to a sense of his responsibilities to the world and explains that though Goethe wrote *Werther* he did not *act* it, recommending him as a model for youth to pattern on. "He understood the divine significance of man's destiny, which is work. Man the worker is the only man fit to live."[47] After being nearly executed for a murder committed by another, Percy goes to Germany and writes a real tragedy with which to redeem his first failure. It succeeds on his return to London. "Where is the poet's reward?" moralizes Lewes, "in activity, in creation, in the healthy employment of his faculties."[48]

Isola meanwhile has become engaged to a friend of Percy's, but he heroically gives her up when he learns that she and Percy still love one another.

And now our hero's troubles are o'er. He is happy, his bride stands at the altar beside him. . . . After many wanderings on the rugged highway, he had reached the happy valley. [His life] is now one of activity and happiness: the true ideal of an author's life: He has bitterly expiated his early error, and in that expiation recovered the purity and independence of mind, the confidence in his mission and reliance on his means of fulfilling it without which a man may indeed become rich and popular, but no man may become a great author. . . . He has won his spurs. His genius has begun to take its flight far above the reach of other wings. . . . His genius is free to operate untrammeled upon the materials afforded him by experience. He has felt and he has thought: he has dreamed and he has suffered. He is now to "preach from the text of his own errors"—to make his experience incarnate in song.[49]

He has walked up through mists but he has reached a certain height. . . . The storms are below him. . . . The poor, dreamy boy, self-taught, self-aided, has risen into power. He wields a pen. And the pen, in our age, weighs heavier in the social scale than the sword of a Norman baron.[50]

Thus Lewes, whom Carlyle called "the prince of journalists," prophesied truly concerning the importance of that new profession in a new England. This artless novel of his points it out only incidentally, but what permanent autobiographical or other value the book may have, lies as much in this as in the more labored moralizings about the development of young prodigals, and the life-journey of the hero-prodigal in particular. *Meister* is echoed and suggested plentifully throughout, and Carlyle's gospel of work also; but this apprenticeship of Ranthorpe's is distinctly a professional, almost a technical one, in the art of being a complete poet and literary man. The art of living in general is only suggested, in spite of sundry sensational episodes (such as the murder of Mr. Thornton), which are supposed to contribute to the hero's general culture.

Lewes's other Candidate for Truth is a religious, not a journalistic one—Armand in *The Apprenticeship of Life*, the fragment of a novel which he began to publish in his new magazine, the *Leader*, March 30, 1850. "In modern fiction," says Espinasse, "from Miss Jewsbury's *Zoe* to Mrs. Humphry Ward's *Robert Elsmere* when the religious belief of the hero is transformed, he is usually made to pass from faith to doubt. Lewes's hero undergoes the reverse operation."[51] Armand, in the first episode of the story, called "The Initiation of Faith," is a young sceptic, the son of a freethinking French baron of the Restoration. He is converted to Christianity by his Greek friend Stavros Frangipoli, whose lack of orthodoxy makes him able to understand Armand's difficulties in belief. He emphasizes to him the universal nature of Christianity and its appeal to all mankind, and Armand is converted. He is cast out from home on account of this by his uncle, and goes to Paris, Lewes moralizing at this point upon the necessity of forming one's own creed.

In the second episode, "The Initiation of Love," Armand is rescued from starvation by his cousin Hortense, a handsome widow of thirty-three. She is a believer in St. Simon's doctrine that love is the only bond of marriage. She had decided not to love or to marry but she falls in love with Armand and finally gives way to her feeling. They are married and Lewes interpolates a chapter on love. Hortense's grandmother teaches her "the lesson of life" which is to be unselfish, and Hortense, much as she loves Armand, vows that she will even lay down her love for Armand, if it should be necessary.

There are some chapters on the state of France and the events leading up to the Revolution of 1830, about Charles X's foolishness, and about the Brothers, a secret society founded by Armand and Frangipoli, the Greek. There is an episode of Bonapartist intrigue, with the killing of a police spy. Armand has fallen in love with Adrienne, the daughter of General Laboissière, and has developed beyond Hortense. He needs "some larger soul" and finds it in Adrienne. "All progressive natures," Lewes points out, "are inconstant, hence the notorious inconsistency of poets and artists." Adrienne at first dislikes him for his Republican views, but their friendship grows and finally they recognize that they are in love. His moral code thus shaken, Armand is forced to modify his opinions according to his experience, and has gone one step further in his apprenticeship.

The King is threatened with death and Adrienne's father is arrested, and Adrienne and Armand give way to their love. Lewes interpolates a passage reminiscent of Scott's *Life Journey of Prince Legion* as well as of *Wilhelm Meister* and the morality plays: "To make my hero understand life I am forced to make him pass through all the great typical dilemmas of life so that at the close we may say of him, 'He learned from all he suffered.' "

Overpowered at a meeting which called for the assassination of the King, Armand is arrested but frees himself and escapes. Hortense, finding that Armand loves someone else, determines to free him, remembering her vow to give up even her love for him. She writes him that she is about to die, but instead of dying she becomes a Sister of Charity. "By making Armand believe he was free, it made him free."

Episode the third was to be "The Initiation of Work" but this was, unfortunately, never written; so we cannot know how Lewes intended to terminate this religious and political and amatory apprenticeship. Having been a pioneer in the novel of journalistic and literary apprenticeship, Lewes again broke an almost new path in the novel of religious conversion or controversy which became during the nineteenth century almost a type in itself, culminating in *Robert Elsmere* and *The Way of All Flesh* and *Father and Son.* Froude and Geraldine Jewsbury, and—in some ways— Kingsley, had been before him in the field by a very few years, but the first two are echoes of the Oxford movement and their heroes progress more conventionally from faith to doubt instead of in the reverse direction. Kingsley's novels were preëminently social in purpose. But Lewes, agile little positivist man of science and philosopher that he was, gives us at last a convincing apprentice hero as alert and independent as the author himself, and as able as his creator to "learn from all he suffered."

3. JAMES ANTHONY FROUDE

Froude's checkered career brought him about 1850 into Geraldine Jewsbury's circle at Manchester, along with George Lewes, and he and Geraldine became great friends, in spite of her first mistaken estimate of him quoted above. By the time Geraldine met him, his ill-fated *Nemesis of Faith* (1849) had been published, banned, and burned, but he had written before this, under the influence of Newman, a first feeble novel called *Shadows of the Clouds* (1847). We cannot blame his father, the archdeacon, for buying up and destroying almost the whole edition, though this worthy man was no doubt thinking more of its religious heresies than of its literary weakness.

The hero of this somewhat unfortunate effort,

Edward Fowler, is to some extent Froude himself, and his story is summarized by Hutchinson as follows:

Edward Fowler, a precocious child of weak moral stamina, with an unsympathetic father of unbending severity, is sent to Westminster School, where he is subjected to such bullying and harshness by his schoolfellows and masters that his character degenerates and he becomes a liar and a craven. After three years of school life he is removed and put under private tuition before proceeding to Oxford, where he works hard for a time, then falls into debt and is consequently disappointed in a love-affair; though his last hours (he dies young of course) are cheered by the presence of the lady of his affections, who has meanwhile married somebody else. Incidentally he takes part in the *Lives of the English Saints* at Newman's invitation.[52]

Between 1842 and 1844, Froude "discovers Lessing, Neander, and Schleiermacher"[53] and passes from Carlyle to Goethe, before he writes this story, but we cannot lay the blame even upon *Werther*, far less upon *Wilhelm Meister*, which we have held responsible for so much. Edward does nothing, and goes into a decline gently regretful,

to feel that I have to go with no work done to follow me, without one single point to look back upon in which I have made the earth better or happier by my presence in it. . . . As I understand it, the question will be rather, What are you? What have you made of yourself?—then one by one what are the specific things you have done? By a subtle enough but exact enough power, each thing you do leaves its indelible scar upon you, and remains recorded, like two stones in a piece of masonry, not separate but in a collective result.[54]

He indicates here a kind of consciousness that work and development are indeed the important things but his life has been a negative one. There is no apprenticeship worth mentioning. To be sure, during the latter part of his Oxford life

he was learning, not for college honors, but to *know;* to make himself a man, and to raise himself above the beings whose playthings he had been so long;[55]

and at the beginning of his illness he reviews his past and writes to his friend:

To have been obliged so many times to be taught and taught the same thing over and over, each time forgetting the meaning of the word and having to look it out again in the dictionary of suffering. . . . One ceases to wonder at the little use other men's experience is to us, when one thinks how very often one's own has to be repeated.[56]

But unlike the ordinary apprentice hero he learns from his experience too late to do anything about it. Submission to God's will is the sum and substance of the book's message; the hero has worked out no scheme of action that will adjust him to the world; he is one of the failures.

The same "thoughtful, speculative, agreeable young man" as Caroline Fox found him, wrote yet another progress toward truth, but this time from faith to doubt. *The Nemesis of Faith* was discussed by Geraldine Jewsbury in the *Westminster Review* for January, 1850, in an article called "Religious Faith and Scepticism," which Lewes helped her to publish. She called it

a very powerful picture of the struggle of a religiously disposed sceptic . . . it is "a voice of crying heard and loud lament" but nothing more; there is no attempt to discover by what right this state of things exists. Doubt is treated as a painful phenomenon, and not as a legitimate phasis in the transition of humanity from one condition to another: therefore the work is oppressive and painful; it suggests nothing; there is no outlet from it—not even into the wilderness where one might at least breathe—for the author insists on setting his face toward the Past.   And yet his book is constructed like a town in which every street should be a *cul de sac*.[57]

She goes on to recommend "modesty and reserve" during periods of spiritual transition, and deprecates

the fashion of writing sceptical books, full of sentimental regret and interesting struggle . . . the man who begins his utterance in sincerity, may end by enjoying his sorrows and draping himself becomingly in his "doubts," "sorrows," "positions" or whatever may chance to be the point in which the interest of society has been enlisted.[58]

Carlyle also felt this way about the book and expressed himself even more strongly.[59]   But the book had more sympathetic readers here and there, Lord Houghton being one:

It is a sort of religious anti-religious *Wilhelm Meister*, and balances itself between fact and fiction in an uncomfortable manner, though with great ability, and has caused the poor man to lose his fellowship and a college in Van Diemen's Land and to fall into utter poverty.[60]

Froude in this much-discussed book paints a weak and inconsistent young man, Markham Sutherland, whose trouble is, as Froude remarks in his preface to the second edition, that "exactly where the direct action of his heart upon himself is required as the complement of the intellect, there his thought as well as

his action breaks down."[61]   He indulges in speculation, having swung away from Newman, to Carlyle,
and enters "the battle-field of action" and fails.   He
proves only that "man is a real man, and can live and
act manfully in this world, not in the strength of
opinions, not according to what he thinks, but according to what he *is*."   "Times are changed," muses
Froude sadly.   "This is an age of fact—it believes
only in experience—it is jealous and enquiring."[62]
So Markham cannot believe in the supernatural origin
of the Bible, though he is religiously disposed by
nature and the loss of his faith is therefore the more
tragic.   "To a man in his case," Froude points out
in the manner of Carlyle, "employment grasped
strongly and vigorously is the only resource."[63]   But
Markham is too weak to grasp it though he recognizes
the fact that one must learn life by living and that,
as his father tells him, "you cannot dream yourself
into a character; you must hammer and forge yourself one.[64]

He takes orders, against his better instincts, only
to leave the ministry when his doubts become known
and he confesses them to his bishop.   The old creeds
are dead, he writes mournfully to his friend Arthur,
and voices here the plaintive nineteenth-century
outcry,

Once, once for all, if you would save your heart from breaking, learn
this lesson—once for all you must cease, in this world, to believe in
the eternity of any creed or form at all.   Whatever grows in time is
a child of time, and is born and lives, and dies at its appointed day
like ourselves. . . . Life is change, to cease to change is to cease

to live; yet if you may shed a tear beside the deathbed of an old friend, let not your heart be silent on the dissolving of a faith.[65]

To how many readers of Froude's day this melancholy half-acceptance of uncertainty as the inevitable, must have come as the echo of their own experience! Here was one candidate for truth who went down in the fray. Faith ought to have been Sutherland's salvation—it was his Nemesis—it destroyed him.

He tries philosophy as a substitute but finds no support in it. He drifts to Italy on account of poor health, and writes a long autobiography entitled *Confessions of a Sceptic* which he sends back to his friend, and which describes minutely his early struggles and religious experiences at home and at school. his home life, his progress toward Newman and pseudo-Catholicism, his need to face facts honestly after he reads Carlyle's *French Revolution*, and his slipping toward a kind of passive agnosticism. "For me this world was neither so high nor so low as the Church would have it." Men are neither "God's children nor the Devil's children, but children of men."[66]

But at Como all is lost. He meets the beautiful Helen Leonard, another man's wife, and falls in love with her, and she with him, in her unsuspecting and somewhat stupid husband's absence. They are only half conscious of sin and try to stifle a sense of guilt (we are led to believe that if Markham had been really religious this would not have happened) and so they drift along for a time. Finally Mrs. Leonard's little girl of three, Annie, takes cold while they are all out sailing, and dies. This is a judgment upon them for their wickedness. Markham is about to commit suicide when he is saved and persuaded into the Catholic Church by Frederic Mornington, who is Newman in a thin disguise. Helen meanwhile goes into a convent and dies (though unreconciled with some aspects of the Church), happy. Markham, however, had been too sudden a convert, and doubt soon attacks him again. "He sank down into the barren waste, and the dry sands rolled over him where he lay; and no living being was left behind him on earth, who would not mourn over the day which brought life to Markham Sutherland."[67]

These two gloomy failures, Edward Fowler and Markham Sutherland, represent the intensest form of Victorian, post-Oxford movement, religious heart-searching which, in the very nature of the case, must come to nothing in the end. No real apprenticeship and no adjustment to the changing world are possible for such natures as these, vacillating, idealistic, afraid of reality, lacking in gusto. They are Candidates for Truth indeed, but their spiritual suffering teaches them nothing but a blind and bewildered submission to forces they do not understand, which they can only define as "God's will." More modern heroes may end more prosaically in submission to the inevitable Commonplace (like the hero of Somerset Maugham's *Of Human Bondage*), but they have at least tasted life on the way to it. Kingsley's heroes and the creations of the inimitable Geraldine Jewsbury are no more satisfying than Froude's from an artistic point of view, perhaps, but they are more convincing.

They have not missed so much along the route of their life-pilgrimage.

4. Geraldine Endsor Jewsbury

The incomparable Miss Jewsbury may not have been an eminent Victorian, but she was such a picturesque one that it seems a slip on the part of the hungry biographers to have passed her by. Artless and eager she was, yet shrewd and modern in many ways, decidedly a "clever" woman, as that word was used during her period—well-read, independent, unconventional, a strong feminist before feminism really came into its own—yet full of sentimentalities and as easily led as a child by anyone she adored as she did Jane Carlyle. Miss Jewsbury's biography would provide not only a rich study of the period, but of a vibrant, dramatic personality that revealed itself, all too unreservedly for the reader's complete comfort sometimes, in her letters to Jane Carlyle and in her novels and magazine articles. It may be this lack of reticence about her love affairs, her moods and emotional states, her health and her fears for Jane's welfare, that has scared away possible biographers; she is too "easy," there is nothing subtle about her[68].

Yet a certain charm is present in her very frankness and her fearless outlook on life. "There is a great deal that wants saying about matrimony. Who dare say it?" she writes to Jane. She attempted to say some of it in *Constance Herbert* (1855) and *The Sorrows of Gentility* (1856) but for Jane's sake was willing to make concessions to decency in *Zoe*, where she had herself felt no lack of it.

However, my dear, there shall be a liberal distribution of spotted muslin, only, will you tell me where it is to be applied.   It is no use "leaving it to our own consciences."   Our sympathies are imperfect on that point.[69]

She was intent on getting the thing said that seemed to her to be crying for utterance in these circulating-library, rather melodramatic novels of hers, and the more prudish standards of her Victorian audience did not assert themselves until the more careful Jane called her attention to them.   She was willing, however, to attain a higher standard of correct writing, under Jane's admonitions.   She had thought such things "came by nature" but "the Devil is in it if I do not contrive to mend my faults,"[70] she adds gallantly.   Her devotion to Jane knew no bounds and had no reserves.   She hates sewing but she makes Jane an eider-down quilt for her feet in cold weather.[71] She resolves pathetically to be "more conformable and more proper-behaved in my manners and conversation, in order to be more of a credit to you!"[72]   But it is an effort; she is not at her best in a state of artificial calm.   "I am never witty . . . except when I am ready to cut my throat; when I am at ease I am stupid and content."[73]

Her unquenchable thirst for experience and curiosity about life are, after all, the significant things about her.   It may be only a circus that captures her imagination, but she sees a giraffe there for the first time, and off she goes about the poor, pretty giraffe, looking like a captive princess; there was something quite pathetic in her appearance and I wished her well dead with all my heart!   But she was apparently in the enjoyment of excellent health and resignation.   [She looked like] something from between the regions of truth and fiction.[74]

Geraldine is anxious to see behind the scenes of the circus, too.

I like to know the processes of things and I was . . . curious to know what sort of souls resided in bodies of men who spent their lives in turning forty-four somersaults in succession.[75]

Her keen interests included all sorts of reading—Rabelais in the original French, German newspapers which she forwards to Jane Carlyle, *Paracelsus*, Emerson, whose indebtedness to Carlyle she spots at once, Newman's sermons, *John Buncle*, the letters of Horace Walpole, Niebuhr, Fichte's *Scholar*, Chateaubriand, *Jane Eyre* (which she does not care for, preferring Lewes's novels), Margaret Fuller (she views this lady's excessive emphasis on self-culture with a penetrating and slightly disapproving eye);[76] Ellis's *Early English Metrical Romances* ("My word!   One's ancestors were not at all stupid," is her reflection on these,)[77] and finally White's *Natural History of Selborne*.   The cause of women was always near her heart and she states their true position of dependence with a rare and courageous honesty for 1849, but with a forward look:

I believe we are touching on better days, when women will have a genuine normal life of their own to lead. . . . Women will be taught not to feel their destiny *manqué* if they remain single.   They will be

able to be friends and companions in a way they cannot be now. All
the strength of their feelings and thoughts will not run into love.
. . . I do not feel either you [Jane Carlyle] or I are to be called
failures. We are indications of a development of womanhood
which as yet is not recognized. It has, so far, no ready-made
channels to run in, but still, we have looked and tried and found that
the present rules for women will not hold us—that something better
and stronger is needed. . . . There are women to come after us
who will approach nearer the fulness of the measure of the stature of
woman's nature. I regard myself as a mere faint indication . . . of
certain higher qualities and possibilities that lie in women, and all
the eccentricities and mistakes and miseries and absurdities I have
made, are only the consequences of an imperfect formation, an im-
mature growth.[78]

This, for as strong a sentimentalist as Miss Jewsbury undoubtedly was, shows an amazing degree of
insight not only into the position of women but into
her own nature, and lets us see, once again, how unsafe
it is to generalize unduly about the minds of our
Victorian sisters. Whatever may have been her
shortcomings, Geraldine was at least thoroughly alive.
Jane might be unfeeling and careless about writing
to her or coming to visit her; she may be worried half
to death because she feels that Carlyle does not
appreciate Jane, is too absorbed in *Oliver Cromwell*
and expects Jane to make the house comfortable on
"next to nothing,"—her own love affairs may be
devastating enough to cause an acute degree of mental
anguish; her health may be poor, her household
affairs all too exacting, her writing not going on as well
as she could wish—no matter! Life is worth living.
"I hope I am not going to die, but to live to see the
end of all the great things that are coming to pass in

the world. . . . The next few years will be worth
seeing."[79]　She lived until 1880, almost as long as
Carlyle himself, and fourteen years longer than Jane,
whose friendship was the one great, abiding joy of her
life.　The record of it in Geraldine's letters (Jane's
were destroyed according to an agreement between
them) confused, exclamatory, childish as these sometimes are, forms, nevertheless, one of those profoundly
touching personal portraits that we would not lose.
A spontaneous, generous, vivid human being is
brought back to us out of the mid-century; we see a
little better, because of her, how the world of the
fifties looked to a woman who faced it, not without
qualms and deep misgivings, but also with a gallant
acceptance, a challenge to the future.　"The next
few years will be worth seeing."　We may be sure
that Miss Jewsbury, for one, found them so.

Such a woman as this, writing novels, would
naturally be a pioneer.　Geraldine's *Zoe* (1845) was
a forerunner of *The Nemesis of Faith* and *Robert
Elsmere* and all their tribe, and her *Marian Withers*
(1851) anticipated Mrs. Gaskell's *North and South* by
four years.　*The Half Sisters* (1848) is a ringing and
tempestuous sermon on the Carlylean text of the
gospel of work before this had found incorporation in
novel form at anyone else's hands.　*Zoe* and *The
Half Sisters* bear some traces of the apprentice theme.
Geraldine read German, but Carlyle and not Goethe
was her guiding star, and reminiscences of *Meister*
are very faint in both of these books.

Miss Jewsbury's *Zoe, or The History of Two Lives,*

was "the first novel in which the hero's career is made dependent on the victory of modern scepticism over ancient belief."[80]   Everard Burrows, the timid, sensitive younger son of a Catholic father, who has destined him for the Church, is treated unsympathetically by a hard, able French mother after his father dies, and depends chiefly upon Father Martin, the priest who has charge of his education and his brother's.   But the kindly priest dies of typhus and Everard and his brother Louis are sent to Bruges to school.   On his way to the English College in Rome to study for the priesthood, Everard, aged seventeen, visits an uncle in Paris, and "a new era in life" opens for him.   It is the pre-Revolutionary period in France and our hero meets, like Arthur Coningsby, Sterling's hero, with all the notables, including Grimm and d'Holbach. But he learns something:

He was introduced to a perfumed, brilliant, luxurious version of that hard, mysterious reality called *Life*. He mixed in female society for the first time; hitherto he had seen no women but his mother and her attendants. . . . He was entering on the heritage of *himself* and felt endowed with new gifts and perceptions.[81]

He has a chance to escape from the priesthood by working for a relative who is a rich India merchant, but in spite of doubts he prefers to go on to Rome and does so.   "Be discreet," everyone tells him, "and you will become a great man."   But the English College chills him; his emotions are pent up; his adolescent sense of power has no outlet, but he learns from the example of companions the danger of being "divided against himself."

Zoe, the illegitimate daughter of George Cleveland, an English officer, and a Greek girl, has been adopted by her uncle, an English clergyman. He "makes a scholar of her," as his sister fails to make her a housewife. Her "tropical organization," as Geraldine calls it, may be something like her authoress's own. She is a generous person, "on too large a scale, both for good and evil, to have room for spite." She refuses to marry the obvious young squire, and her father comes and takes her away to Bordeaux. On the Rhine boat she meets her future husband, Gifford, who is charmed by "the stamp of genius" that her "masculine education" has given her, and she marries him. To marry her he has had to resign his intention of joining the priesthood. They have two children, and while they go on a journey for Zoe's health to Bath and London, the story shifts back, in its temperamental way, to Everard.

After five years at the college he has become interested in metaphysics (this is always the sign, in these faith-to-doubt novels, of the beginning of the end)! He passes through phases of Jesuitism, humility, a struggle to conquer "gross and grovelling sensuality." But the "bloom of reverence and awe" is gone from religion for him. He is ordained to the priesthood, but his religion is slowly slipping from him. He is made a professor in the college.

Gifford meanwhile has become the leader of the Catholic party in London, and Zoe, a great social success. She develops a taste for experience and for deceiving people about the really earnest nature which is hers; she cultivates many famous admirers among the men of her day.

Everard reads the Encyclopedists and writes a book which is answered by no less a person than Diderot. He is having Robert Elsmere's experience: he finds that Christianity—"revealed religion"—as far as external evidences go, is no sounder than any other; the Church is only a form. His agony is just as intense as Elsmere's and a good deal longer. He develops brain-fever and a feeling of guilt and mortal sin. His yearning for God remains unsatisfied, but some deliverance is supplied by natural beauty which inspires in him "speechless devotion." Thus ends Volume One.

He explains to the Superior what his difficulties are, but they are not thought important, and Everard is sent to Paris on a church mission by the Pope himself. He is considered for the headship of the Catholic college that Gifford, Zoe's husband, is to found in Devonshire, and falls in love with Zoe as soon as he goes there. He rescues her from a fire and declares his passion. Overcome with remorse, Everard reaches a crisis. He has "acquired and done nothing with his acquirements." He has lacked purpose and "frittered away his integrity" for the sake of expediency and comfort, and has been neither honest in teaching young minds to believe, nor "sincere in telling them to doubt." He resigns his priesthood and the presidency of the college, reaching at thirty-eight the conclusion that "To love rightly, is the highest morality of which mankind is capable."[82]

He goes to a wild district of southern Wales to practise applied social Christianity among the savage miners of the district. The influence of the rising sect of Wesleyan revival preachers spoils the schools he has established and the people's confidence in him. He is driven out. He writes a book embodying his newer convictions, but when published it arouses only horror and slander.

The Giffords go abroad. Zoe is now a changed woman and has "more of a high pagan virtue about her than anything approaching to modern Unitarian morality."[83] Gifford, her husband, dies, and thus ends Volume Two.

Everard meanwhile has offers from friends of posts which he will not accept since they seem to him to involve compromise. He travels through Germany with a friend and finds many of his radical views a matter of course there. He meets with great minds that stimulate his thought, and decides to stay there. (Miss Jewsbury had only a cursory knowledge of Germany at first hand, but her worship of it as the home of real philosophy and advanced thinking was in line with the prevailing English opinion.) He can now exercise his powers and find peace. "We spend half our strength in beating the air" (in serving an apprenticeship, in fact), and the important thing is to "discover our own work."[84] In the wasted efforts to do so consists "the weariness of life." His funds fail him and he learns the bitterness of poverty. He is appointed to a librarian's post and publishes with success his philosophic history which he has been working on. Now he has won "honor, consideration, friends."

Mirabeau has been all this while a devoted suitor of Zoe, but departs in a rage when her mother-love conquers, and she will not leave her child for him. Everard comes painfully home, a broken man through illness and his blighted and hopeless love for Zoe. But she has gone to Italy, and he dies before she can reach him.

Miss Jewsbury attempted here to give the struggles and development of two characters, a man and a woman, and show how they profited by their apprenticeships to life; but she has more material than she can handle and might better have confined her efforts either to Everard or Zoe. Her interest in feminism leads her into the most inopportune digressions about the value of education for women, contrasts between the intellectual and the domestic woman, woman's place in the home; all interesting enough in themselves but spoiling the effect of her story. The apprenticeship theme is never explicit, but the book does consist in showing how the two main characters are built by life, the man chiefly by his religious experience, the woman by her social one. In contrast to Froude's feeble heroes, Everard and his struggle seem lifelike and convincing though theatrical. There is the vitality and zest in the book which pervade everything Geraldine's dynamic personality touched.

She had difficulty in constructing the book.

What are we sent into this world at all for? What ought we to do with our life? The whole book is to ask that question or rather to

suggest it.   I am sure I know of nothing that is worth doing.   What
can we set Everard to work upon?   I have taken him as far as I
can. . . .   I can set him up with no new doctrines to begin to lead
the remainder of his life-time. . . .   Let him die in the consciousness that he has failed in his task. . . .   I cannot make him up
into any theory of utility or usefulness to mankind.   I cannot
even make out his scheme of morality for him.   He must grow shape-
less and vague and pass away, leaving all sorts of inconsistencies to
be reconciled. . . .   My God!   I would give the rest of the years
of my life to be able to know why it is that Life is given us, and I
would say it and leave it behind me. [85]

Miss Jewsbury had a tendency to ask of Carlyle
and others just such large, appalling questions to
which there was no answer.   It made Carlyle admire
her honesty and spiritual strenuousness, but after a
while it made him uncomfortable.   Presumably Jane,
to whom this letter was addressed, found no answer
either.   Geraldine herself, in living out her own life
to the full, probably found as good an answer as any.

The Half Sisters is devoted to the gospel of work
rather than to any idea of apprenticeship, but the
latter comes in incidentally.   Bianca, the successful
actress (modeled on Charlotte Cushman, the American
actress, who became a good friend of Miss Jewsbury's)
is contrasted with her feebler half-sister, Alice, who is
a sweet, idle, feminine clinging-vine.   (Here again
comes Geraldine's favorite topic of the education of
women!)   Bianca loves the undependable but attractive Conrad Percy who has befriended her during her
early professional struggles; Alice marries John
Bryant, the successful iron-master, older than she, and
the typical gruff Victorian husband, solid, domestic,

but so engrossed in his business that he neglects his wife. Conrad Percy falls in love with Alice, in the course of time, after he has found Bianca too strong-minded and vehement in her feelings. Alice dies of the disgrace, forgiven by her husband, and Conrad becomes a "religious." But Bianca's rise in her profession is the really interesting element in the book. At sixteen she starts with a circus, then through Conrad's kind offices she has an opportunity in a real theater, and begins to educate herself by reading Shakespeare. A great Shakespearean actor, an elderly man who eventually leaves her all his fortune, takes an interest in her and acts as a kind of professional mentor. Bianca has "a broad, practical way of viewing things and stripping them of the atmosphere that distorted them"[86] some of Miss Jewsbury's own downright honesty, in short. She is, like Miss Jewsbury, fearfully in earnest. Love and friendship are great responsibilities, not to be lightly undertaken. She reads eagerly—Hazlitt, Schlegel, Schiller, and Goethe. Her love for Conrad stimulates her acting for a while, but her old mentor reminds her that she should not depend on this stimulus, but act for the art's sake itself. "Art alone is worthy of the dedication of a life-time." Other idols are of clay, but he warns her that she will learn this only by experience. "Through how much suffering will you not have to pass before you believe this! I had hoped you would be led by an easier path; but excellence can be perfected by suffering alone." . . . "It is out of struggles like these," she finds, "that any achievement must come, conquered and carried captive from the realms of madness and darkness. We must take our reason as well as our life in our hand, and be ready to lose both, if we would desire to attain to that which is invisible."[87]

She has a great triumph in the part of Juliet. Conrad sees her, but no longer loves her. She finally learns that she had been mistaken in him, and marries Lord Melton, who appreciates her deep sincerity of character, and the too dependent position of women who have no work to do. He is, in fact, a philosopher after Miss Jewsbury's (and Carlyle's) own heart:

> To convert our life's pilgrimage into a "search after happiness" seems to me drivelling. . . . What is *life* in its very essence but the *power to struggle?* . . . Man must not be divided against himself, but free to wrestle erect and manful against all the difficulties that beset him.[88]

Lord Melton's sister, Lady Vernon, who runs sensible schools for middle-class girls, gives Miss Jewsbury another chance to show ways in which women may be actively useful. "I have found something at which I can work heartily," she tells Bianca.

> There is a great fuss about giving women a negative purity of mind, but there is no care taken to give them any strong antiseptic qualities, whereby they may resist evil.[89]

But when Bianca marries Melton, Miss Jewsbury makes a concession to her public. She makes Bianca give up her dubious profession at Lady Vernon's request! However, she manages her house well because she is naturally intelligent and can turn her hand to anything. We behold her crocheting a cushion for her new sister-in-law and reflecting as follows:

Sorow is our matriculation in humanity and no one who has received its mysterious baptism would ever wish to have been spared what has been laid upon him.[90]

She continues Lady Vernon's school after that lady's death and founds others on its model. She and Lord Melton have several children who "inherited the sound characters of their parents," and Geraldine closes the symphony with the quotation:

Gentleness, wisdom, virtue, and endurance—
These are the seals of that most firm assurance,
Which bars the pit over Destruction's strength.

As a novel, *The Half Sisters* is less successful than *Zoe*, but as a feminist document of 1848 it is of immense interest. Miss Jewsbury could never keep off her favorite topic for very long at a time in any of her novels, and the conversations of the characters during their long Victorian evenings are often devoted to this theme. Education by life is the backbone of most of her books, and shows a strong tincture of Carlyle here and there. No one of this group of novelists used the old life-journey or search-for-adjustment theme more interestingly than Miss Jewsbury, who combined it with her own passionate interest in the position of women, and gave the old pattern some fresh material to work upon. The character of Bianca is perhaps the only woman apprentice in fiction, until we come to Esther Waters and Tess, and both of these are social studies rather than studies in learning from life. Miss Jewsbury had blazed a new path and was quite unconscious of it.

5. CHARLES KINGSLEY

In the same decade with Miss Jewsbury's theatrical heroes and heroines, and contemporary too with the apprentices of Lewes and Froude, two earnest Christian seekers after truth start upon their way. Both of them are geniuses, though of different sorts; both are deeply indebted to Carlyle (his name appears frequently in Kingsley's novels) and his discontent with the existing state of affairs colors their outlook on life as it did Kingsley's. Both of them pass through various stages of development which are more closely related to those that Teufelsdröckh experiences, than to Wilhelm Meister's.

Not that Kingsley did not appreciate the Germans. He read them and made an extensive trip through Germany in 1851 when on a vacation from Eversley. His letters rave over the beauty and charm of the country and the good qualities of its inhabitants.

Really this Germany is a wonderful country—though its population are not members of the Church of England—and as noble, simple, shrewd, kindly hearts in it, as man would wish to see. I cannot tell you what moral good this whole journey has done me.[91]

We can well believe that it shook him out of his strenuous insularity a little, but he had written these two books before he went.

The first of them, *Yeast,* is full of F. D. Maurice, Kingsley's master, even more than Carlyle, and its hero (Lancelot Smith) goes through a chaotic and mixed apprenticeship indeed. In the beginning of the book he is an introspective adolescent who keeps a journal, reads *Manfred,* and writes thereupon, "Doubted whether I should live long." He is in "the fifth act of the Werterian stage" and is undergoing sentimental measles. Byron and Shelley are beginning to pall and he is reading Bulwer "and worshipping *Ernest Maltravers.*" Then he leaves Bulwer for

old ballads and romances and Mr. Carlyle's reviews; was next alternately chivalry-mad and Germany-mad; was now reading hard at physical science, and on the whole trying to become a great man without any very clear notion of what a great man ought to be.[92]

He had not got much education from college, but was a "gentleman" and of a truly religious cast of mind. Colonel Bracebridge, a more finished and successful man-of-the-world type, is Lancelot's ideal because he seems superior to the huge, awkward

Titan-cub . . . still in a state of convulsive dyspepsia, swallowing formulae and daily well-nigh choked; diseased throughout with that morbid self-consciousness and lust of praise, for which God prepares, with his elect, a bitter cure. Alas! poor Lancelot! an unlicked bear with all his sorrows before him![93]

He is of course in love with the Squire's lovely, prudish, High-Church daughter, Argemone Lavington—a maiden after Kingsley's own heart, according to that poem of his that has become the subject of so much unseemly laughter since his own day. There is no chance of his marrying her; he has no money and no expectations of any. The pious, Evangelical, social-minded gamekeeper, Tregarva, becomes a friend of Lancelot's, and teaches him to consider the needs of the poor. Lancelot is also engaged in a correspondence with his cousin Luke, who is thinking of going over to Rome, thereby giving Kingsley the opportunity of speaking his mind on this point. Lancelot is injured while hunting, and during his convalescence reads *Chartism* and is profoundly impressed by its warning.[94] Tregarva loses his position with the squire because of a supposedly libellous poem upon landlords called "A Rough Rhyme on a Rough Matter": "The merry brown hares came leaping," etc. Tregarva stands for "the kingdom of God on earth" and gives Kingsley a chance to discuss the ill effects of the new Poor Law, the low tastes of the poor, and the evil results of overwork on human nature.

Lancelot is ruined financially because of the failure of his uncle's bank, whereupon he inveighs against the evils of a selfish, money-grabbing society. He cannot affiliate himself with any political party. "He had the unhappiest knack (as all geniuses have) of seeing connexions, humorous or awful, between the most seemingly antipodal things."[95] He meets Claude Mellot the painter, a cheerful bohemian, and his mysterious eastern wife. Tregarva has now become a city missionary. A mysterious Stranger appears now and then, by whom Lancelot is to be led and who is a friend of Mellot's. Lancelot and Tregarva join forces. Lancelot would like to learn to paint and the

Stranger half encourages him; Mellot and his wife are his pupils.   Argemone meanwhile dies of typhus contracted while doing good to the village poor and Lancelot must forget his sorrow in labor, "but at what?" All his doubts and hopes and perceptions have led only to this Carlylean question.   He writes a few articles for magazines but has "nothing to say" and "his melancholy paralyzed him more and more." He carries a trunk for the Stranger for sixpence, a symbol perhaps of the worthiness of manual labor. He discovers that great materials are latent in modern England but the "inspiring spirit" (or yeast) is lacking.   The Stranger will take Lancelot and Tregarva to his mysterious, nameless country, since Lancelot has tried all teachers in vain, renounced all his idols and admits he is nothing.   They will seek "Jesus Christ *the Man*" and in this step Lancelot's real education has at last begun.   And here Kingsley leaves it, not saying whether they are going to seek a "Caucasian Utopia" or some other island of the blest. He has "given his readers yeast" he says, and they "can bake with it themselves."[96]

Kingsley wanted the book to

show the feelings which are working in the age, in a fragmentary and turbid state. [Lancelot is] to be raised above his mere faith in nature by the simple Christianity of Tregarva, at the same time that he is taught by him that true democracy which considers the beautiful the heritage of the poor as well as of the rich; and Tregarva in his turn becomes the type of English art-hating Puritan gradually convinced of the divine mission of art and of its being the rightful child not of Poetry but of Protestantism alone. Thus I think Lancelot, having grafted on his own naturalism the Christianity of

Tregarva, the classicism of Mellot, and the spiritual symbolism of Luke, ought to be in a state to become the mesothetic artist of the future and beat each of his tutors at their own weapons.[97]

No wonder that the story is confused or that Kingsley got lost among the symbols of his own creation. But the familiar development-through-life pattern is apparent through the confusion, even though the author had it in mind only as secondary to his social and religious purpose in writing the book.

Mrs. Carlyle was less lyrical than Geraldine Jewsbury over *Alton Locke*. She called it "The Devil Among the Tailors" and wrote to her husband after she had read it:

All the indignation against existing things strikes somehow so numbly—like your father whipping the bad children under the bed-clothes! But the old Scotchman is capital—only that there never was and never will be *such* an old Scotchman. I wonder what will come of Kingsley—go mad perhaps.[98]

Some scenes of the book make Jane Carlyle seem justified in her conjecture as to Kingsley's future, especially the dream-like phantasmagoria towards the end which sound like a poor imitation of De Quincey. But the hero is the most "real and earnest" of this whole collection. He is a genius too, but different from Lancelot Smith. The book is written in auto-biographical form, by the hero, Alton Locke. He has a severe Calvinist background of poverty, and is apprenticed early to a tailor, in whose shop prevail the fearful conditions of sweated labor that Kingsley wrote the whole book to protest against. Crossthwaite the Chartist becomes his protector and awakener to the conditions among the working class. But he is a bitter and severe mentor and Alton realizes it:

Well for me that it was not from him my mind received the first lessons in self-development.   For guides did come to me in time, though not such perhaps as either my mother or my readers would have chosen for me.[99]

Alton has a great zeal for book-learning and makes the friendship of the Scotchman, Sandy Mackaye, who lends him books from his stall, and helps him to learn Latin. The self-development motif is stressed throughout. "Who'll teach a man anything," says Sandy, "except himself?   A man kens just as much as he's taught himsel, and nae mair."[100] Alton has all the weaknesses of genius, and makes many missteps in his ambition to become "the people's poet." But "perhaps the very struggle and sorrows of a poor genius may teach him more than ever wealth and prosperity could."[101] He declares himself a free-thinker, is banished from his mother's house, and goes to live with Sandy Mackaye. He goes to visit his cousin George at Cambridge and gets a glimpse of a different world, sees beautiful pictures, and falls in love with the dean's lovely daughter. "This book," he reminds us, "is the history of my mental growth, and my mistakes, as well as my discoveries, are steps in that development and may bear a lesson in them."[102] Sandy reminds him, when he laments his hopeless love, that those who seek their own pleasure are not worthy of the people's great cause, and the dean too speaks of the value of affliction to poets. On the whole, Alton gets more than his share of advice, even compared to his much-advised brother-apprentices; Kingsley is so anxious to leave no possible angle unpresented. Alton learns that "true poetry begins at home" and that he must draw his material from the London slums as a Cockney poet should, and not from imitating Tennyson. But he suffers from "the peculiar melancholy of intellectual youth which Mr. Carlyle has christened forever by one of his immortal nicknames—Wertherism. I battened on my own melancholy."[103] He goes to Cambridge again and the dean says his poems are worth publishing but he must learn science to be "a poet for these days." Alton becomes a hack writer for *The Weekly War-whoop*, and soon discovers the unscrupulous ways of popular journalism and demagoguery, and denounces O'Flynn, the editor of the paper, and loses his job. Sandy rejoices that he has learned this lesson, and that he will accept work on an innocuous popular journal "of the Howitt and Eliza Cook school."

His poems are published after he has compromised "the Cause" by cutting out, at the dean's behest, some of the more radical and incendiary passages. This disgraces him in Sandy's eyes, and eventually in his own. He has deserted his class and weakly succumbed to flattery. He tries to redeem himself by speaking at a peasants' rising in the country, but his speech only rouses the mob to riot and plunder and he is imprisoned for three years. He keeps apart

from the other prisoners and reads and worships
"mere intellect." When he gets out, a workers'
revolution is pending. Sandy dies. At his deathbed
Alton meets Lady Ellerton, the dean's older daughter,
who is really his best friend, and not Lillian, the
younger and more selfish daughter with whom he has
been in love all along. She warns him against rash
action, but the uprising comes off. The revolution
is lost and the charter too. To add to Alton's
despair, he finds that his cousin George and Lillian
are in love and about to be married.

He has an attack of brain-fever during which his
past mistakes become clear to him in a series of
symbolic visions, in which the necessity of work for
others to replace selfish endeavor, is brought home to
him. The prophetess in his dream says to him:

Your penance is accomplished. You have learned what it is to be
a man. You have lost your life and saved it.[104]

He finds that Lady Ellerton has nursed him through
this illness and saved his life. She has watched his
progress all along and helped him in ways unknown
to him until now. He really loves her, and not her
sister. But she will not marry him. She is dedicated
to preaching the cause of Christ, the true conservative
and demagogue and reformer, the champion of the
poor. Sandy has left Alton Locke and the ex-
Chartist, Crossthwaite, enough money to emigrate to
Texas and they do so. Alton, enfeebled by his prison
term and his illness, writes his autobiography on the
way across to the new world, and dies.

This apprenticeship comes to little in the end, as the hero is not allowed the chance to work out in actual living what he has learned by his reverses, any more than Kingsley's other hero of this type, Lancelot Smith in *Yeast*. But the idea, well-worn by this time, and subjected to much softening and bending at the hands of the author's stern social and religious purpose, is present in something like its old familiar form—the wayward and gifted young man, the humorous, detached mentor in the shape of Sandy Mackaye, who lets him make his own mistakes in his own way, the extremists and charlatans like Crossthwaite and O'Flynn whom he meets upon his moral pilgrimage, the mistaken belief that he can take everyone's advice and compromise with his own genius and loyalty to his class, the false starts at things he is not really fitted to do, and his blindness in his love of the wrong woman—all this runs true to form.

The novel of religious controversy, foreshadowed by Geraldine Jewsbury, Froude, and even by George Lewes in his *Apprenticeship to Life*, came at the close of the century to its best-known culmination in the novels of Mrs. Humphry Ward, *Robert Elsmere* (1888) and *David Grieve* (1891). Samuel Butler's *Way of All Flesh* may also be put in this class, different as its whole tone is from anything that Mrs. Ward ever wrote. But these novels, though they have a tinge of the apprentice theme, really form a group by themselves, not only because of their later date but because they have shown the learning-from-life idea in a more highly specialized form than their predecessors just mentioned. The religious development of the hero is predominant in them, although they show some traces of the other theme, and the experiences he is put through are all narrowed down to their effect on his specifically religious doubts and struggles. They form a study in themselves, taken in connection with the Oxford movement and with some of the semi-religious apprenticeships discussed in this chapter.

CHAPTER IX

MEREDITH AND THE MODERNS

Plus ça change, plus c'est la même chose.

TOWARDS the end of the century, a slightly different phase of the old youth's-encounter idea begins to be emphasized in the apprenticeship novels—the theme of the younger against the older generation, or at least a break between the two. To some extent, of course, this situation is a venerable one. Ever since the time of the Prodigal Son, some younger member of almost every family has made his voice heard as decisively and abruptly as that well-known character of the Scriptures, saying, "Father, give me the portion of goods that falleth to me," and has then proceeded to follow still further the time-honored example—"And not many days after the younger son gathered all together, and took his journey into a far country, and there wasted his substance with riotous living." Even Parsifal leaves the sheltered life with his mother in the forest for his own encounter with the world, in which the maternal advice—prompted by over-solicitude—is more of a hindrance than a help to him. Bunyan's Christian, like many another zealous pilgrim, is a source of great distress to his family. His experience, in all its stages, has been repeated through countless generations:

At this his relations were sore amazed . . . because they thought
that some frenzy distemper had got into his head; therefore, it drawing
toward night, and they hoping that sleep might settle his brains,
with all haste they got him to bed. But the night was as trouble-
some to him as the day; wherefore, instead of sleeping, he spent it in
sighs and tears. So when the morning was come, they would know
how he did. He told them "Worse and worse": he also set to talking to them again, but they began to be hardened. They also thought
to drive away his distemper by harsh and surly carriage to him;
sometimes they would deride, sometimes they would chide, and
sometimes they would quite neglect him. Wherefore he began to
retire himself to his chamber to pray for and pity them, and also to
condole his own misery; he would also walk solitarily in the fields,
sometimes reading, sometimes praying; and thus for some days he
spent his time.[1]

In the significant words, "But they began to be
hardened," lies the key to the age-long conflict. Not
all families will, like Christian's, relent in the end.

These enthusiasms for life, eternal or otherwise,
which the seeker may only find in a far country or the
middle of the plain or at Arthur's court—somewhere,
at all events, remote from home—have never been
taken quietly by families. Wilhelm Meister's practical merchant father remonstrates with his son about
his foolish enthusiasm for the theater, and with really
praiseworthy forbearance sends him on a business
trip to distract his mind from his disastrous love affair
—a trip from which the vague young man never does
return to the parental roof. But this is almost the
only case on record where the trip was instigated by
the family, which is strange when one considers how
trying the younger generation can make itself in the
home circle. Wilhelm has been disdainful about the

narrow, monotonous, provincial middle-class life of his home town long before he leaves. *Mein Herz hat schon lange meiner Eltern Haus verlassen*, he tells his friend.[2]

The Byronic heroes of Bulwer and Disraeli are either orphaned young and therefore independent, or they may have a parent of superhuman patience and foresight, like Contarini's father or the elder Chillingly, who recognizes the latent genius of his child and supplies him with money and good advice for his travels. Sometimes, as in *Vivian Grey* and *Pelham*, the parent is made the vehicle for all the cryptic summaries of life which the author himself has gained from his worldly experience. At all events, the struggle between the generations in these novels seldom assumes a serious tone, except for purposes of theatrical effect, when mysteries of birth, revenges, hates, flights abroad, are scattered with a liberal hand, as in Bulwer's *The Disowned*.

The hero of Carlyle's *Sartor*, like Melchisedek— that Biblical hero so pathetically envied by Butler's Ernest Pontifex—is practically a "born orphan." He is left at the cottage of his foster-parents in a basket by a "Mysterious Stranger" and Carlyle thus avoids the necessity for making him transgress the laws of filial piety when he sends him out into the world, for we never hear of his parents after that, except in a brief mention of his foster-father's death. "Does anyone know his own parents?" reflects Carlyle. Even our father in heaven, he reminds us, we behold only with the spiritual eye.[3] The young Diogenes

comes into very little conflict with his elders. There
is a rosy light over his childhood, and though he was
too rigorously brought up, he does not linger over this
in resentment. He thinks that probably it did him
good.

As might be expected, the group of strenuous spirits
whose novels were described in the preceding chapter
have made more of this possible adjunct to the
apprentice theme. Alton Locke and his mother part
in bitterness on the religious issue, when Alton becomes a freethinker and can no longer abide her
canting Methodist friends. She forbids him the
house and refuses to see him again before she dies.
Religion, again, is the cause of the conflict between
father and son in *The Nemesis of Faith*, and in *Zoe*,
although a fundamental psychological and temperamental difference is the more radical source of it.
Arthur Coningsby, in Sterling's novel of that name,
leaves his family and his *fiancée* because of his political
heterodoxy and sympathy with the French Revolution. In Lewes's *Ranthorpe* the young hero forsakes
his home because of his father's antipathy to poetry,
and writing in general, as a profession for him. The
young man will not keep on working as a clerk when
he feels that his creative genius in literature is being
cramped, and he is one of the earliest of the long line
of temperamental young heroes who set out to justify
their existence by the pen, returning in triumph to
the philistine family that prophesied a dark future.
In this group as a whole, however, religion comes most
prominently to the fore as the cause for hostility

between old and young, and is still more clearly the bone of contention in such later books as *Father and Son* and that most masterly and devastating study of antagonism within the family, *The Way of All Flesh*, in which Ernest gives this succinct and ruthless summary of the eternal struggle,

A man first quarrels with his father about three-quarters of a year before he is born. It is then he insists on setting up a separate establishment; when this has once been agreed to, the more complete the separation for ever after the better for both.[4]

In the more modern novels discussed at the end of this chapter, the conflict is worked out with an increasingly elaborate knowledge of psychology, and a sharpening sense of the dramatic values inherent in the rasping of one temperament on another—long, slow, relentless. The subdued state of almost unbearable tension it produces has been used with growing skill by still more modern writers like D. H. Lawrence, and the rich harvest that, for better or for worse, the novelist may reap from the discoveries of the Freudian psychology has scarcely begun to be realized.

Coming to the last of the Victorian novelists who used the old apprenticeship pattern in a whole group of novels—namely, George Meredith—we come also to one who was magnificently outspoken in his treatment of the family situation. Dr. Shrapnel in *Beauchamp's Career* states the case for the young in ringing tones:

A man's uncles, aunts and cousins have no claim on him at all, except for help in necessity, which he can grant and they require. None—

wife, children, parents, relatives—none has a claim to bar his judgment and his actions. Sound the conscience and sink the family!
With a clear conscience, it is best to leave the family to its own
debates. No man ever did brave work who held counsel with his
family. The family view of a man's fit conduct is the weak point of
the country. It is no other view than "Better thy condition for our
sakes." . . . Resolution taken, consult the family means—waste
your time! Those who go to it want an excuse for altering their
minds. The family view is everlastingly the shopkeeper's.[5]

With this battle cry of "Sound the conscience and sink
the family!" Meredith's three apprentice heroes
have more or less to do. Richard Feverel, Evan Harrington, and Nevil Beauchamp would all have done
well to live up to it more completely than they did; the
success of their efforts toward fulfilling their destinies
in active living is measured by the firmness with
which they held to it. All three books form studies
of ardent and gifted youth in conflict with the world.
All three heroes are at odds with an environment
created and ruled by their elders; they succeed according to the strength of their resistance to it. Richard
is unable to "sink the family" at all, and meets with
disaster. Evan copes with it a little better, and
although his agonies are on a less tragic scale than
Richard's, he pays with a full measure of them for his
feebleness in holding out against the forces of his
elders. Nevil Beauchamp puts up the best fight of
the three, and is in a fair way to reap the fruits of his
consistent defiance when Meredith sees fit to strike
him down, for the artistic purposes of a tragic *dénouement*. With these three the ancient strife becomes

for the first time explicit and elaborate as fiction material.

In all three there are faint echoes of Goethe's and Carlyle's ideas of the pilgrim hero journeying into far countries, learning from life as he goes, and finally settling down to practical, useful living. But on the whole, Meredith's heroes point forward to the modern world and to what we are pleased to call the new psychology. They are not of Wertherian or Byronic lineage; they are more practical, flesh-and-blood young men than most of their predecessors, and it is significant—as well as something of a relief—that none of them is a literary genius. They are crossed in love, to be sure, and encounter some of the traditional obstacles that beset the path of all apprentices. They have that fatal attractiveness to women which is common to the whole long line of their brethren with whom we have been concerned. Each has several women watching over his welfare, maternally or otherwise, and Beauchamp has no less than three in love with him throughout the course of the story. All three heroes are romantic and incurable idealists, but they are not especially temperamental or introspective young people. The modern scientific point of view begins to show in the fact that they are attached more firmly to their backgrounds and shown to be products of their early training and environment. Their vagaries begin to be accounted for psychologically, and as individual developments, not merely as typical stages of a common life-pilgrimage. They are allowed to run their course more freely than earlier heroes; Meredith does not force them in the end to adjust themselves to the world in terms of any set code of values that is his, or that proves any religious or social thesis. There is even the suggestion of futility and uncertainty that later characterizes so many novels dealing with the eternal struggle for adjustment; we are allowed to glimpse for a moment the possibility that perhaps there *is* no solution, no adjustment at all—that the struggle itself is everything, justifying itself in varying degrees, according to the grasp and the perception and the capacity for living of him who struggles.

Richard Feverel is, in a way, the negative of the apprenticeship idea. The mentors and counsellors who appear in all these novels—in this case the hero's father and "the wise youth Adrian"—loom so large that they stifle any impulse to experiment, and therefore any real apprenticeship, by means of their famous system. Richard is not permitted to "live himself into" the world, to develop normally, to make his own compromise with life by the trial-and-error method, as the true apprentice does. The book is a kind of *Erziehungsroman*, but an object lesson in the *wrong* sort of education. The foil to the idealistic hero is not merely, as in so many preceding novels of this type, a sturdy, common-sense extravert who counsels hardheadedness and a cheerful, practical philosophy. Adrian is "an epicurean of our modern notions. To satisfy his appetites without rashly staking his character, was the wise youth's problem for life. . . . Adrian Harley had mastered his philosophy at the early age of one-and-twenty. Many would be glad to say the same at that age twice-told: they carry in their breasts a burden with which Adrian's was not loaded."[6]   This man helps to superintend the education of Richard, but it is the father who makes the most serious mistake, in wishing to be Providence to his son.[7]   He plays his part too earnestly, heavily, and rigidly.   There is in him nothing of the amiable resignation that has helped the fathers of so many apprentices to bear bravely and even with amusement the early waywardness of their offspring, and nothing either of the grim arbitrariness of the religious bigot, or of the father who will turn his son from the door rather than make a sacrifice to him of some dearly loved principle.   Sir Austin is more dangerous than some of these cruder fathers of fiction precisely because he knows, at least for a long time, how to keep his son's affection and loyalty, how to play upon his sympathies, and how the son's temperament will react to varying degrees of pressure, neglect, and coercion.   He shows how the path of the apprentice in the world of modern fiction may be darkened and obstructed by half-understood theories about adolescent psychology, a theme which later novelists than Meredith have developed and used with shattering effect.

This misguided pair, Adrian and Sir Austin, watch Richard's first encounter with the problem of how to take the consequences of his own actions, and Adrian speaks the apostrophe to Experience usually found somewhere in all these novels.

This will be his first nibble at experience, old Time's fruit, hateful
to the palate of Youth, for which season only hath it any nourishment! Experience! You know Coleridge's capital simile? Mournful you call it? Well! all wisdom is mournful.[8]

Richard learns affection for people less fortunate than
himself through his pity for Tom, the farm boy, who
is willing to go to prison for Richard's guilt in burning
the farmer's rick. He goes through a phase of hero
worship in the traditional manner of his kind and this
impressionable period "when the young savage grows
into higher influences" his father marks as the period
of "spiritual seed-time." He nourishes in the boy
the ambition for statesmanship and tells him, "First
be virtuous and then serve your country with heart
and soul." But so much concentration on his education spoils him a little. "The boy with a Destiny
was growing up a trifle too conscious of it."[9] He
passes through a more introspective and imaginative
phase:

He relinquished the material world to young Ralph and retired into
himself, where he was growing to be lord of kingdoms: where Beauty
was his handmaid and History his minister.[10]

But promising as he seems to be, his father watches
him no less closely, and even then does not know he is
writing poetry in secret. When he discovers it and
makes Richard destroy his work because "no Feverel
has ever written poetry" there is an end, as Meredith
points out, to all true confidence between father and
son.

During what his father calls the Magnetic Age,

"the Age of violent attractions, when to hear mention of love is dangerous, and to see it, a communication of the disease," our hero falls in love with Lucy. His father, hoping to force his confidence, warns him of the nature of his ordeal:

You are mounting to the table-land of life, where mimic battles are changed to real ones. And you come upon it laden equally with force to create and to destroy. . . . There are women in the world, my son. . . . It is when you encounter them that you are thoroughly on trial. It is when you know them that life is either a mockery to you, or, as some find it, a gift of blessedness. They are our ordeal. Love of any human object is the soul's ordeal; and they are ours, loving them or not.[11]

But separated from Lucy, Richard lives through a severe illness, and his first freshness is gone: "In the heart of the young man died the Spring Primose." The early stages of what might have been a real instead of a directed apprenticeship are past.

Like most apprentice heroes, Richard has a faculty for letting things happen to him, and Meredith believes in this.

By this you perceive the true hero, whether he be a prince or a pot-boy, that he does not plot; Fortune does all for him. He may be compared to one to whom, in an electric circle, it is given to carry the *battery*. We caper and grimace at his will; yet not his the will, not his the power. 'Tis all Fortune's, whose puppet he is. She deals her dispensations through him. Yea, though our capers be never so comical, he laughs not. Intent upon his own business, the true hero asks little services of us here and there. . . . Probably he is the elect of Fortune because of that notable faculty of being intent upon his own business: "which is," says the Pilgrim's Scrip, "with men to be valued equal to that force which in water *makes a stream*."[12]

They are indeed "intent upon their own business," all these heroes, and Beauchamp is perhaps the first who is not thoroughly self-absorbed in his apprenticeship. Richard, at any rate, is sunk in his own misery for a while, until his father, like Wilhelm Meister's, suggests a little traveling. Richard uses this opportunity to rejoin Lucy by a stratagem and crosses his Rubicon; he marries her, against his father's wishes and without his knowledge. The real world at last lies before him, as before every young man sooner or later.

Only when they stand on the opposite bank, [philosophizes Meredith] do they see what a leap they have taken. The shores they have relinquished shrink to an infinite remoteness. There they have dreamed; here they must act. There lie youth and irresolution: here manhood and purpose. . . . Richard Feverel was now crossing the River of his Ordeal. Already the mists were stealing over the land he had left: his life was cut in two, and he breathed but the air that met his nostrils. His father, his father's love, his boyhood and ambition, were shadowy. His poetic dreams had taken a living attainable shape.[13]

He allows himself gradually to be separated from Lucy, learns all sorts of society as the true apprentice should, and decides, "Something I will do. A man must deserve to live. . . ."[14] In a fit of quixotic chivalry he rescues his mother from what he considers her unjust degradation, but that is all. Looking back, he views himself as a failure. "He began to think that the life lying behind him was the life of a fool. What had he done in it? He had burnt a rick and got married!"[15] In this desperate state of mind he takes up with the "Enchantress," Mrs. Mount, a somewhat melodramatic lady of dubious character, whom Richard stands by because the world has condemned her. "He knew the world now, the young man said." But remorse grips him, and he is further humbled by the death of Clare, who has loved him secretly all her life. With his usual talent for flying to extremes, Richard's exaggerated sense of his impurity forbids him to return to Lucy, who has meanwhile borne him a son. He longs for work:

Often wretchedly he watches the young men of his own age trooping to their work. Not cloud-work theirs! Work solid, unambitious, fruitful.[16]

But his education has ruined him; he is the perfect dilettante, as Wilhelm Meister might have been if he had not graduated from the theater into real life. Again like Wilhelm Meister, Richard first feels at one with humanity and himself through the knowledge that he is a father:

And though he knew it not, he was striking the keynotes of Nature. But he did know of a singular harmony that suddenly burst over his whole being.[17]

However, this is not allowed to be his salvation. He foolishly undertakes a duel on account of a fancied slight to his wife's honor, just when he is on the point of being reunited with Lucy and his child under his father's roof. The bitterness of his position is fully borne in upon him.

Now first he tasted hard earthly misery. . . . He had the precision of speech, the bearing of a man of thirty. Indeed he had all that the necessity for cloaking an infinite misery gives.[18]

His suffering has matured him, as it has done in the case of many another apprentice. His father recognizes this, and gives him—though too late—his formal freedom from the system, just as the watchers over Wilhelm's progress through his early experience acknowledged in the *Lehrbrief* his coming-of-age:

> I decreed that you should experience self-denial and learn something of your fellows of both sexes, before settling into a state that must have been otherwise precarious, however excellent the woman who is your mate. My System with you would have been otherwise imperfect, and you would have felt the effects of it. It is over now. You are a man. The dangers to which your nature was open are, I trust, at an end. I wish you to be happy, and I give you both my blessing, and pray God to conduct and strengthen you both.[19]

But Lucy dies and "Richard will never be what he promised." He is never allowed to put into practical living the lessons he has learned from the world; he is thwarted until it is too late for his apprenticeship to take effect.

Evan Harrington goes through what might be called a snob's progress. True to the apprentice type, he is a somewhat feeble character to begin with:

> He has little character for the moment. Most youths are like Pope's women; they have no character at all. And indeed a character that does not wait for circumstances to shape it is of small worth in the race that must be run. To be set too early, is to take the work out of the hands of the Sculptor who fashions men. Happily a youth is always at school . . .[20]

Evan's apprenticeship consists mainly in sacrificing his pride and his vanity to what is still more fundamental in him—his hatred of hypocrisy and loyalty to honest social standards. "No more disguises for me!" he tells his socially ambitious sister, the countess. He publicly acknowledges his origin as a tailor's son, but in falling in love with Rose, who is above him in social station, he blindly allows himself to be put into a false position and to be forced into a breach of confidence when he does not declare his parentage to her family. But in the congenial environment of the upper classes he sincerely ceases to be aware of "the shades of Tailordom" and so, in one sense, he is honest enough. He at length resolves to break with Rose, but "it is thus that young men occasionally design to burst from the circle of the passions, and think that they have done it, when indeed they are but making the circle more swiftly."[21] He makes a second resolve of renunciation, but from self-love and his deep dislike of playing "second fiddle" rather than love of Rose. But she will not let him demean himself, and he rises to her demands upon him; he finally learns much from his limited circle of experience:

This shall be said of him: that he can play second fiddle without looking foolish, which, for my part, I call a greater triumph than if he were performing the heroics we are more accustomed to. He has steady eyes, can gaze at the right level into the eyes of others, and commands a tongue which is neither struck dumb nor set in a flutter by any startling question.[22]

He even reaches the point at which he no longer cares what people will say, and to this extent, surely, his apprenticeship has not been in vain—elementary or trivial as the lessons he has learned may seem: "The tattle we shall hear we shall outlive," he tells his sister, "I care extremely for the good opinion of men, but I prefer my own; and I do not lose it because my father was in trade."[23]   He develops a sense of humor as he goes on.   After an imaginary duel with a nobleman who has insulted him, "he turned upon himself with laughter, discovering a most wholesome power, barely to be suspected in him yet."   Of course he becomes financially independent, Rose's family is reconciled to their marriage, and Rose herself breaks her engagement with the nobleman, Laxley, to marry Evan.   Of his three apprenticeships, this is the only one that Meredith has allowed to end happily, perhaps because of its comparatively superficial nature.

The most robust hero of this trio is of course Nevil Beauchamp.   He is the most exuberant and effective idealist of the three, and his apprenticeship takes the new form of activity and protest against the existing order by means of political radicalism.   His predecessors had registered their protests a little differently; they had, as all apprentices have done, found themselves rebels against family, friends, (when these merely counselled expediency) and the *status quo* which cramped their self-expression in the arts, in love, in religion.   But with the possible exception of Alton Locke, the Chartist, none of them had struck with the full force of Beauchamp's reforming zeal against the social foundations of the world with which they found themselves in conflict.   Their attacks were more limited in range and less fundamental. For the most part, they had asserted themselves by starting out to see the world, not to change it.   Beauchamp is the first of the moderns in being self-assured enough to know—or to feel that he knows—what is good for large numbers of other people.   He looks upon the contemporary scene, not as something from which to draw increasing personal power, spiritual and mental, with a view to building up a well-rounded life within its borders, but as a set of symptoms which he must do his best to correct.   Meredith has realized the possibilities that this situation affords for the apprentice novel.   The array of obstacles that the world presents to such an idealistic and sensitive hero who is out to reform it, has not changed materially since the nineteenth century, with its somewhat newly developed social conscience, made such a situation possible.   Countless modern novels bear witness to the drama of this type of apprenticeship, many of them ending, as does *Beauchamp's Career*, with emphasis on the pitiful futility of the unequal struggle, and the tragedy of youth defeated.

His early enthusiasm for his country and for gallant action on behalf of it, sounds the keynote of his character.   Hero-worship and his devotion to the Gospel of Work proclaim him the ardent reader of Carlyle that he is.

These traits of his were regarded as characteristics hopeful rather than the reverse; none of his friends and relatives foresaw danger in them.   He was a capital boy for his elders to trot out and banter.[24]

The older generation with which Nevil finally finds himself in conflict is represented by his uncle, the Hon. Everard Romfrey, "in person a noticeable gentleman,

in mind a medieval baron, in politics a crotchety un-
intelligible Whig." He sends Nevil to sea at fourteen,
against the boy's wishes and natural tastes.

Somewhere he [Nevil] had got hold of Manchester sarcasms concerning glory. . . . He really disliked war and the sword; and scorning
the prospect of an idle life, confessing that his abilities barely adapted
him for a sailor's, he was opposed to the career opened to him almost
to the extreme of shrinking and terror.[25]

His uncle is no help to him in his efforts to think about
the people of England and the privileges of the nobility. Nevil opposes the war in which England is
engaged and stands up for those who oppose it, and
defends the interests of the poor, much to his uncle's
rage. And here Meredith takes the opportunity of
apologizing for and explaining his new type of apprentice hero.

To be a public favorite is his last thought. Beauchamp-ism . . . is
the obverse of Byronism, and rarely woos your sympathy, shuns the
statuesque pathetic, or any kind of posturing. For Beauchamp will
not even look at happiness to mourn its absence. . . . His faith is
in working and fighting. . . . Meantime the exhibition of a hero
whom circumstances overcome, and who does not weep or ask you
for a tear, who continually rfeits attractiveness by declining to
better his own fortunes, must run the chances of a novelty during
the interregnum,[26]

until, in short, the more romantic and alluring type
has had its day.

Nevil distinguishes himself in the war and his uncle
becomes more hopeful of him. "He shines in action,
and he'll find that out and leave others the palaver-
ing." But he is still at war with his country after

the peace and runs as Radical M. P. for Bevisham and is defeated after a gruelling campaign honestly fought on his side.   It teaches him many things about human nature and destroys many of his youthful illusions.

He had taken up arms; he had drunk of the *questioning* cup, that which denieth peace to us, and which projects us upon the missionary search of the How, the Wherefore, and the Why not, ever afterward.   He questioned his justification, and yours, for gratifying tastes in an ill-regulated world of wrong-doing, suffering, sin, and bounties unrighteously dispensed—not sufficiently dispersed.   He said by and by to pleasure, battle today.[27]

As is usual in the case of these heroes, the women who love Nevil try to protect him against his own weaknesses.   He scarcely has time to fall in love, until it is too late to do anything about it, but three devoted women watch closely to ward off from him the harder consequences of his own crusading zeal and his over-earnestness.   His lack of humor, common to many reformers, is one pitfall.   "He seemed to Cecilia too trusting, too simple, considering his cousin's undisguised tone of banter."   But it is hard for crusaders to keep a sense of proportion and especially for as strenuous a fighter as Nevil.   "Does incessant battling keep the intellect clear?"   Jenny Denham very pertinently asks him.[28]   Nevil believes in the independence of women and in their intellectual emancipation, but he is a little absent-minded about them, except in the case of Renée.   Even with her he realizes that "his work in life was much above the love of a woman,"[29] and in this he differs from almost all the rest of our susceptible, philandering heroes.

Nevil's devotion to the radical philosopher, Shrapnel, and his uncle's horsewhipping of this man who is his nephew's idol, leads to Nevil's permanent break with his family. He is strong enough to hold out stubbornly against his equally stubborn uncle on this issue, insisting that he shall apologize to Shrapnel, in order to vindicate the family honor. Of all these apprentices arrayed against the older generation Beauchamp is the only one who seems able to hold his own. His uncle finally capitulates, although he believes that this stage in Nevil's career is merely "greensickness and Shrapnel's the god of it." Meredith does not altogether defend his hero's position, but points out the reasons for it:

An incessant struggle of one man with the world, which position usually ranks his relatives against him, does not conduce to soundness of judgment . . . his relatives are present to assure him that he did not jump out of Jupiter's head or come of the doctor. They hang on him like an ill-conditioned, prickly garment; and if he complains of the irritation they cause him, they one and all denounce his irritable skin. Fretted by his relatives he cannot be much of a giant.[30]

Cut by his old friends for his opinions, and considered a political maniac by his uncle, Nevil fortunately inherits money from his great-aunt, to start his radical paper *The Dawn*, which is designed to educate the people. He has a childlike reliance on "effort and outspeaking" and "wants to jam the business of two or three centuries into a lifetime."[31] But when he falls dangerously ill, his critics are softened by remorse. "The fellow had bothered the world, but the world without him would be a heavy matter. . . . If our England is to keep her place, she must have him, and many of him."[32]

After his recovery and his marriage to Jenny Denham, Shrapnel's niece, he sets off with his wife and Shrapnel himself, on a long sea-voyage that is to hasten his convalescence. He is haunted by a sense of the failure of his past efforts, and of the increased knowledge and activity that is demanded of him in future. He has accomplished hardly anything, his uncle feels:

"He hasn't marched on London with a couple of hundred thousand men: no, he hasn't done that," the Earl said, glancing back in his mind through Beauchamp's career. "And he escapes what Stukely calls his nation's scourge, in the shape of a statue turned out by an English chisel. No: we haven't had much public excitement out of him. But one thing he did do: *he got me down on my knees.*"[33]

He dies rescuing an insignificant little boy from drowning, thus making the final concession to futility, as Meredith understood it.

Among some novels of our own day, which it is possible to treat only briefly here, the ancient theme recurs. The various guises in which it may be found are too numerous to deal with exhaustively. In the literature of discontinuity, it appears in such novels as Virginia Woolf's *Jacob's Room*, in Dorothy Richardson's long Odyssey of Miriam that began with *Pointed Roofs*, and in James Joyce's *Portrait of the Artist as a Young Man*, and *Ulysses*. It is a far cry indeed from *Wilhelm Meister* to these intrepid and disillusioned adventurers striving to orient themselves in a modern world seething with unrest. But the tenacity with which the old form for the novel of youth's eternal experience has held on its way, out of the tranquil depths of the eighteenth century and into the dust and turmoil of today, is singularly impressive.

A group of pre-war English novels better illustrates the modern use of the idea than the more experimental school represented by the titles just cited. Arnold Bennett's *Clayhanger* gives the father-and-son conflict at its sharpest, and takes Edwin through "His Vocation" for architecture, thwarted by his father's tyranny that keeps him in the printing business in the Five Towns; "His Love" for Hilda Lessways; "His Freedom" through his father's breakdown; and finally "His Start in Life" after his father's death and Hilda's return. He makes the gesture of acceptance in the end: "He braced himself to the exquisite burden of life." The grim provincial background of industrial northern England in the seventies, the relentless, realistic way in which the father's early experience is made to react on the life of the son, Edwin's own weaknesses accentuated by the heavy dominance of the father's personality, all show how effectively the old pattern may be used with the addition of modern scene-painting and psychology, and how the commonplace young man begins to hold our interest as the hero, because of his very commonplaceness. There is almost a return in some of these modern novels to the typical figures of the moral allegory, at least so far as the central figure is concerned; the hero by his excessive drabness and adolescent foolishness, is more than the ordinary young man—he is Everyman.

J. D. Beresford's *The Early History of Jacob Stahl* and *A Candidate for Truth* look upon youth in the modern world from the angle of a slightly more romantic and gifted hero, who is a quarter Jewish. Influenced by the whole modern trend of thought in general and by Samuel Butler in particular, Beresford has tried to account for Jacob's sense of being "different." His Irish-German parentage is to help explain it.

A strange convention of races and conflicting tendencies this that lies behind Jacob Stahl and his brother Eric, but the laws of heredity are hard to understand. That primary inclination to deviate from the original type upsets all calculation from the outset.[34]

Jacob is essentially ethical, and has a plastic and resilient mind that sees "fitness or appropriateness in the proportions of life." He is somewhat vain and conceited in spite of what we should now call an inferiority complex, and battens on approval and encouragement. His commonsense brother Eric is the foil that all such heroes need, and at first scoffs at Jacob's growing taste and gift for literature.

Eric understood books in terms of literature; Jacob wanted to understand books in terms of life. . . . Jacob was for the evaluation of the constant, he wanted to understand life.[35]

He lacks initiative but grows in the ability to diagnose his own weaknesses. He becomes a good bluffer at advertising, for which he has no real interest, and being imaginative he leaps over the intermediate practical steps to revel in dreams of attainment. He is egotistical, timid, passive, dreading change, and yet chafes at being miscast in his profession. His adolescent susceptibility to the appeal of sentimental moral uplift in the personality of Cecil Barker, the reformer, is characteristic. He finds that he has no theories.

He had been a looker-on; his experience, bitter though it had been in some ways, had not been directive. He had been an observer of life, detached, condemning or appraising without a positive test.[36]

But he is open-minded and eager to learn.

My experience is beginning to crystallize into ideas, into theories.

In making up his mind whether or not to take Betty away with him, he faces the age-old dominance of Fear, as Teufelsdröckh and so many others have faced it before him. "Fear, the root Evil!" He sees it is "despicably easy to be good" and decides he will and must do the hard thing. "Jacob was ever at the beginning of life."[37] He belongs to the modern world in his recognition of the "old ideal of a self-sacrifice that was not purposive, and the new ideal of a courage to grasp and hold,"[38] whereas the great moments of the earlier heroes had been chiefly those of renunciation. But the perennial strain of something faintly Carlylean is felt at the close of his history. "The Renewal of Effort" is what Jacob is dedicated to, after all. He is always reaching after eternal values

and never resting.   But we are led to believe that he
becomes a successful writer.   The literary young man
is an almost irresistible temptation to this group of
modern novelists.

"*Fortitude:* being a true and faithful account of
the education of an adventurer," is the significant
title of one of Hugh Walpole's earliest novels.   Young
Peter Westcott who has literary ambitions, leaves his
savage old Cornish father and the harsh environment
of his desolate childhood to go to London, where he
finally writes one good novel.   His wife, his child,
and all hope of further success in his work are one
by one taken from him.   He is obsessed by the hostile,
negative forces of his grim inheritance which his father
and the old house in Cornwall represent.   They
exercise a sinister power over his life whenever his
will is weakened, but in the end he triumphs over
them.   The conquest of his fear of them is the theme
of the book.   Though crushed by defeat and sorrow,
and utterly bereft of all that makes life worth living,
he wins a spiritual victory out of despair.   The Carlyle note is fairly distinct here, unconscious though
the author may have been that he was sounding it.
The purification by sorrow has again bridged the gap
between Goethe and the modern age via Carlyle.

Although Compton Mackenzie expressly denies any
autobiographical intent in his *Youth's Encounter* and
Sinister Street, we may surmise that the usual quota of
the author's own experience went into these novels as
into so many others of the same type.   These two
books take Michael Fane from early nursery days

through public school and Oxford, some varieties of religious experience, and several love episodes. "The theme of these two stories," writes Mackenzie in his "Epilogical Letter" to *Sinister Street*, "is the youth of a man who presumably will be a priest. . . . My intention, however, was not to write a life, but the prologue of a life. He is growing up on the last page, and for me his interest begins to fade. He may have before him a thousand new adventures; he may become a Benedictine monk: he may become a society preacher. I have given you as fully as I could the various influences that went to mold him."[39] The increasing interest in the *process*, in "becoming," that Morley noted as characteristic of the Victorian age, is noticeable here as in so many similar novels, which stress the formative years of the hero rather than his adult life. Michael thus summarizes his own youth:

All that I have done and experienced so far would not scratch this stone. I have been concerned for the happiness of other people without gratitude for the privilege of service. I have been given knowledge and I fancied I was given disillusion. If now I offer myself to God very humbly, I give myself to the service of man.[40]

In Somerset Maugham's *Of Human Bondage*, we have one of the best novels of this modern group and the closest parallel to the old apprentice tradition. Philip Carey, made oversensitive by the deformity of a clubfoot, has something like the Goethian ideal of life as an artistic medium to be shaped creatively into an individual and satisfying pattern. But he makes the inevitable false starts. He passes through a religious phase and its accompanying disillusion and loss of faith; he goes to Germany and becomes less provincial in learning something about the characters who live in his *Pension;* he tries to become an account-ant and gives it up in despair and disgust; he goes to Paris to learn to paint, and learns many other things, among them, that he will never be a painter.   His ideas, however, begin to take shape.

Of late Philip had been captivated by an idea that since one had only one life it was important to make a success of it, but he did not count success by the acquiring of money or the achieving of fame; he did not quite know yet what he meant by it, perhaps variety of experience and the making the most of his abilities.

He discovers that "One profits more by the mis-takes one makes off one's own bat than by doing the right thing on somebody else's advice,"[42] an idea that many apprentices have reached before him, and that none proved more conclusively than Wilhelm Meister himself.   Philip becomes involved in his unfortunate affair with Mildred, and his struggle to shake off this obsession, or to cope with it, is one of the main factors in his spiritual development.

With him it was the conduct of his life as a whole that perplexed him.   That was his means of self-expression, and what he must do with it was not clear.[43]

He gets his first taste of raw life when he decides to become a doctor and sees the people passing through the hospital clinic and finds he has some gift for win-ning their confidence.   He makes new friends who give him a romantic and restless desire to go to Spain. Through the paintings of El Greco he experiences a renewal of his inner life:

He seemed to see that a man need not leave his life to chance, but that his will was powerful; he seemed to see that self-control might be as passionate and as active as the surrender to passion; he seemed to see that the inward life might be as manifold, as varied, as rich with experience, as the life of one who conquered realms and explored unknown lands.[44]

He passes through the inevitable spiritual crisis, the equivalent of Carlyle's Everlasting Nay in the Rue St. Thomas de l'Enfer. Life is meaningless, though one may still make of it, for one's own pleasure solely, an aesthetic pattern. He decides that the mystery and color of life will only be revealed fully to him in strange countries which he must travel and experience for himself, soaking up new impressions. But he loves Sally, the motherly, normal, kindly girl who asks nothing of him, and who will be the healthy mother of his children. He feels a great compassion for human beings, and no longer resents the treachery of friends, or the deformity which in some ways has warped his own life hitherto, for he sees that "the normal is the rarest thing in the world. Everyone had some defect, of body or of mind."[45] Instead of going on the travels that had captivated his imagination, he will marry Sally and have what he really wants—a wife and a home and love. He reaches Wilhelm Meister's conclusion almost in Wilhelm's very words:

America was here and now. It seemed to him that all his life he had followed the ideals that other people . . . had instilled into him, and never the desires of his own heart. . . . He had lived always in the future, and the present always, always had slipped through his fingers. . . . He thought of his desire to make a design, intricate and beautiful, out of the myriad, meaningless facts of life: had he not seen also that the simplest pattern, that in which a man was born, worked, married, had children, and died, was likewise the most perfect? It might be that to surrender to happiness was to accept defeat, but it was a defeat better than many victories.[46]

He had, in fact, not remembered the words that Wilhelm reads over the door of Nathalie's castle: *Gedenke zu leben!* or the words of Imlac the Sage, "While you are making the choice of life, you neglect to live." He is the only one of this particular group of modern apprentice heroes who like Goethe's hero, deliberately accepts the commonplace instead of the romantic destiny.

With *Tono-Bungay*, that great modern epic of Waste, there is bound up the story of one of the most relentless and honest of modern apprenticeships, as it was lived by George Ponderevo. As the housekeeper's son on the great estate of Bladesover, he early becomes a questioner of injustice. Like so many others of his kind he wanders about asking the eternal question: "But after all, *why* . . .?" All these apprentice heroes are cursed with enough sharpness of observation to want to get at the reasons for things, and this is one reason why their lives are almost invariably unhappy. George sees in the old system of Bladesover something that "illuminates England; it has become all that is spacious, dignified, pretentious, and truly conservative in English life. It is my social datum."[47] Leaving it, he becomes an atheist

and an outlaw, spiritually speaking, and is apprenticed to his uncle who is a chemist, and becomes later
the famous inventor of Tono-Bungay. During these
years as an actual apprentice, George studies and
grows mentally. His idea is to work and to learn.

I thought I was destined to do something definite to a world that had
a definite purpose. I did not understand then, as I do now, that
life was to consist largely in the world's doing things to me. Young
people never do seem to understand that aspect of things.[48]

(In fact, the essentially passive rôle of this type of
novel-hero is almost never obvious to the hero himself.) He comes up to London and matriculates at
the University of London for the science degree. He
has grown up. "You're a man, George," his Aunt
Susan tells him.

His uncle has started Tono-Bungay on its great
career, and George goes into the business with him,
and makes his blundering and unsuitable marriage
with Marion, ending it finally with divorce. Instead
of regarding it in the light of one of the inevitable
"false starts" made by all such heroes, Wells, reminis-
cing in his hero's words, is inclined to blame the waste
and folly of it on the community which let them "come
together so accidentally and so blindly,"[49] without
any guidance whatever. His purely sensual relationship with Effie is only a temporary one, and the tragic
figure of Beatrice is destined to form the greatest
sorrow of his life, so that we may consider him even
more unfortunate than the average apprentice in his
relations with women, educational though they are.

He develops in his other social relationships more successfully, and becomes in his middle thirties "restless and full of vague enterprise." It comes over him that "the perplexing thing about life is the irresoluble complexity of reality, of things and relations alike. Nothing is simple."[50] He sees his life for the first time as a whole, passing through one of those moments of revelation common to these pilgrims of adversity.

As I regard it all now in this retrospect, it seems to me as if in those days of disgust and abandoned aims I discovered myself for the first time. Before that I had seen only the world and things in it, had sought them self-forgetful of all but my impulse. Now I found myself *grouped*, with a system of appetites and satisfactions, with much work to do—and no desire, it seemed, left in me.[51]

He seeks and partially finds salvation in scientific truth which is, after all, "always there." But he faces the bitterness of the fact that there is no ultimate solution, only degrees of adjustment to the inevitable.

All my life has been at bottom, *seeking*, disbelieving always, dissatisfied always with the thing seen and the thing believed, seeking something in toil, in force, in danger, something whose name and nature I do not clearly understand, something beautiful, worshipful, enduring, mine profoundly and fundamentally, and the utter redemption of myself; I don't know,—all I can tell you is that it is something I have ever failed to find.[52]

And here Wells has stated the case for countless modern apprentices, showing the bitterness of their lot in a world where the conditions of living have become so complicated that their aspirations, however high they may be, cannot but lead them toward a horizon that grows more and more dim. The mazes through which they pass in pursuit of it, and the torturing sense of possibilities almost within their grasp, make the ultimate sense of failure harder to bear.   Failure and discouragement for Wilhelm Meister, for Teufelsdröckh, for Ernest Maltravers were simple things compared to the multiple forms they may assume for the modern hero wandering in confusion and obscurity through an industrialized, mechanized universe.

George takes up the work of building gliders, and reforms his way of easy living in order to make himself fit for the demands his work makes upon him. He undertakes on behalf of his uncle's business the wild-goose chase after the mysterious tropical deposit of Quap, commits a murder in the course of it, and returns to find his uncle has failed, and that the monumental house the old man had begun to build is now only

the compactest image and sample of all that passes for Progress, of all the advertisement-inflated spending, the aimless building up and pulling down, the enterprise and promise of my age. . . . For this futility in its end, for an epoch of such futility, the solemn scroll of history had unfolded. . . . "Great God!" I cried, "but is this Life?" . . . This was Life! It came to one like a revelation, a revelation at once incredible and indisputable of the abysmal folly of our being.[53]

He rescues his uncle from his creditors by flying with him across the Channel in the new glider he has just built, and cares for him until his death in France soon afterward. He returns to England and to Beatrice, but she too has been spoilt by the wealth and wastefulness of her life in this modern world, and feeling unworthy and unable to help him with his problems, refuses to marry him.   He sees that she is right, but

then, indeed, I tasted the ultimate bitterness of life.   For the first time I felt utter futility, and was wrung by emotion that begot no action, by shame and pity beyond words.[54]

Everything passes, he concludes, England and human achievement, men, and nations.   The progress toward the acceptance of uncertainty which the histories of all his brother-apprentices has unrolled before us, is now ended.   The next step may be the glorification of change for its own sake, but for the time being the circle is complete.   The long losing fight for permanence, stability, security, peace—is over.   The Victorians waged it bravely, stoically, wringing a certain victory out of their defeat, as is the way of all fighters for causes doomed from the beginning to be lost. And we leave the long line of apprentice heroes they have created, and their modern followers in the novel, with this most courageous of their number, of whom Wells has written—the scientific, complicated, modern man who has learned from his apprenticeship to life to face futility, defeat, and despair with the conviction, or the hope, that alone can make them tolerable:

Through the confusion something drives, something that is at once human achievement and the most inhuman of existing things Something comes out of it. . . .[55]

EPILOGUE

IN LOOKING back upon the long procession of
youthful adventurers shaped and taught by life,
and forward, from this modern group of them, to the
possibilities of their future development in the novel,
one cannot but be struck by the extraordinary flexibil-
ity of this old and still vital theme. The forms that
it may assume in adapting itself to an even more
complex world than ours, are infinite, and pass beyond
our conjecture. But we can safely predict for it an
even more rich and varied life than it has lived between
Goethe's time and ours.

The tracing of its often vague and obscure progress,
which this book has attempted to compass, may
indeed raise in the reader's mind the question, "What
of it, when all is said and done?"—that fatal, and quite
justifiable question to which, so often, there is no answer. A given complex of literary ideas and forms
may seem scarcely worth tracing. The interweaving
of German and English thought, and its resulting
expression in fiction, may seem unimportant, and
much of the fiction itself trivial and second-rate.
But as a record of the dauntless capacity for growth
and adaptation that is in the human spirit, the course
of the apprenticeship theme may still merit its
small share of tolerant attention. Today in this
post-war world we are perhaps, as so many have

called us, the children of disillusion and unbelief We may have little confidence left in human benevolence, human intelligence, generosity, or justice. But the courage of Youth moving gallantly down the generations to face Experience, inevitable and worn with repetition though the encounter may be, can still—if we have time to see it—reveal to our incredulous eyes some distant glimpses of an austere and imperishable beauty.

NOTES

CHAPTER I

1. *Pilgrim's Progress*, Chapter I.
2. Compton Mackenzie, 1913.
3. J. D. Beresford, 1911.
4. See Melitta Gerhard: *Der deutsche Entwicklungsroman bis zu Goethe's Wilhelm Meister* (Parsifal, Simplicissimus, Agathon, Wilhelm Meister), Niemeyer, Halle, 1926.
5. For a discussion of these forms in the German novel, see *Reallexikon der deutschen Literaturgeschichte*, Berlin 1925–26, Vol. I, p. 141, article *Bildungsroman*, by Christine Touaillon, which defines the *Bildungsroman* as a "Roman welcher die seelische Entwicklung eines Menschen von den Anfängen bis zur Erreichung einer bestimmten Lebensausbildung darstellt." See also Max Wundt: *Goethes Wilhelm Meister und die Entwicklung des modernen Lebensideals*, Berlin und Leipzig, Göschen, 1913.
6. *Sartor Resartus*, Chapter VI.
7. *Ibid.*, Chapter II.
8. *Ibid.*, Chapter VI.
9. *Ibid.*, Chapter VIII, "Natural Supernaturalism."
10. *Tono-Bungay*, Book IV, Chapter III.

CHAPTER II

1. *Dichtung und Wahrheit*, II, p. 334.
2. *Ibid.*, II, p. 436.
3. Wundt, *Goethe's Wilhelm Meister*, pp. 76–79.
4. *Dichtung und Wahrheit*, VIII.
5. *Kalligone*, p. 221.
6. *Ibid.*, p. 129.
7. *Wilhelm Meister*, Book VIII, Chapter VII.
8. *Dichtung und Wahrheit*, II, p. 351.
9. *Dichtung und Wahrheit* with regard to Goethe's early training: I, Chapter 4; II, Chapters 6 and 7.
10. Diderot, *Oeuvres Complètes*, ed. Assézat, Vol. II, p. 342.

11. Schiller's letter to Goethe, January 7, 1795.
12. Diderot, ed. Assézat, Vol. XV, p. 35.
13. *Ibid.*
14. *Dichtung und Wahrheit*, Part III, Book XI.
15. Eckermann, *Gespräche mit Goethe*, Brockhaus, Leipzig, 1923, II, p. 81.
16. *Dichtung und Wahrheit*, Part III, Book XI, p. 6.
17. *Ibid.*, Part II, Books VII, VIII, and X; Part III, Book XII.
18. January 25, 1813.
19. Weimar ed. of Goethe's *Werke, Tag und Jahreshefte*, Vol. XXXVI, pp. 311–46.
20. Elson, *Wieland and Shaftesbury*, p. 38.
21. *Ibid.*, p. 34.
22. "Erfahrung," writes Goethe in *Dichtung und Wahrheit*, Part II, Book XV, "war also abermals das allgemeine Lösungswort, und jedermann tat die Augen auf so gut er konnte."
23. *Ferneres über Weltliteratur.*
24. *Dichtung und Wahrheit*, Part II, Book XI; Part III, Books XIV and XV; Part IV, Book XX, and many others.
25. Eckermann, *Gespräche*, I, p. 87; also *Dichtung und Wahrheit*, Part III, Book XIII.
26. Book V, Chapter VII.
27. Ellinger, *Goethe-Jahrbuch*, Vol. IX, 1888.
28. Wieland, *Agathon*, Vol. II, pp. 77 ff.
29. "Dass man in einem grossen Wirkungskreise zwar mehr schimmern, aber in einem kleinen mehr Gutes schaffen kann." (*Agathon*, Vol. II, final chapter.)
30. Lessing's *Werke*, ed. Lachmann-Muncker, Vol. X, p. 80, December, 1767.
31. Wieland wants to show "Wie weit es ein Sterblicher durch die Kräften der Natur . . . bringen konnte; wie viel die äusserlichen Umstände an unserer Art zu denken. . . . Anteil haben, und wie es natürlicherweise nicht wohl möglich sei, anders als durch Erfahrung, Fehltritte, unermüdete Bearbeitung unserer selbst . . . ein weiser und guter Mensch zu werden." (*Agathon*, Introduction, p. 16.)
32. *Tag und Jahreshefte*, Weimar ed., XXXV, pp. 2–25.
33. Kuno Francke, *History of German Literature*, p. 356.
34. Recently republished, in the translation by P. E. Matheson, by the Oxford University Press (World's Classics, No. 299).
35. *Reiser*-"traveler."

36. *Reisen eines Deutschen in England, 1782.* A reprint of the English translation of 1795 was published 1924 by the Oxford University Press, with an introduction by P. E. Matheson.
37. For complete life of Moritz see introduction to reprint of *Anton Reiser* (Georg Müller, München and Leipzig, 1911) by Dr. Fred B. Hardt.
38. Goethe, *Briefe*, ed. Stein, III, p. 165.
39. *Anton Reiser*, pp. 339–40.
40. *Anton Reiser*, p. 232.
41. *Ibid.*, p. 415.
42. *Ibid.*, p. 261.
43. *Ibid.*, p. 301.
44. *Ibid.*, p. 313.
45. *Ibid.*, pp. 236, 319.
46. *Ibid.*, p. 244.
47. *Ibid.*, pp. 243, 307.
48. *Ibid.*, p. 368.
49. *Ibid.*, Part II, p. 105.
50. See Hans Berendt, *Goethes Wilhelm Meister: Ein Beitrag zur Entstehungsgeschichte*, Dortmund, 1911.

CHAPTER III

1. Letter to Goethe, July 8, 1796.
2. *Briefe*, ed. Stein, III, p. 364, December 7, 1783.
3. By Berendt, in *Goethes Wilhelm Meister*.
4. Gräf, *Goethe über seine Dichtungen*, I, p. 706.
5. Letter of Goethe to Merck, August 5, 1778, quoted by Gräf, I, p. 708.
6. Letter to Frau von Stein, Gräf, I, p. 709.
7. Gräf, I, p. 712.
8. *Ibid.*, pp. 715–16.
9. "Heute hab ich endlich das sechste Buch geendigt. Möge es Euch so viel Freude machen als es mir Sorge gemacht hat, ich darf nicht sagen Mühe. Denn die ist nicht bei diesen Arbeiten, aber wenn man so genau weiss was man will, ist man in der Ausführung niemals mit sich selbst zufrieden." (To Frau von Stein, November 11, 1785, quoted by Gräf, I, p. 727.)
10. *Italienische Reise*, October 2, 1787, Gräf, I, p. 739.
11. Erich Schmidt, *Richardson, Rousseau und Goethe*, Jena, 1875.
12. "Nicht um gut zu werden, sondern nur einmal als eine Pseudo-Confession mir vom Herzen und Halse zu kommen." (Gräf, I, p. 744.)

13. Goethe said, "Dass er nicht mehr fähig wäre sich seiner ersten Jugendeindrücke so lebhaft zu erinnern . . . denn die Lebhaftigkeit des Gedächtnisses, mit welcher er den *Meister* vor fünfzehn Jahren entworfen habe, sei ihm nun bei der Ausfeilung ganz fremd geworden." (Gräf, I, p. 753.)

14. "Mit *Wilhelm Meister* ging es mir noch schlimmer," Goethe wrote Schultz in 1829. "Die Puppen waren den Gebildeten zu gering, die Komödianten den 'Gentlemen' zu schlechte Gesellschaft, die Mädchen zu lose; hauptsächlich aber hiess es, es sei kein *Werther*." (Gräf, I, p. 1051.)

15. Eckermann, *Gespräche*, December 25, 1825.

16. J. O. E. Donner, *Der Einfluss Wilhelm Meisters auf den Roman der Romantiker*, Helsingfors, 1893.

17. Thomas Carlyle, *Early Letters*, ed. Norton, II, p. 223.

18. "A greater voice still,—the greatest voice of the century,—came to us in those youthful years through Carlyle: the voice of Goethe. To this day . . . I read the *Wilhelm Meister* with more pleasure in Carlyle's translation than in the original. The large liberal view of human life in *Wilhelm Meister*, how novel it was to the Englishman in those days! and it was salutary, too, and educative for him doubtless, as well as novel. But what moved us most in *Wilhelm Meister* was that which, after all, will always move the young most,—the poetry, the eloquence." (*Discourses in America:* Essay on Emerson.)

19. Goethe, *Tag und Jahreshefte von 1780–1786*, Weimar edition, Vol. XXXV, Chapter VIII, pp. 2–25. Quoted by Gräf, I, pp. 928–29: " . . . einem dunkeln Vorgefühl der grossen Wahrheit: Dass der Mensch oft etwas versuchen möchte, wozu ihm Anlage von der Natur versagt ist. . . . Ein inneres Gefühl warnt ihn abzustehen, er kann aber mit sich nicht ins Klare kommen, und wird auf falschem Wege zu falschem Zwecke getrieben, ohne dass er weiss, wie es zugeht. . . . Geht ihm hierüber von Zeit zu Zeit ein halbes Licht auf, so entsteht ein Gefühl das an Verzweiflung gränzt, und doch lässt er sich wieder gelegentlich von der Welle, nur halb widerstrebend, fortreissen. Gar viele vergeuden hiedurch den schönsten Teil ihres Lebens, und verfallen zuletzt in wundersamen Trübsinn. Und doch ist es möglich, dass alle die falschen Schritte zu einem unschätzbaren Guten hinführen: eine Ahnung, die sich in *Wilhelm Meister* immer mehr entfaltet, aufklärt, und bestätigt, ja zuletzt mit klaren Worten ausspricht; 'Du kommst mir vor wie Saul, der Sohn Kis, der ausging seines Vater's Eselinnen zu suchen, und ein Königreich fand.' "

20. Eckermann, *Gespräche*, V, January 18, 1825: "Es gehört dieses Werk übrigens zu den incalculabelsten Productionen, wozu mir fasst selbst der Schlüssel fehlt. Man sucht einen Mittelpunkt, und das ist schwer und nicht einmal gut. Ich sollte meinen, ein reiches, mannichfaltiges Leben, das unsern Augen vorübergeht, wäre auch an sich etwas, ohne ausgesprochene Tendenz, die doch blos für den Begriff ist. Will man aber dergleichen durchaus, so halte man sich an die Worte Friedrich's, die er am Ende an unsern Helden richtet, indem er sagt, 'Du kommst mir vor wie Saul, der Sohn Kis, der ausging seines Vaters Eselinnen zu suchen, und ein Königreich fand.' Hieran halte man sich. Denn im Grunde scheint doch das Ganze nichts Anderes sagen zu wollen, als dass der Mensch, trotz aller Dummheiten und Verwirrungen, von einer höhern Hand geleitet, doch zum glücklichen Ziel gelange."

CHAPTER IV

1 Quoted by Alford, p. 11.
2. *Monthly Review*, XXVII, pp. 543–44.
3. *Ibid.*, pp. 549–51.
4. Taylor, *Historic Survey*, III, pp. 348–49.
5. See *Diaries* of H. C. R., ed. Sadler, and Edith J. Morley, *Crabb Robinson in Germany, 1800–1805*, Oxford University Press, 1929.
6. Carré, *Revue Germanique*, 1912, p. 386.
7. Morley, *Crabb Robinson in Germany*, p. 65. The spelling and punctuation are Robinson's.
8. Carré, *Revue Germanique*, 1912, p. 387, note (translated).
9. Henry Crabb Robinson, MS *Diary* I, p. 158, quoted by Carré, *op. cit.*, p. 401.
10. Mme de Staël, *De l'Allemagne*, Vol. II, Chapter XXVIII.
11. See Haney, Dunstan, Stokoe, and Margraf.
12. Quoted by Stokoe, *German Influences in the English Romantic Period*, p. 136.
13. Dykes Campbell, p. 260.
14. *Ibid.*, p. 96.
15. Robinson, *Diaries*, II, p. 274; III, pp. 486–87.
16. *Ibid.*, I, p. 389.
17. *Ibid.*, I, p. 305.
18. *Table Talk*, ed. Shedd, p. 424.
19. Campbell, p. 249, note 3. The opening of the story of Maxilian was borrowed from *Der Goldene Topf*, by E. T. A. Hoffmann, 1814.
20. *Works*, ed. Shedd, IV, p. 436.

21. *Ibid.*, p. 445.
22. *Ibid.*, p. 451.
23. *Ibid.*, p. 452.
24. Brandl, *Coleridge und die englische Romantik*, p. 419.
25. *Works*, ed. Shedd, V, p. 569.
26. But Goethe's works were in Shelley's library in 1820. (Medwin, *Shelley*, II, p. 31.)
27. See Shelley's *Journals* for December 8, 1814.
28. Stokoe, pp. 162–63.
29. By Meusch, Heller, *et al.*
30. Robinson, *Diaries*, I, p. 482.
31. Harper, *Life of Wordsworth*, I, pp. 364, 378.
32. *Ibid.*, I, p. 375.
33. Robinson, *Diaries*, II, p. 224, February 25, 1822.
34. *Ibid.*, III, p. 10, July 13, 1832.
35. Wordsworth, *Prose Works*, III, p. 435, August 26, 1841.
36. *Ibid.*, p. 465.
37. Emerson, *English Traits*, p. 21, 1833.

Chapter V

1. *Love Letters of Jane Welsh and Thomas Carlyle*, II, p. 334.
2. *Early Letters of Thomas Carlyle*, ed. Norton, Vol. I, p. 233, April 10, 1819.
3. D. A. Wilson, II, p. 165.
4. *Early Letters*, I, p. 119.
5. *Ibid.*, p. 209.
6. *Ibid.*, p. 213.
7. *Ibid.*, p. 227.
8. Wilson, I, p. 201.
9. *Early Letters*, I, p. 233.
10. Wilson, I, p. 206.
11. *Early Letters*, I, p. 287.
12. *Ibid.*, January 8, 1819.
13. Wilson, I, p. 222.
14. *Reminiscences*, ed. Froude, p. 166.
15. Wilson, I, p. 221.
16. William Allingham, *Diary*, p. 253.
17. Wilson, I, p. 221.
18. Emerson, *Journals*, for 1834, June 26, p. 313.
19. *Wilhelm Meister*, Book VI.

20. Espinasse, *Literary Recollections*, p. 202.
21. Wilson, I, p. 237.
22. J. M. Carré, *Goethe en Angleterre.*
23. Wilson, I, p. 277.
24. *Love Letters*, I, p. 122, December 16, 1822.
25. *Ibid.*, I, pp. 273–74, August 31, 1823.
26. *Early Letters*, II, pp. 183–84.
27. *Ibid.*, p. 191.
28. *Ibid.*, p. 219.
29. *Ibid.*, p. 223.
30. *Love Letters*, I, p. 292.
31. *Early Letters*, II, pp. 268–69.
32. *Love Letters*, I, p. 346.
33. *Ibid.*, p. 349.
34. *Ibid.*, p. 352.
35. *Ibid.*, p. 357.
36. *Early Letters*, II, p. 279.
37. *Love Letters*, I, p. 387.
38. *Early Letters*, II, p. 302.
39. *Monthly Review*, 1825, Vol. VI, pp. 528–33.
40. Preface to First Edition of Carlyle's Translation of *Wilhelm Meister.*
41. *Historic Survey*, III, pp. 632–87.
42. *Ibid.*, III, p. 362.
43. *Ibid.*, III, p. 378.
44. *Ibid.*
45. See Eckermann, *Gespräche*, pp. 159, 220, 399.
46. Carré, *Revue Germanique*, January-February, 1912, pp. 35–39.
47. Espinasse, *Literary Recollections*, p. 220.
48. *Goethe-Zelter Correspondence*, XI, p. 260.
49. *Letters*, ed. Norton, I, p. 44.
50. *Ibid.*, I, p. 62.
51. *Ibid.*
52. Wilson, II, p. 19.
53. *Ibid.*
54. *Ibid.*, II, p. 15.
55. *Wotton Reinfred*, Chapter I, p. 3.
56. *Ibid.*
57. *Ibid.*, Chapter II, p. 13.
58. *Ibid.*, p. 21.
59. *Ibid.*, p. 24.

60. *Ibid.*, p. 33.
61. *Ibid.*, p. 53.
62. *Ibid.*, p. 61.
63. *Ibid.*, p. 68.
64. *Ibid.*, p. 85.
65. *Ibid.*, p. 95.
66. *Ibid.*, p. 100.
67. *Ibid.*, p. 109.
68. Wilson, II, p. 62.
69. *Ibid.*, II, p. 63.
70. *Ibid.*, II, pp. 132, 225.
71. *Ibid.*, p. 177.
72. *Letters*, ed. Norton, I, p. 271.
73. *Ibid.*, II, p. 105.
74. *Sartor Resartus*, Everyman Edition, p. 74.
75. *Ibid.*, p. 77.
76. *Ibid.*, p. 74.
77. *Ibid.*, pp. 69, 73.
78. *Ibid.*, p. 82.
79. *Ibid.*, pp. 91–92.
80. *Wilhelm Meister*, Meyer's Klassiker Ausgabe, Vol. I. p. 319.
81. *Ibid.*, I, p. 458.
82. *Sartor*, p. 104.
83. *Ibid.*, p. 125.
84. *Ibid.*, p. 129.
85. *Ibid.*, p. 133.
86. *Ibid.*, p. 142.
87. *Wilhelm Meister*, II, p. 78.
88. *Sartor*, p. 153.
89. *Carlyle's Letters*, ed. Norton, II, p. 123.
90. *Sartor*, p. 155.
91. *Wilhelm Meister*, II, p. 204.
92. *Sartor*, p. 155.

CHAPTER VI

1. *John Forster and His Friendships*, p. 152.
2. *Life of Edward Bulwer, First Lord Lytton*, by the Earl of Lytton, London, 1913, II, p. 119.
3. *Ibid.*, I, p. 28.
4. *Ibid.*, II, p. 119.

5. *Ibid.*, I, p. 81.
6. *Ibid.*, I, p. 76.
7. *Ibid.*, I, p. 88.
8. *Life, Letters and Literary Remains of Edward Bulwer,* by Robert Lytton, London, 1883, II, p. 98.
9. Goldhan, pp. 268–91; Carré, *Goethe en Angleterre,* Part III, Chapter II, p. 205.
10. Preface to 1835 edition of *Pelham.*
11. *Miscellaneous Prose Works,* II, p. 154.
12. Preface to *Pelham,* p. iv.
13. *Life, Letters and Literary Remains,* II, p. 3.
14. *Life of Edward Bulwer,* II, p. 13.
15. *Pelham,* pp. 51 ff.
16. *Ibid.*, p. 135.
17. *Ibid.*, p. 148
18. *Ibid.*, p. 168
19. *Ibid.*, p. 171
20. *Ibid.*, p. 446
21. *Ibid.*, p. 447
22. *New Monthly Magazine,* Part I, 1828, Vol. XXII, p. 576.
23. *Fraser's Magazine,* August, 1831, Vol. IV, p. 912. Also December, 1831, Vol. IV, pp. 520–26, and August, 1832, Vol. VI, p. 112. For later attacks on Bulwer, Vols. V, VI, VII, VIII, XIII, XVII.
24. *Life, Letters and Literary Remains,* II, pp. 205–6.
25. Goldhan, p. 307.
26. *Life, Letters and Literary Remains,* II, pp. 206 ff.
27. Preface to Knebworth Edition of *The Disowned,* 1852.
28. *The Disowned,* pp. 124, 156.
29. *Westminster Review,* January, 1829, Vol. X, pp. 173–91, No. 19.
30. *The Quarterly Review,* Oct.–Dec., 1832, Vol. XLVIII, p. 393. See also *New Monthly Magazine,* 1835, Part III, Vol. XLV, pp. 14–16.
31. Monypenny, *Disraeli,* I, 203–4.
32. *Lord Beaconsfield's Correspondence with his Sister,* p. 10, August, 1832.
33. *Ibid.*, p. 12.
34. *Ibid.*, p. 11.
35. Monypenny, I, p. 235.
36. *Ibid.*, I, p. 235.
37. *Edinburgh Review,* April, 1832, Vol. XLV, p. 208.
38. *Fraser's Magazine,* February, 1832, Vol. V, pp. 107–12.
39. *Edinburgh Review,* April, 1847, Vol. LXXXV, p. 475.

40. Wilson, II, p. 265.
41. *Ibid.*, II, p. 268.
42. Carlyle, *New Letters*, I, p. 16.
43. *Ibid.*, I, p. 188, July 14, 1836.
44. *Letters of Thomas Carlyle to John Stuart Mill*, p. 74.
45. Espinasse, p. 215.
46. Wilson, II, p. 222.
47. Espinasse, p. 125.
48. *New Letters*, II, p. 325, February 5, 1876.
49. *New Monthly Magazine*, 1832, Part I, p. 429, Section 3.
50. *Ibid.*, July, 1832, Part II, Vol. 35, pp. 27–28.
51. *Godolphin*, Preface, p. x.
52. *Ibid.*, p. 29.
53. *Ibid.*, p. 41.
54. *Ibid.*, p. 62.
55. *Ibid.*, p. 104.
56. *Ibid.*
57. *Ibid.*, pp. 106–7.
58. *Ibid.*, p. 111.
59. *Ibid.*, p. 143.
60. *Ibid.*, p. 184.
61. *Ibid.*, p. 249.
62. *Ibid.*, p. 330.
63. *New Monthly Magazine*, 1833, Part I, pp. 146 ff.
64. *Ernest Maltravers*, Preface, p. iii.
65. *Ibid.*, p. ix.
66. *Ibid.*, p. 61.
67. *Ibid.*, p. 66.
68. *Ibid.*, p. 69.
69. *Ibid.*, p. 90.
70. *Ibid.*, p. 96.
71. *Ibid.*, p. 104.
72. *Ibid.*, p. 135.
73. *Ibid.*, p. 136.
74. *Ibid.*, p. 197.
75. *Ibid.*, p. 201.
76. *Ibid.*, p. 248.
77. *Ibid.*, p. 255.
78. *Alice*, p. 237.
79. *Ibid.*, pp. 261–62.

80. *Ibid.*, 423.
81. *Life of Edward Bulwer*, II, 480–81 (1872).
82. *Kenelm Chillingly*, p. 31.
83. *Ibid.*, p. 52.
84. *Ibid.*, pp. 157–58.
85. *Ibid.*, p. 230.
86. *Ibid.*, p. 291.
87. *Ibid.*, p. 295.
88. *Ibid.*, p. 306.
89. *Ibid.*, p. 506.
90. *Ibid.*, pp. 507 ff.
91. Trollope, *Autobiography*, XIII, pp. 225–26.

CHAPTER VII

1. *Fraser's Magazine*, May, 1833, Vol. VII, p. 602, "Gallery of Literary Characters," No. 36.
2. *Diaries of Henry Crabb Robinson*, ed. Sadler, II, Chapter XIII, p. 237.
3. Monypenny, *Benjamin Disraeli*, I, pp. 42 ff.
4. *Ibid.*, I, p. 70.
5. *Ibid.*, I, p. 113.
6. *Vivian Grey*, Hughenden edition, pp. 51, 53, 57, 63.
7. Monypenny, I, p. 258, August 15, 1834.
8. Maurois, *Disraeli*, p. 218.
9. *Ibid.*, p. 304
10. Monypenny, I, p. 192
11. *Ibid.*, I, p. 236.
12. *Vivian Grey*, Chapter VI, p. 16.
13. *Ibid.*, Chapter VII, p. 17
14. *Ibid.*, Chapter VII, p. 21.
15. *Ibid.*, Book V, Chapter I, p. 165.
16. *Ibid.*, Book VI, Chapter VII, p. 370.
17. *Edinburgh Review*, April, 1853, Vol. XCVII, p. 427.
18. Monypenny, I, p. 176, Chapter IX.
19. Emerson, *Natural History of Intellect*, Papers from the *Dial*, p. 196: *Europe and European Books*.
20. Emerson, *Journals*, 1842, Vol. VI, p. 228.
21. *Ibid.*, 1837, Vol. IV, p. 216.
22. *Ibid.*, 1844, Vol. VI, p. 526.
23. *Ibid.*, 1862, Vol. IX, p. 420.

24. *Ibid.*, 1848, Vol. VII, p. 503.
25. Cabot, *Memoir*, Vol. II, p. 532.
26. Disraeli later mistakenly attributed Goethe's praise of *Vivian Grey* to *Contarini*.
27. *Contarini Fleming*, Preface to Hughenden Edition.
28. Reviews of *Contarini* appear in *Literary Gazette*, May 12, 1832, Vol. XIV, p. 289; in *New Monthly Magazine*, Vol. XXXVI, p. 297; Vol. XLIX, p. 532; Vol. XXXVIII, p. 140; Vol. LXXVI, p. 249; in *Edinburgh Review*, Vol. XCVII, p. 428.
29. Monypenny, I, p. 192.
30. *Contarini Fleming*, Chapter XIII, p. 58.
31. *Ibid.*, Part III, Chapter I, p. 370.
32. *Lothair*, Chapter XVII, p. 19.
33. *Ibid.*, Chapter LIX, p. 315.
34. *Ibid.*, Chapter LXXVI, p. 402.
35. *Ibid.*
36. *Ibid.*, Chapter LXXIX, p. 422.
37. *Ibid.*, Chapter LXXXIX, p. 483.
38. *Tremaine; De Vere; De Clifford*, etc., by Plumer Ward.
39. Trollope, *Autobiography*, p. 233.
40. Speare, *The Political Novel;* Sichel, *Disraeli*, pp. 85, 119.
41. Wilson, *Carlyle on Cromwell and Others*, p. 203. Quotation from letter of 1843 from J. Arnould in *Robert Browning and A. Domett*, p. 70.
42. Emerson, *Journals*, 1841, pp. 515–16.
43. *Ibid.*, 1848, pp. 511–12.
44. *Ibid.*, 1840, pp. 445–46.

CHAPTER VIII

1. John Sterling

1. The last volume of J. D. Beresford's modern apprentice novel, *Jacob Stahl*, is called *A Candidate for Truth*.
2. *Letters of Geraldine Jewsbury to Jane Carlyle*, p. 292.
3. Caroline Fox, *Memories of Old Friends*.
4. Morley, *Recollections*, I, p. 71.
5. *Ibid.*, I, p. 69.
6. Wilson, *Carlyle at His Zenith*, Chapter 14, p. 367.
7. *Memories of Old Friends*, p. 109.
8. *Ibid.*, p. 82.
9. Wilson, *Carlyle on Cromwell*, pp. 409–10.

10. Carlyle, *Life of Sterling*, Part I, Chapter V, p. 33.
11. *Ibid.*, Conclusion, p. 235.
12. *Ibid.*, Part II, Chapter II, p. 91.
13. *Ibid.*, pp. 233–34.
14. *London and Westminster Review*, 1839.
15. *Foreign Quarterly Review*, 1842.
16. *Essays and Tales*, Vol. I, p. 413.
17. *Arthur Coningsby*, Vol. I, p. 247.
18. *Ibid.*, I, pp. 275–76.
19. *Ibid.*, II, p. 285.
20. *Ibid.*, III, p. 110.
21. *Ibid.*, III, p. 353.
22. *Ibid.*, III, p. 368.
23. *Ibid.*, III, p. 371.
24. *Ibid.*, III, p. 396.
25. *Life of Sterling*, Part I, Chapter XV, p. 82.

2. George Henry Lewes

26. Scott, *Autobiographical Notes*, II, p. 245.
27. *Ibid.*, I, p. 131.
28. *Ibid.*, I, p. 133.
29. *Ranthorpe*, Chapter VI, p. 239.
30. *British and Foreign Review*, Vol. XIV, No. 27, pp. 78–135.
31. *Correspondence of Sir Arthur Helps*, p. 40.
32. Espinasse, p. 282.
33. *British and Foreign Review*, Vol. XIV, p. 99.
34. *Ibid.*, pp. 114–15.
35. *Life of Goethe*, Book VI, Chapter II, pp. 397–405.
36. *British and Foreign Review*, Vol. XIV, p. 130.
37. *Fortnightly Review*, Vol. III, No. 15, 1865, December 15, p. 352.
38. *Ibid.*, Vols. I, II, 1865.
39. Espinasse, pp. 294–95.
40. Mrs. Gaskell's *Life of Charlotte Brontë*.
41. Espinasse, p. 278.
42. *New Monthly Magazine*, 1847, Vol. LXXX, Part II, p. 250.
43. *Ranthorpe*, p. 71.
44. *Ibid.*, p. 96.
45. *Ibid.*
46. *Ibid.*
47. *Ibid.*, p. 145.

48. *Ibid.*, p. 240.
49. *Ibid.*, pp. 303–7.
50. *Ibid.*, p. 307.
51. Espinasse, p. 291.

3. James Anthony Froude

52. *Nemesis of Faith,* Introduction, p. xii.
53. *Ibid.*, p. xvii.
54. Froude, *Shadows of the Clouds,* p. 115.
55. *Ibid.*, p. 76.
56. *Ibid.*, p. 119.
57. Quoted by Espinasse, pp. 141–42.
58. *Ibid.*, p. 142.
59. *New Letters of Thomas Carlyle,* II, p. 59, 1848.
60. Quoted by Espinasse, p. 139.
61. Preface to *Nemesis of Faith,* p. xlix.
62. *Ibid.*, p. li.
63. *Ibid.*, p. xlvii.
64. *Nemesis of Faith,* p. 5.
65. *Ibid.*, p. 36.
66. *Ibid.*, p. 178.
67. *Ibid.*, p. 248.

4. Geraldine Endsor Jewsbury

68. Mrs. Virginia Woolf has indicated some of the possibilities in her article, "A Friend of Jane Carlyle's," *Bookman,* February, 1929.
69. Jewsbury, *Letters to Jane Welsh Carlyle,* p. 146.
70. *Ibid.*, p. 122.
71. *Ibid.*, pp. 41, 101.
72. *Ibid.*, p. 31.
73. *Ibid.*, p. 196.
74. *Ibid.*, p. 97.
75. *Ibid.*, p. 99.
76. *Ibid.*, p. 336.
77. *Ibid.*, p. 384.
78. *Ibid.*, pp. 347–48.
79. *Ibid.*, p. 337.
80. Espinasse, p. 136.
81. Geraldine Jewsbury, *Zoe,* I, p. 79.
82. *Ibid.*, II, p. 261.

83. *Ibid.*, II, p. 306.
84. *Ibid.*, III, p. 29.
85. Geraldine Jewsbury, *Letters to Jane Welsh Carlyle*, pp. 148–51.
86. Geraldine Jewsbury, *The Half-Sisters*, p. 97.
87. *Ibid.*, pp. 122–24.
88. *Ibid.*, p. 186.
89. *Ibid.*, p. 171.
90. *Ibid.*

5. Charles Kingsley

91. *Letters and Memories of His Life*, ed. Mrs. Kingsley, I, p. 296.
92. Charles Kingsley, *Yeast*, p. 3.
93. *Ibid.*, p. 11.
94. *Ibid.*, p. 86.
95. *Ibid.*, p. 233.
96. *Ibid.*, p. 322.
97. *Letters and Memories of His Life*, I, pp. 219–20.
98. Quoted by Wilson, *Carlyle at His Zenith*, Chapter XXXIV, p. 217
99. Kingsley, *Alton Locke*, p. 24.
100. *Ibid.*, p. 29.
101. *Ibid.*, p. 43.
102. *Ibid.*, p. 62.
103. *Ibid.*, p. 86.
104. *Ibid.*, p. 327.

Chapter IX

1. *Pilgrim's Progress*, Chapter I.
2. *Wilhelm Meister*, Book I, Chapter XVI.
3. *Sartor Resartus*, Book II, Chapter I.
4. Samuel Butler, *The Way of All Flesh*, Chapter LXXVII.
5. George Meredith, *Beauchamp's Career*, Chapter XII.
6. *Richard Feverel*, Chapter I, p. 7.
7. *Ibid.*, IV, p. 28.
8. *Ibid.*, VI, p. 38.
9. *Ibid.*, XII, p. 77.
10. *Ibid.*, XII, p. 79.
11. *Ibid.*, XXI, p. 151.
12. *Ibid.*, XXV, p. 180.
13. *Ibid.*, XXIX, p. 233.
14. *Ibid.*, XXXIV, p. 301.

15. *Ibid.*, XXXVIII, p. 353.
16. *Ibid.*, XLII, p. 420.
17. *Ibid.*, XLII, p. 423.
18. *Ibid.*, XLIV, p. 440.
19. *Ibid.*, XLIV, p. 443.
20. *Evan Harrington*, Chapter VI, p. 50.
21. *Ibid.*, XVIII, p. 184.
22. *Ibid.*, XXXI, pp. 328.
23. *Ibid.*, XXXIII, p. 535.
24. *Beauchamp's Career*, Chapter I, p. 11.
25. *Ibid.*, II, p. 8.
26. *Ibid.*, IV, p. 32.
27. *Ibid.*, XV, p. 130.
28. *Ibid.*, XXVII, p. 247.
29. *Ibid.*, XXIV, p. 207.
30. *Ibid.*, XXXIX, p. 364.
31. *Ibid.*, XLVIII, p. 458.
32. *Ibid.*, L, p. 481.
33. *Ibid.*, LV, p. 514.
34. J. D. Beresford, *Jacob Stahl*, p. 14.
35. *Ibid.*, p. 334.
36. *Ibid.*, p. 348.
37. *Ibid.*, p. 481.
38. *Ibid.*, p. 485.
39. Compton Mackenzie, *Sinister Street*, pp. 656–57.
40. *Ibid.*, p. 653.
41. W. Somerset Maugham, *Of Human Bondage*, Chapter L, p. 256.
42. *Ibid.*, LII, p. 268.
43. *Ibid.*, LXV, p. 331.
44. *Ibid.*, LXXXVIII, p. 465.
45. *Ibid.*, CXXI, p. 644.
46. *Ibid.*, CXXII, p. 647.
47. H. G. Wells, *Tono-Bungay*, Book I, Chapter II, Section 8.
48. *Ibid.*, Chapter III, Section 2.
49. *Ibid.*, Book II, Chapter IV, Section 1.
50. *Ibid.*, Section 9.
51. *Ibid.*, Section 10.
52. *Ibid.*, Section 10.
53. *Ibid.*, Book IV, Chapter I, Section 2.
54. *Ibid.*, Book IV, Chapter II, Section 4.
55. *Ibid.*, Book IV, Chapter III, Section 3.

BIBLIOGRAPHY

CHAPTERS II AND III

BERENDT, HANS: Goethes Wilhelm Meister. Dortmund, Ruhfus, 1911.

BERGER, ARNOLD E.: Werther, Faust, und die Anfänge des Wilhelm Meister. Nord und Süd, Band 47, 1888, IV, 353.

BIELSCHOWSKY, A.: Goethe; sein Leben und seine Werke. München, 1911, 2 vols.

BILLETER, GUSTAV, ED.: Wilhelm Meisters theatralische Sendung. Zürich, 1910.

BOUCKE, E. A.: Goethes Weltanschauung auf historischer Grundlage. Stuttgart, 1907.

BRANDES, GEORG: Wolfgang Goethe. New York, Maurice, 1925, 2 vols.

BRAUN, J. W., ED.: Goethe im Urteile seiner Zeitgenossen, 1773–1812. Berlin, Luckhardt, 1885.

BROWN, P. HUME: Life of Goethe. New York, Holt, 1920, 2 vols.

BUNYAN, JOHN: The Pilgrim's Progress. London, Routledge.

CARRÉ, JEAN-MARIE: Goethe en Angleterre. Paris, Plon-Nourrit, 1920.

CERVANTES: Don Quixote. London, Cassell, ed. Clark.

CRU, R. LOYALTY: Diderot and English Thought. New York, Columbia University Press, 1913.

DIDEROT, DENIS: Oeuvres complètes, Vols. 2, 3, 14, 15. Paris, Garnier, 1875, ed. Assézat.

DODSLEY'S OLD PLAYS, ED. HAZLITT: Interlude of Youth, 1425; Castle of Perseverance, 14th Century; Mundus et Infans, ca. 1500; Interlude of the Four Elements, ca. 1500; Lusty Iuventus, 1547–53.

DONNER, J. O. E.: Der Einfluss *Wilhelm Meisters* auf den Roman der Romantiker. Helsingfors, 1893.

ECKERMANN, J. P.: Gespräche mit Goethe. Leipzig, 1896, ed. Von der Linden.

ELLINGER, GEORG: Der Einfluss von Scarrons *Roman Comique* auf Goethes *Wilhelm Meister*. Goethe-Jahrbuch, IX, 1888, 188–97.

ELSON, CHARLES: Wieland and Shaftesbury. New York, Columbia University Press, 1913.

FIELDING, HENRY: Tom Jones.

——— Joseph Andrews.

FRANCKE, KUNO: A History of German Literature. New York, Holt, 1911.

GEIGER, L., ED.: Goethe-Jahrbuch. Frankfurt.

GOETHE, JOHANN WOLFGANG VON: Werke, Weimar Ausgabe, Vols. 36, 40. Weimar, 1887–.

―――― Werke, ed. Karl Heinemann, Vols. 9, 10, 12, 13, 14, 15. Bibliographisches Institut, Leipzig und Wien, 1905–7, Meyers Klassiker-Ausgabe.

―――― Briefe, ed. Philipp Stein. Berlin, 1913, 8 vols.

GOLDSMITH, OLIVER: The Vicar of Wakefield.

―――― The Traveler.

―――― The Deserted Village.

GRÄF, H. G., ED.: Goethe über seine Dichtungen, Erster Teil, Band II, 696–1071. Frankfurt, 1902.

―――― Jahrbuch der Goethe-Gesellschaft. Weimar, 1914–.

GUNDOLF, F.: Goethe. Berlin, Bondi, 1922, 11'' Auflage.

HERDER, J. G.: Werke, ed. Suphan. Berlin, Weidemann, 1880.

HETTNER, HERMANN: Geschichte der Literatur im achtzehnten Jahrhundert. Braunschweig, 1894, 4'' Auflage.

JACOBI, FRIEDRICH HEINRICH: Woldemar. Leipzig, Fleischer, 1826.

JOHNSON, SAMUEL: Rasselas.

LESSING, GOTTHOLD EPHRAIM: Werke, ed. Lachmann-Muncker, Vols. IX, X. Stuttgart, Göschen, 1894.

LEVY, S.: Goethe und Oliver Goldsmith. Goethe-Jahrbuch, 1885, Band VI, 281.

MACKENZIE, HENRY: The Man of Feeling.

MACPHERSON, JAMES: Ossian.

MAYNC, HARRY, ED.: Wilhelm Meisters theatralische Sendung. Stuttgart und Berlin, Cotta, 1911.

MEYER, RICHARD M.: Goethe. Berlin, Bondi, 1913, Volksausgabe.

―――― Wilhelm Meisters Lehrjahre und der Kampf gegen den Dilettantismus. Euphorion, II, 1895.

MIELKE, HELLMUTH: Der deutsche Roman. Dresden, Reissner, 1912.

MINOR, JACOB: Die Anfänge des Wilhelm Meister. Goethe-Jahrbuch, IX, 1888, 163–87.

MORITZ, KARL PHILIPP: Anton Reiser: ein psychologischer Roman. Berlin, Maurer, 1785.

RALEIGH, SIR WALTER: The English Novel. London, Murray, 1895, 2d ed.

RICHARDSON, SAMUEL: Clarissa Harlowe.

ROUSSEAU, JEAN JACQUES: La Nouvelle Héloise.

―――― Confessions.

―――― Émile.

SCHILLER, FRIEDRICH: Briefwechsel zwischen Schiller und Goethe, 2 Bände, 1794–1805. Stuttgart, Cotta, 1870.

——— Briefwechsel zwischen Schiller und Körner, 2 Bände, 1784–1805. Stuttgart, Cotta, 1892.

——— Briefe, ed. Fritz Jonas. Stuttgart, Cotta, 1892, 7 Bände.

SCHLEGEL, A. W. UND FRIEDRICH: Charakteristiken und Kritiken, Vol. I, 132–69, "Charakteristik des Wilhelm Meisters." Königsberg, Nicolovius, 1801.

SCHMIDT, ERICH: Richardson, Rousseau und Goethe. Jena, Frommann, 1875.

SMOLLETT, TOBIAS: Roderick Random.

——— Humphrey Clinker.

STERNE, LAURENCE: A Sentimental Journey.

SUPHAN, BERNHARD: Goethe und Barbara Schulthess. Goethe-Jahrbuch, XLII, 1892, 149–62.

SWIFT, JONATHAN: Gulliver's Travels.

VOLTAIRE: Candide. New York, Boni and Liveright, Modern Library edition.

WIELAND, CHRISTOPH MARTIN: Agathon. Stuttgart, Cotta, ed. Muncker.

——— Don Sylvio.

WUNDT, MAX: Goethes Wilhelm Meister und die Entwicklung des modernen Lebensideals. Berlin und Leipzig, Göschen, 1913.

XENOPHON, TRANSL. W. MILLER: Cyropedia. London, Heinemann, 1914.

YOUNG, EDWARD: Night Thoughts.

CHAPTER IV

ALFORD, R. G.: Goethe's Earliest Critics in England. English Goethe Society, Vol. VII, 1893.

CAMPBELL, J. DYKES: Samuel Taylor Coleridge. London, Macmillan, 1894.

CARRÉ, JEAN-MARIE: Bibliographie de Goethe en Angleterre. Paris, Plon-Nourrit, 1920. Articles in Revue Germanique, 1912.

COLERIDGE, S. T.: Works, ed. Shedd, Vols. IV, V. New York, Harper, 1853. Biographia Literaria. New York, Dutton, Everyman ed.

DE QUINCEY, THOMAS: Goethe as Reflected in His Novel of Wilhelm Meister. London Magazine, 1824.

——— Goethe (article for Encyclopaedia Britannica). Encyclopaedia Britannica, 7th edition, 1838–39.

DOWDEN, EDWARD: Life of P. B. Shelley. London, 1886, 2 vols.

DROOP, A.: Die Belesenheit P. B. Shelleys. Weimar, 1906.

DUNSTAN, A. C.: The German Influence on Coleridge. Modern Language Review, Vols. 17, 18, July, 1922, and April, 1923.

EMERSON, R. W.: English Traits. Boston, Houghton Mifflin, 1893.

GOETHE, J. W. VON: Kunst und Altertum. Stuttgart, Cotta, 1827, 6 Bände.

HANEY, J. L.: The German Influence on Coleridge. Philadelphia, 1902.

——— German Literature in England before 1790. Americana Germanica, IV, 1902, p. 130.

HARPER, GEORGE MCLEAN: William Wordsworth, 2 vols. London, Murray, 1916.

HOGG, T. J.: A Biography of Percy Bysshe Shelley. London, 1858, n. d.

MARGRAF, E.: Einfluss der deutschen Literatur auf die englische. Leipzig, 1901.

MEUSCH, R. A. J.: Goethe and Wordsworth. English Goethe Society, Vol. VII, 1893.

PRICE, LAWRENCE MARSDEN. English-German Literary Influences (Bibliography and Survey). Berkeley, University of California Press, 1919.

ROBBERDS, J. W.: A Memoir of the Life and Writings of the Late William Taylor of Norwich. London, Murray, 1843, 2 vols.

ROBINSON, HENRY CRABB: Diaries, ed. Sadler. London, Macmillan, 1869, 3 vols.

——— Correspondence of Henry Crabb Robinson with the Wordsworth Circle, 1808–66, edited by Edith Morley. Oxford, Clarendon Press, 1927, 2 vols.

STAËL, MME DE: De l'Allemagne. Paris, Garnier, 2 vols., n. d.

STOKOE, F. W.: German Influence in the English Romantic Period, 1788–1818. Cambridge University Press, 1926.

TAYLOR, WILLIAM: Historic Survey of German Poetry. London, Treuttel and Würtz, 1828–30, 3 vols.

WORDSWORTH, WILLIAM: Prose Works of, ed. Alexander B. Grosart. London, Moxon, 1876, 3 vols.

CHAPTER V

CARLYLE, JANE WELSH: Love Letters of Jane Welsh and Thomas Carlyle. New York, John Lane, 1909, 2 vols.

CARLYLE, THOMAS: Critical and Miscellaneous Essays. London, Chapman and Hall, 3 vols.

——— Early Letters of, ed. C. E. Norton. London, Macmillan, 1886, 2 vols.

CARLYLE, THOMAS: Last Words of Thomas Carlyle. New York, Appleton, 1892 (Centennial Memorial Edition).

—— Letters of, ed. C. E. Norton. London, Macmillan, 1888, 2 vols.

—— New Letters of, ed. Alexander Carlyle. London and New York, John Lane, Bodley Head, 1904.

—— Reminiscences, ed. J. A. Froude. New York, Scribner, 1881.

—— Sartor Resartus. New York, Dutton, Everyman edition.

—— Wilhelm Meister's Apprenticeship and Travels, translated from the German of Goethe. New York, Scribner, 1908, 2 vols.

CARRÉ, JEAN-MARIE: Quelques lettres inédites de William Taylor, S. T. Coleridge et Carlyle à Henry Crabb Robinson sur la littérature allemande. Revue Germanique, 1912, Janvier-Février, pp. 35–49.

GOETHE, J. W. VON: Briefwechsel zwischen Goethe und Zelter. Berlin, 1834, ed. Riemer.

—— Goethe-Carlyle Correspondence. London, Macmillan, 1887, ed. Norton.

KRAEGER, H.: Carlyle's deutsche Studien und der Wotton Reinfred. Anglia Beiblatt, IX, 1898, 193–219.

LORENZ, A. C.: Diogenes Teufelsdröckh und Thomas Carlyle. Leipzig, Noske, 1913.

NEFF, EMERY E.: Carlyle and Mill. New York, Columbia University Press, 1924.

RALLI, AUGUSTUS: Guide to Carlyle. London, Allen & Unwin, 1920.

STREULI, WILHELM: Thomas Carlyle als Vermittler deutscher Literatur und deutschen Geistes. Zürich, Schulthess, 1895.

TAYLOR, WILLIAM: Review of Wilhelm Meisters Lehrjahre. Monthly Review, 1798.

—— Review of Wilhelm Meisters Lehrjahre, as translated by Carlyle. Monthly Review, 1825.

TICKNOR, GEORGE: Life, Letters and Journals. Boston and New York, Houghton Mifflin, 1909, 2 vols.

WILSON, DANIEL ALEXANDER: Carlyle till Marriage. New York, Dutton, 1923.

—— Carlyle to the French Revolution. New York, Dutton, 1924.

—— Carlyle on Cromwell and Others. New York, Dutton, 1925.

CHAPTER VI

DISRAELI, RALPH, ED.: Lord Beaconsfield's Correspondence with His Sister, 1832–1852. 1885.

ESPINASSE, FRANCIS: Literary Recollections. New York, Dodd Mead, 1893.

FONBLANQUE, ED.: The Life and Labors of Albany Fonblanque. London, Bentley, 1874.

FORSTER, JOHN. The Life of Charles Dickens. Philadelphia, Lippincott, 1874, 3 vols.

GOLDHAN, H.: Ueber die Einwirkung des Goethischen Werthers und Wilhelm Meisters auf die Entwicklung Edward Bulwers. Halle, Niemeyer, 1894 (Reprinted in Anglia, XVI, Neue Folge, IV, 1893–94).

LANDON, LETITIA ELIZABETH: Romance and Reality. London, Bentley, 1852.

LYTTON, SIR EDWARD BULWER: Falkland. London, Routledge, 1852, Knebworth edition.

—— Pelham. London, Routledge, 1840.

—— The Disowned. London, Routledge, 1877.

—— Conversations with an Ambitious Student. New York, Harper, 1832.

—— Godolphin. London, Routledege, Knebworth ed.

—— Review of Contarini Fleming. New Monthly Magazine, July, 1832, Part II, Vol. 35, p. 27 ff.

—— Asmodeus at Large, etc. New Monthly Magazine, 1832 *passim.*

—— Ernest Maltravers. London, Routledge, 1840, Knebworth ed.

—— Alice, or The Mysteries. London, Routledge, 1840, Knebworth ed.

—— Miscellaneous Prose Works. London, Bentley, 1868, 3 vols.

—— Kenelm Chillingly. London, Routledge, 1897.

LYTTON, ROBERT BULWER: The Life, Letters, and Literary Remains of Edward Bulwer, Lord Lytton. London, Kegan Paul Trench, 1883, 2 vols.

LYTTON, EARL OF: The Life of Edward Bulwer, First Lord Lytton. London, Macmillan, 1913, 2 vols.

McCARTHY, JUSTIN: Portraits of the Sixties. New York, Harper, 1903.

MACKENZIE, R. SHELTON, ED.: The Fraserian Papers of the Late William Maginn. New York, Redfield, 1857.

MARTINEAU, HARRIET: Autobiography, Vol. I. Boston, 1877.

PRICE, LAWRENCE MARSDEN: Karl Gutzkow and Bulwer Lytton. Journal of English and Germanic Philology, XVI, 1917, 397 ff.

RENTON, RICHARD: John Forster and His Friendships. London, Chapman and Hall, 1912.

SCHMIDT, JULIAN: Bilder aus dem geistigen Leben unserer Zeit. Leipzig, Duncker, 1870.

SHORE, W. TEIGNMOUTH: D'Orsay, or the Complete Dandy. London, John Long, 1911.

THACKERAY, W. M.: Yellowplush Papers and Burlesques. Boston, Dana Estes, n. d.

TROLLOPE, ANTHONY: Autobiography. New York, Harper, 1883.

WILLIS, N. P.: Pencillings by the Way. London, John Macrone, 1835

CHAPTER VII

CABOT, JAMES ELLIOT: A Memoir of R. W. Emerson. New York, Houghton Mifflin, 1887, 2 vols.

DISRAELI, BENJAMIN: Vivian Grey. London, Longmans Green, 1881, Hughenden edition.

—— Contarini Fleming.

—— Lothair.

EMERSON, R. W.: Journals, Vols. 4, 5, 6, 7. New York, Houghton Mifflin, 1910–13.

—— Natural History of Intellect and Other Papers. New York, Houghton Mifflin, 1894.

FRASER, SIR WILLIAM: Disraeli and His Day. London, Kegan Paul, 1891.

HENLEY, W. E.: Views and Reviews, Vol. I. London, David Nutt, 1908.

MAUROIS, ANDRÉ: La Vie de Disraeli. Paris, Gallimard, 1927.

MELVILLE, LEWIS: Life and Letters of William Beckford. New York, Duffield, 1910.

MONYPENNY AND BUCKLE: Life of Benjamin Disraeli. New York, Macmillan, 1910, 6 vols.

PHIPPS, HON. EDMUND: Memoirs of the Political and Literary Life of Robert Plumer Ward, Esq. London, John Murray, 1850, 2 vols.

"PUNCH": Benjamin Disraeli: In upwards of 100 Cartoons from the Collection of "Mr. Punch." London, Punch Office, 1878.

SADLEIR, MICHAEL: Excursions in Victorian Bibliography. London, Chaundy and Cox, 1922.

SICHEL, WALTER: Disraeli: A Study in Personality and Ideas. London, Methuen, 1904.

SMILES, SAMUEL: Memoirs and Correspondence of the Late John Murray. London, Murray, 1891.

SPEARE, MORRIS EDMUND: The Political Novel. New York, Oxford University Press, 1924.

STEPHEN, LESLIE: Hours in a Library. New York, Putnam, 1907.

STRACHEY, LYTTON: Queen Victoria. New York, Harcourt Brace, 1921.

SWINNERTON, FRANK: Disraeli as a Novelist. London Mercury, XVII, no. 99, Jan. 1928, 260–72.

VICTORIA, QUEEN: The Letters of Queen Victoria, Second Series, 1862–78, ed. G. E. Buckle. New York, Longmans Green, 1926, 2 vols.

CHAPTER VIII

1. John Sterling

CARLYLE, THOMAS: The Life of John Sterling. London, Chapman and Hall, n. d.

ESPINASSE, FRANCIS: Literary Recollections. New York, Dodd Mead, 1893.

FOX, CAROLINE: Memories of Old Friends. Philadelphia, Lippincott, 1882.

GILFILLAN, GEORGE: Second Gallery of Literary Portraits. New York, Appleton, 1850.

STERLING, JOHN: Essays and Tales, ed. Hare. London, J. W. Parker, 1848.

―――― Arthur Coningsby. London, Effingham Wilson, 1833.

WILSON, D. A.: Carlyle at His Zenith. New York, Dutton, 1927.

2. George Henry Lewes

COLVIN, SIDNEY: Memories and Notes of Persons and Places, 1852–1912. London, Edward Arnold, 1921.

DUNCAN, DAVID: Life and Letters of Herbert Spencer. London, Methuen, 1908.

ELIOT, GEORGE: Life as Related in Her Journals, ed. Cross. London, Blackwood, 3 vols., n. d.

GASKELL, MRS.: Life of Charlotte Brontë. London, Smith Elder, 1882.

HARRISON, FREDERIC: Autobiographic Memoirs, 1831–1910. London, Macmillan, 1911, 2 vols.

HELPS, SIR ARTHUR: Correspondence, ed. E. A. Helps. London, John Lane, 1917.

JACKS, L. P.: Life and Letters of Stopford Brooke. London, John Murray, 1917, 2 vols.

LAYARD, GEORGE SOMES: Mrs. Lynn Linton. London, Methuen, 1901.

LEWES, GEORGE HENRY: Apprenticeship of Life. The Leader, 1850–51 (Brit. Mus.).

―――― The Character and Works of Goethe. British and Foreign Review, Vol. 14, 1843, p. 78.

―――― Life and Works of Goethe. London, Smith Elder, 1890, 4th ed.

―――― The Leader, ed. Vols. 4, 5, 7, 8, 1853–57.

―――― The Fortnightly Review, ed. Vols. 1–4, 1865–66.

―――― Ranthorpe. Leipzig, Tauchnitz, 1847.

LINTON, ELIZA LYNN: Reminiscences of Dickens, Thackeray, George Eliot, etc. London, Hodder & Stoughton, n. d.

MAITLAND, FREDERIC WILLIAM: Life and Letters of Leslie Stephen. New York, Putnam, 1906.

MORLEY, JOHN: Recollections, Vol. I. New York, Macmillan, 1917. 2 vols.

ROSS, JANET: Three Generations of English Women. London, T. Fisher Unwin, 1893.

SCOTT, WILLIAM BELL: Autobiographic Notes, 1830–82. London, Osgood McIlvaine, 1892, 2 vols.

SPENCER, HERBERT: An Autobiography. New York, Appleton, 1904.

3. James Anthony Froude

FROUDE, J. A.: Nemesis of Faith. London and New York, Walter Scott Publishing Co., n. d.

———— Shadows of the Clouds. London, John Ollivier, 1847.

JEWSBURY, GERALDINE: Religious Faith and Skepticism (Review of *Nemesis of Faith*). Westminster Review, 1849.

4. Geraldine Endsor Jewsbury

CARLYLE, JANE WELSH: New Letters and Memorials of Jane Welsh Carlyle. London and New York, John Lane, Bodley Head, 1903.

ESPINASSE, FRANCIS: Literary Recollections. New York, Dodd Mead, 1893.

JEWSBURY, GERALDINE: Selections from Her Letters to Jane Welsh Carlyle, 1841–52, ed. Mrs. Alexander Ireland. London, Longmans Green, 1892.

———— Zoe: The Story of Two Lives. London, Chapman and Hall, 1845.

———— The Half Sisters. London, Chapman and Hall, 1854.

MERCER, EDMUND: Geraldine E. Jewsbury. Manchester Quarterly, 1898, Vol. XVII, pp. 301–20.

WILSON, D. A.: Carlyle on Cromwell (pp. 213–17). New York, Dutton, 1925.

———— Carlyle at His Zenith (pp. 103, 308). New York, Dutton, 1927.

5. Charles Kingsley

KINGSLEY, CHARLES: His Letters and Memories of His Life, ed. by Mrs. Kingsley. London, Kegan Paul, 1878, 2 vols.

———— Alton Locke. New York, Frank Lovell, n. d.

———— Yeast. London, Macmillan, 1879.

MAURICE, J. F.: Life of F. D. Maurice. New York, Scribner, 1884, 2 vols.

Conclusion

BUTLER, SAMUEL: The Way of All Flesh. New York, Dutton, 1916.
WARD, MRS. HUMPHRY: Robert Elsmere. London, Macmillan, 1888.
—— David Grieve. London, Murray, 1911.

CHAPTER IX

BENNETT, ARNOLD: Clayhanger. New York, Doran, 1910.
BERESFORD, J. D.: The Early History of Jacob Stahl. New York, Doran, 1911.
—— A Candidate for Truth. New York, Doran, 1912.
MACKENZIE, COMPTON: Youth's Encounter. New York, Appleton, 1921.
—— Sinister Street. New York, Appleton, 1922.
MAUGHAM, W. SOMERSET: Of Human Bondage. New York, Doran, 1915.
MEREDITH, GEORGE: The Ordeal of Richard Feverel. New York, Scribner, 1915, revised ed.
—— Evan Harrington. New York, Scribner, 1916, revised ed.
—— Beauchamp's Career. New York, Scribner, 1916, revised ed.
WALPOLE, HUGH: Fortitude. New York, Doran, 1913.
WELLS, H. G.: Tono-Bungay. New York, Duffield, 1928, Sandgate ed.

INDEX

A

Action, gospel of, 184, 195, 197, 198

Adjustment, struggle for, 205, 213

Agathon, Wieland, 23, 28, 166
effect upon *Meister*, 23

Alice, or The Mysteries, Bulwer, 129, 168–70

Alroy, Disraeli, 144, 178, 179, 184

Alton Locke, Kingsley, 206, 256–60, 265

Anton Reiser, Moritz, 31

Apprentice novel, 4
in England, 6, 127

Apprenticeship of a Master, The, 68

Apprenticeship of Life, Lewes, 221, 223, 228–31, 260

Apprenticeships before *Wilhelm Meister*, 16–40

Arthur Coningsby, John Sterling, 215–20

Artist as separate and unique personality, 17

Asmodeus at Large, Bulwer, 150

Atlas, 139

Autobiographical nature of *Wilhelm Meister*, 42, 62

Autobiographical novel, Carlyle's desire to write, 92

Autobiographical tone in English apprentice novel, 7, 14, 128

Autobiography, Bulwer's, 131, 161, 176

Autobiography in Disraeli's novels, 183, 188, 190

B

Background, 3
English, 127, 128, 203–10
of Bulwer's novels, 129, 153, 169, 173, 175

Beauchamp's Career, Meredith, 266, 277–82

Beckendorff, portrait of, 187, 188, 189, 190

Bennett, Arnold, 283

Beresford, J. D., 284

Bildung, 131, 192, 223

Bildungsroman, 6, 23

Billeter, Gustav, 44

Bismarck and Disraeli, 183

Blessington, Lady, 180, 182

British and Foreign Review, 222

Bulwer, Edward, *see* Lytton

Bunyan, John, quoted, 263

Butler, Samuel, 260, 284

Byron, George Noel Gordon, 78, 94
influence upon apprentice novels, 9, 139, 143, 189

C

Candidate for Truth, A, J. D. Beresford, 284

Candidates for Truth, 202–61

Candidate, Voltaire, 27

Carlyle, Jane Welsh, 82, 84, 92, 96, 104
and Geraldine Jewsbury, 238, 241, 242

323

DATE DUE